American Gun

ALSO BY CHRIS KYLE

American Sniper

American Gun

A History of the U.S. in Ten Firearms

Chris Kyle

WITH WILLIAM DOYLE
AND EDITORIAL CONTRIBUTIONS BY JIM DEFELICE
FOREWORD AND AFTERWORD BY TAYA KYLE

HARPER LUXE

An Imprint of HarperCollins*Publishers*

Grateful acknowledgement is made to the following for the images that appear in this book. The Kyle family: pages xiii, 187, and 335. Library of Congress: pages 17, 23, 31, 36, 38, 44, 50, 55, 57, 61, 65, 78, 85, 89, 93, 96, 109, 113, 125, 129, 134, 138, 147, 152, 155, 159, 170, 173, 180, 193, 199, 204 (top left and bottom right), 210, 224, 228, 233 (top), 260 (middle and bottom), 268, 287, and 299. Steven Noble: pages 1, 41, 75, 112, 150, 189, 217, 252, 284, 310 and 359–370. Peter Hubbard: page 79 (bottom). Don Troiani (www.historicalimagebank.com): page 12. Brimstone Pistoleros: page 52. Paramount Pictures: page 144. Wikipedia: pages 166 and 260 (top). Robert Kowalewski: page 306 (bottom). U.S. Patent Office: page 202 (top). Browning Arms Company: page 204 (top right, bottom left). *American Rifleman:* 202 (bottom). United Artists Corporation: page 220 (bottom). FBI: page 235. National Archives: pages 246, 256, 273, 277, and 280. U.S. Army: pages 281 (photo by Sgt. John Heinrich), 312, and 321. GhostsofDC. org: page 289. Smith & Wesson: page 295. Glock Ges.m.b.H: page 306 (top). Colt's Manufacturing Company: page 327 (top). U.S. Marine Corps: page 330 (photo by Cpl. Albert F. Hunt). U.S. National Guard: page 338 (painting by James Deitz). Camp Patriot (elk hunt, 2008): page 356.

HarperCollins books may be purchased for educational, business, or sales promotional use. For information, please e-mail the Special Markets Department at SPsales@harpercollins.com.

FIRST HARPERLUXE EDITION

HarperLuxe™ is a trademark of HarperCollins Publishers

Library of Congress Cataloging-in-Publication Data is available upon request.

ISBN: 978-0-06-225368-2

13 14 ID/RRD 10 9 8 7 6 5 4 3 2 1

This book is dedicated to Chris's family and friends, from all walks of life and throughout the world . . .

And to you, Chris. I am proud of you. I love you.
—Taya

American Gun

Contents

Foreword
by Taya Kyle

"I would love for people to be able to think of me as a guy who stood up for what he believed in and helped make a difference for veterans. You know, somebody who cared so much about them that he wanted them taken care of."

—Chris Kyle, January 28, 2013

Like many young boys, Chris first developed his sense of justice playing in the outdoors. He and his brother, Jeff, would take sticks and pretend they were guns, fighting imaginary bad guys in the creek bed behind their house. They loved to copy the heroes they saw in the old Western shows and John Wayne movies. Those early battles nurtured a strong desire to protect others from evil and to fight for what was right.

As he got older, Chris's parents taught him about gun safety and the proper use of real guns. He learned to respect firearms as tools that could bring as much harm as good. When he learned to shoot and hunt, he was taught only to kill what he needed for food. He developed an appreciation for the gun as a means of providing for the family while exploring the peaceful essence of nature.

Chris grew up to be a fine cowboy (and a good-looking one at that, if you don't mind me saying). He won championship buckles in rodeos and worked for several years on ranches. His guns were tools to protect himself and the animals in his care against predators ranging from rattlesnakes to coyotes.

After joining the military and becoming a U.S. Navy SEAL, Chris trained as a sniper. He saved countless lives and helped alter the course of history for good. Most of all, he protected other patriotic young men who'd selflessly signed up to serve their country. As Chris often said, "Members of the military voluntarily sign a blank check to the United States of America for a price up to and including their life." His goal was to make the price as low as possible.

While Chris was a warrior, that wasn't all he was. He was a young man full of life and laughter with an easy confident spirit. He was incredibly intelligent. Most of all, he wasn't naive; he knew there might come a time when he couldn't do what was asked of him on

Chris and Taya in Arizona, November 2011.

the battlefield. To do his job, Chris knew he had to let go of his innocence. It was a hefty price, but one Chris would willingly pay time and time again.

When faced with a decision to fire or let an American die, Chris dug deep. He found courage. He was able to use his weapon to save the lives of those he was sent to protect. Many people have told me heart-wrenching stories about how they would not be alive today if it weren't for Chris. He felt a sense of purpose and fulfillment protecting the people around him. He appreciated the guns that helped him do that.

I have been blessed to hear from a U.S. Marine who knew with all certainty that he, and consequently his young daughter, would not be alive today were it not for Chris's service. I have witnessed parents addressing

Chris with tears in their eyes, thanking him for saving the life of their child.

Chris knew the stories of countless people who returned home thanks to his skills. He also knew the pain of loss caused by guns and anguished over those he couldn't save every day of his life. He had to fight to come back from the dark, heavy weight of loss he felt when his friends died on the battlefield. But Chris was strong enough to face the bad head-on; to push through and live with the memories of all the experiences he was given. Somewhere in there, he found a balance.

Life after the military took on a different meaning. Chris and I moved our family to Texas. Chris felt all of us have a duty to serve those who serve us. This meant he began dedicating his time to training interested members of military and law enforcement communities. By sharing the skill set he developed on the battlefield, he was able to continue serving. He encouraged others to share their knowledge as well. Chris's humble nature was present in training. He referred to it as providing "additional tools in an operator's tool belt."

Chris and I were fortunate enough to have the support of many wounded veterans. Chris loved hearing their stories and joking with them the same way he would have had they not been wounded.

They loved it. It was a sign of respect. Chris did *not* view them as wounded. He saw them as we all should: As patriotic, skilled, and above all, men of honor. Many of them thought that the healing they received in the hospital, though important, was exponentially slower than the healing they experienced when they got into the great outdoors. Many service members were out-doorsmen before they served in the military and felt great peace hunting or shooting targets. Chris found a new use for the gun: healing.

In the last year of his short life, Chris was able to reflect on the varied experiences he had with guns and the way he had used them through every stage of his journey. He also loved history. Chris and I loved visit-ing historical sites, and he would spend hours delving into many different aspects of America's past. His face would light up with reverence and appreciation as he shared stories about the Rough Riders and the Texas Rangers lawmen. That passion was one reason he was inspired to write *American Gun.* Chris was so excited to share stories in his new book about individuals whose sacrifices and strength changed history.

He often surprised people with his knowledge. He was incredibly intelligent, but liked to keep that fact close to the vest. I have a smile on my face as I tell you that my husband loved to play down how extraordinary he was. He was humble and embraced his country roots. I cannot tell you how many times he was at a book signing where people would line up for hours to meet him. When they would finally arrive at the table to shake his hand, they would express their nervousness, anticipation, and honor in meeting him. Chris would lean in and say, "I am so sorry. Here you waited all this time and got to the front only to find another dumb redneck standing here." Everyone would laugh and Chris would have put them at ease, as he often did.

As you read *American Gun,* I hope you feel the presence of Chris with you. As you take a walk back in time with him, I hope you feel the excitement he had as you explore the remarkable role these guns had in shaping our great nation. Perhaps you will join me in the memory I have of my handsome husband, a smile as big as the state of Texas, wearing his T-shirt and jeans, twirling his replica pistols in the Old West style as he reflects on his childhood, his love of the Old West, and the country he loved and devoted much of his life to. These are the stories that make up *American Gun.*

God Bless,
Taya

Introduction

More than any other nation in history, the United States has been shaped by the gun. Colonists used firearms to secure their land, then turned them on the King and his men to win their independence. Cowboys and plain folk used revolvers and rifles to survive in the West, putting food on the table, fighting off Indians, and occasionally settling squabbles. After America came of age as a world power, we used guns to beat Hitler and subdue terrorists across the world.

Of course, there is another part to the story—firearms have also torn us apart, literally and figuratively. The Civil War, bank robberies, assassination attempts—the gun has been a tool for bad as well as good.

I first learned how to handle guns from my dad, who started teaching my brother, Jeff, and myself how to hunt and shoot before we could even ride bikes. He taught us to respect weapons as important tools, and part of that respect was knowing just a little bit about the history of the gun. I can't swear that knowing Johann Nicolaus von Dreyse invented the first bolt-action rifle made me a better shot with one, but I do know that the tidbits of information I picked up along the way fired (if you'll excuse the pun) a powerful fascination with our nation's history. One of my proudest possessions is a replica Peacemaker—the famous Colt revolver that defined the Wild West. Take that bad boy in your hand and you're transported back a hundred and fifty years.

There's a saying that to really know someone you have to walk a mile in their shoes. I'd add that to really know our ancestors, we have to put on more than their shoes, which were generally poor-fitting and leaky. Hitch a plow to an ox and work a field for a few hours, and you come away with a whole new appreciation for what your great-great-grandpa did come spring on the Ohio frontier. Pick up a Kentucky long rifle and aim it at fleeing whitetail, and you'll learn real quick about how important it is to use every bit of an animal you harvest; you may not have another one down for quite a while.

When I decided to do this book, I didn't want to write a stodgy textbook, or sound like the teachers who used to put me to sleep in the back of the classroom. I aimed to talk history with the bullets flying: the critical single rifle shot of the Revolutionary War; the climaxes of the Battle of the Alamo and Custer's Last Stand; Abraham Lincoln's personal shooting range on the White House grounds. I wanted to explore some of the greatest U.S. military battles of the twentieth century; the St. Valentine's Day massacre; and the North Hollywood bank robbery and shootout in 1997, which caused American police forces around the country to radically rethink their approach to firearms self-defense, and to gear up for combat.

To write this book, I traveled deep into American history. A team of friends and I read thousands of pages of historical documents, books, journals, military reports, and long-forgotten letters. I talked to firearms historians and reenactors, and I poked around museums and archives on the history of guns in America. I also had the thrill of personally handling and shooting many of these weapons.

I reached back into my own past, recalling gun stories we SEALs traded around a campfire in the middle of the combat zone in Iraq, and the tales my dad told me about our Texas ancestors and the guns they relied on. In the process I've learned to better appreciate the courage of the men and women who made America.

As I got further into this project, it became increasingly clear to me that guns have always been present at the leading edge of American history—often crucially. And along the way, certain revolutionary firearms seemed to shape the story of America more than all others.

I've picked ten guns to serve as the flagship weapons for our tour of America's past. Now, I have to say, it's my personal list. If you're a gun-history buff, you'll agree with some of my choices and disagree with others. I'm sure you'll be scratching your head wondering why in the hell I didn't talk about this Remington or that Smith & Wesson. I understand completely. A top-ten list is tough to settle on, and you may come up with a list of your own you like much better.

But that's enough of a preamble. Let's get 'er done.

—C.K.

PUBLISHER'S NOTE

On February 2, 2013, as this book was nearing its final stages, Chris Kyle was killed. A book may seem a small thing after a tragedy such as this. But *American Gun* was a piece of Chris that lay unfinished; and it was a project that was born out of his passions. For these reasons, there was never a question of whether we would see the book through to publication. Taya Kyle, his incredible wife, affirmed this immediately. She brought in Jim DeFelice, Chris's coauthor on *American Sniper*, to team with William Doyle and wrap up the manuscript. Many of Chris's friends were graciously on call to confirm facts and offer their insights. We believe we got the book right, but any errors are our own.

Lastly, no shadow hangs over these pages, despite the circumstances. Chris was full of more life, humor, and love of country than anyone who'll ever cross your path. That's the spirit you'll be lucky enough to meet as you turn the page.

American Gun

1

The American Long Rifle

"I never in my life saw better rifles (or men who shot better) than those made in America."

—*Colonel George Hanger, a British officer*

On the morning of October 7, 1777, a young rebel named Timothy Murphy spat on his hands and began climbing up a tree in a field not far from Saratoga, New York. His progress was slowed by the weapon he gripped in his hand, but the gun was entirely his reason for getting up in that tree in the first place. Murphy was a Continental Army sergeant and a master marksman—a sniper in so many words. His weapon, a long rifle, was one of the few technologically advanced weapons the ragtag Continentals possessed during the

Revolutionary War. His mission: to find and eliminate high-value targets in the ranks of the Red Coats mustering for attack a few hundred yards away.

Now, I may be a bit partial to Mr. Murphy, who like me was a sniper. But I think it's not much of an exaggeration to say that the good sergeant and the other marksmen with him had the potential to change the Battle of Saratoga, and with that, the whole Revolution. They'd already harassed the daylights out of British General John Burgoyne and his troops. Burgoyne had a master plan to cut the American rebellion in two, slicing down New York's Hudson River Valley. He was marching south; another general was coming north. If the two forces met in the middle, the Revolution was done.

But Burgoyne was having tough going. The Americans were better fighters than he thought. One reason they were whipping him was their tactics. The British army depended on close coordination on the battlefield. It was a thing of beauty to look at, assuming the Red Coats weren't shooting at you. Groups of men marched in perfect precision, took their shots together, and made their bayonet charges like a well-oiled machine. But it all relied on well-trained officers and well-timed orders to keep things moving smoothly.

The Americans aimed to mess that all up by targeting those officers. In modern terms, we'd say they were zeroing in on Burgoyne's command and control. Burgoyne couldn't lead his army without its officers. That's where Murphy and his fellow snipers came in. Their long-range shots sought to leave the Red Coat units headless.

If they could do that in this battle, the whole Revolution might turn around for them. The French king was looking on from the sidelines, wondering if he should support the Americans. If the Americans stopped the Brits here, not only would they have a huge victory, but maybe get some French guns and money to boot.

Not that Murphy was thinking about all that as he climbed the tree. He was just looking for a nice target to fire at.

Very soon, one rode into view: a British officer, buttons gleaming on his red coat. It was General Simon Fraser, the best British leader on the field, and the man commander John Burgoyne was counting on to save the British bacon today.

Murphy aimed, and fired. . . .

While that bullet is sailing toward General Fraser—carrying with it the fate not just of the battle but maybe the entire American Revolution—let's take a look at the weapon that fired it.

American long rifles were adapted for the demands of the New World from designs first produced by European-born gunsmiths in the 1620s. These had grown from the shorter-barreled, larger-caliber Swiss-German Jaeger hunting rifle used in the forests of central Europe. The lighter Americanized guns featured barrels of up to four feet, and often were adorned with nicknames and personalized designs and inscriptions. The biggest difference between muskets and rifles was the "rifling" in the barrels. Rifling is the series of spiraling grooves cut into the bore of the barrel, which cause the projectile to spin on its axis. This spinning would give the projectile enough stability to dramatically enhance the overall accuracy of the gun.

Gun-making was small manufacturing at its best. It was literally a cottage industry: you might have a single master with an apprentice or two creating a weapon for a customer he knew very well from church and the local market. It was a downright poetic activity, as John Dillin put it in his 1924 book *The Kentucky Rifle:* "From a flat bar of soft iron, hand forged into a gun barrel; laboriously bored and rifled with crude tools; fitted with a stock hewn from a maple tree in the neighboring forest; and supplied with a lock hammered

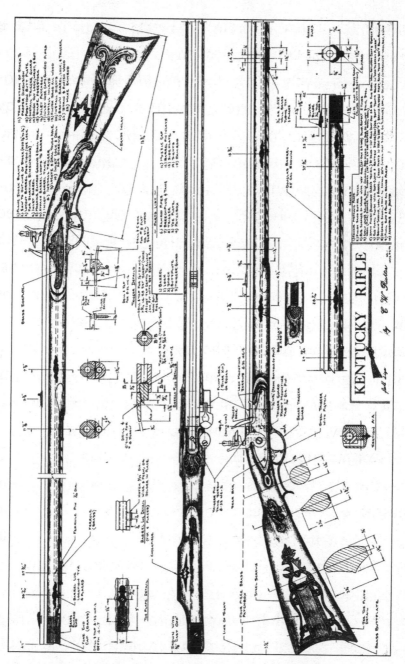

Diagrams of a Kentucky rifle, aka the American long rifle.

to shape on the anvil; an unknown smith, in a shop long since silent, fashioned a rifle which changed the whole course of world history; made possible the settlement of a continent; and ultimately freed our country of foreign domination. Light in weight; graceful in line; economical in consumption of powder and lead; fatally precise; distinctly American; it sprang into immediate popularity; and for a hundred years was a model often slightly varied but never radically changed."

The long rifle was so called because of its lengthy rifled barrel. It was also known as "the Kentucky rifle" ("Kentucky" was once the catch-all word used to describe much of the little-known western wilderness of the Appalachians and beyond) and "the Pennsylvania rifle" (Lancaster and other Pennsylvania towns were a Silicon Valley of innovation and creativity for gunmakers in the 1700s).

When I first fired a vintage "black-powder" flintlock long rifle, I was struck by two things. As a Navy SEAL sniper, I was used to handling weapons weighing in the area of fifteen or sixteen pounds. But the typical American long rifle was around nine pounds, a sleek, surprisingly lightweight gun, more like a precision combat surgical instrument than a battlefield weapon. The process of firing the gun, on the other hand, is incredibly slow. You line up your shot through the superb sighting system and pull the trig-ger. Sparks shower as the flint strikes the frizzen pan. There's a quick flash as the sparks ignite the powder in the pan, and a delayed sensation of contact in the gun. A little bit of smoke puffs from the pan as it ignites. A flash of flame passes through a hole into the breech of the barrel, which kicks off the powder charge behind the patched lead ball. Then a mass of gray smoke blasts out of the end of the barrel. The smoke fills the shooter's whole field of vision. The rifle is so light that the recoil feels more like a push against the shoulder.

Long rifles were first designed and used primarily to kill small-to-medium-sized game on the frontier. Precision was at a premium—a rabbit or deer gave a hunter a relatively short time to fire; by the time you got the weapon reloaded, it would be gone. But rifles would also prove their worth against Indian raids. The bullet—actually a round ball anywhere from .25 to .75 caliber, though usually around .40 to .50—could do a good piece of damage to any target.

(Should I explain what we mean by caliber? In theory it's the measurement of the barrel's bore diam-eter, or in a rifle the size of the grooved interior hole, expressed in fractions of an inch—for instance, 32/100s of an inch equals .32 caliber. But when we're talking about guns in the Revolutionary War era, it's best to remember that the measurements and calibers were not anywhere near as standard as they are today. Bullet making was as much of an art as gun making; precision standardization and mass production were about a hundred years in the future.)

The weapon's longer barrel—extending from 35 inches to over 48 inches (compared to some 30 inches for the average musket)—gave the black powder extra time to burn, boosting the rifle's accuracy and velocity. The long rifle had adjustable sights for long-distance accuracy; like modern rifles, the gun would be "sighted in" by its owner, tuning it not only to his needs and circumstances, but the weapon's own distinct personality.

Since they were made by hand, no two long rifles were exactly alike. Granted, the majority might appear very similar to anyone except their rightful owner. But look closer, and each weapon's uniqueness became obvious. Small variations in the wood furniture or the fittings were of course to be expected. Much larger innovations were also common—Sergeant Murphy, for instance, was believed to have had a double-barreled rifle. It was an over-under design, with one barrel above the other. The arrangement would have made it quicker for him to get off a second shot, a key asset in battle as well as hunting.

Warfare in the late eighteenth century was dominated by a very different gun, the smooth-bore musket. While the firing mechanisms used by muskets and rifles were pretty much the same, the barrels were decidedly not. As the name implies, a smooth-bore musket had a barrel that was smooth, not rifled; fire the gun and its bullet traveled down the tube as quick as it could. By design, the bullet was smaller than the inside of the barrel. This was necessary because deposits of burnt powder and cartridge tended to form on the inside as the weapon was fired. Gunmakers had learned from experience that under battlefield conditions, too tight a fit might lead to the gun misfiring—not a good situation. They designed their bullets to be snug, but not tight.

There was a downside to that. A bullet flying from a musket could only go so far on a given charge. Some of its energy was wasted in that open space around the ball. It also wasn't necessarily that accurate. The farther the bullet got from the gun, the more likely it was to move in any direction but the one the shooter intended. Now, this wasn't a problem at ten feet. But put yourself on a battlefield and engage an army at a few hundred yards, and you begin to see the limitations. Still, the musket was a considerable weapon. Contemporary tactics were organized around it; that's why you see all those lines of soldiers in the historic paintings and reenactments. Truth be told, every important battle in the Revolution centered around those lines of men and their muskets.

The firearms the British used were generally Land Pattern Muskets, known informally as the "Brown Bess." There were a number of variations on the same basic design; the most important was the Short Land Pattern, used by cavalry and other horsemen. Oftentimes, especially early in the war, the Americans used the Brown Bess, too. Later the French shipped large numbers of their various Charleville models. Like the long rifle, the muskets were flintlocks. Pulling the trigger released the flint to strike the frizzen; the spark ignited the gunpowder in the barrel and off went the bullet.

So why didn't everyone use rifles, given their superior accuracy? The biggest problem had to do with how all guns were loaded in those days—through the muzzle. Pushing a bullet straight down a smooth, or nearly smooth, tube is a heck of a lot easier than getting it past one that's rifled, particularly after the fouling caused by firing several rounds without time to clean. Now, I'll give it to you that someone like our friend Murph could get the job done quickly under battle conditions, but Sergeant Murphy and his fellow riflemen were master marksmen, and something of an exception. They also had the advantage of not having to coordinate their fire (shooting on command in one group). A line of riflemen working at different paces would be quickly decimated by the most ragged row of musketmen all firing at the same time. They would load their weapons slower, and without time to clean them, have guns much more likely to jam.

Finally, while they were shorter, muskets generally had the advantage of being outfitted with bayonets. Rifles, originally designed for an entirely different type of job, did not. In many if not all battles, bayonet charges proved more deadly and more decisive than several rounds of gunfire.

But used in the right circumstances, a precision weapon like the rifle could be quite important. Traditionally, snipers have been deployed to take high-value targets at long range. And that's exactly how they were employed in the Revolutionary War.

Which brings us back to our friend Sergeant Murphy, up there in that tree.

Murphy was a member of an elite brigade of riflemen under the command of Daniel Morgan. Colonel Morgan's unit specialized in picking off British officers while they mustered their men on the battlefield. The idea was pretty simple: cut off the enemy's head, and

A member of Morgan's Riflemen, with his tool:
the American long rifle.

he floundered. The massed firing tactics that were so favorable to muskets depended on good coordination, which generally could only be provided by the officers in the field.

Throughout the war, British officers were horrified to see American riflemen like Timothy Murphy intentionally aiming at them. This went beyond even the guerilla tactics that had so decimated the British supply lines down from what is now Canada. To many British officers, deliberately aiming at them rather than firing generally at the mass of men on the front line was nearly akin to a war crime. The upper class that filled the officer ranks had never heard of such behavior before, and they were astounded. To them it seemed repulsive, very un-European tactic.

But it was definitely effective. The British feared the colonial riflemen so much they called them "widow-makers." The best picture of the American long-riflemen comes from the unfortunate British troops who had to face them in battle. British Army Captain Henry Beaufoy wrote that his combat-hardened troops, "when they understood they were opposed by riflemen, they felt a degree of terror never inspired by general action, from the idea that a rifleman always singled out an individual, who was almost certain of being killed or wounded." Another British officer reported that an expert rifleman could hit the head of a man at two hundred yards, and if he "were to get perfect aim at 300 yards at me, standing still, he would most undoubtedly hit me unless it were a very windy day."

But their leaders had not fully absorbed the implications of the tactic, and on this day on the battlefield at Saratoga, several were sitting ducks out in the open, mounted on horses where they could be easily targeted. The most important of them was Simon Fraser, a Scottish aristocrat and British brigadier general who was massing his troops for a fresh charge on what would become known to historians as the Battle of Bemis Heights. Fraser's commander, General Burgoyne, had launched a desperate attempt to break himself free of the rebels surrounding him. Hoping to lure the Americans into a trap, he sent Fraser against the left side of the American line. If Fraser's troops could break the Americans' will, the British might escape westward, and live to fight another day.

The battles at Saratoga have become the subject of legends and not a little propaganda on the part of the participants. But there's no doubt that Murphy was up in the tree, and it's more than a little likely that he and a few of his brothers-in-arms spotted General Fraser on horseback as he began rallying his troops for a charge.

Murphy would have been about three hundred yards away—a good distance in those days, and probably far enough that Fraser didn't feel in any danger at that early stage of the war.

As his rifle hammer dropped, Murphy's firearm's complex process of ignition unfolded, a fragile procedure that is nowhere near as fast as the firing of a modern cartridge arm. Murphy held steady throughout that long second and a half. He handled the gun like it was an extension of himself, and when loading it would have made sure to use the most efficient charge possible. The bullet would have made a sharp crack as it flew, its sonic reflections echoing against the nearby trees and ground.

It missed, though. Instead of hitting the general, it lightly nicked his horse.

Sergeant Murphy pulled a catch to flip up the preloaded bottom barrel. He performed a quick series of complex mental calculations, trying to adjust his aim for wind, altitude, and for the inevitable vertical and lateral drift of the bullet, which at this far distance could be severe.

Then he fired again. The second bullet missed, this one also barely clipping the general's horse. I imagine he had some choice words going through his head. Nothing bad on Murphy—we all miss sometimes.

At this point, Murphy either would have paused to begin the time-consuming process of reloading his flintlock long rifle, which even for a crack shot like Murphy could have taken as long as thirty seconds, or more likely, someone would have passed him up another, preloaded long rifle.

In any event, Sergeant Timothy Murphy sighted down his barrel for a third shot, then squeezed the trigger. The bullet flew. Legend has it that this one found its target, squarely hitting Fraser in his midsection. In those days, a gut shot was both painful and nearly always fatal. Fraser slipped from his horse, mortally wounded.

Although it's difficult if not downright impossible to definitively know whether it was Murphy's bullet that struck the British general, one person above all apparently credited him with the kill: Fraser himself. Taken away to safety too late by two of his aides, the British officer spoke of seeing the American rifleman who shot him, far off in the distance, sitting in a tree.

Fraser's death marked the final turning point of the battle. It deprived Burgoyne of his best lieutenant, and shortly after he was shot, the British troops fell back in retreat. Burgoyne's position was now hopeless. Ten days later, he and six thousand British troops surrendered to the Americans, handing them a critical victory. Impressed, the French soon pitched in to offer crucial help to the Americans.

Sergeant Murphy's boss, Daniel Morgan, is probably a guy you never learned about in history class, but he is one interesting character. He quit the Army

British General Burgoyne surrendering to George Washington at Saratoga, October 1777. Daniel Morgan, whose riflemen emerged as the heroes of the battle, is depicted at center in white.

after Saratoga because he felt he was passed over for a promotion. But he was soon back in action, and finally received his appointment to brigadier general in 1780. A short time later, he became one of the Revolution's most important generals, one of the guys we probably couldn't have won independence without.

Morgan wasn't the only commander of riflemen in the war, and he didn't just lead riflemen, but he did both very well. Credit where credit is due: individual riflemen played a small but important role in skirmishes and battles all across the continent. And employing what we would now call guerilla tactics, their hit-and-run raids kept the British off-balance throughout.

But let's focus on Morgan and his crew. He had a bunch of riflemen besides our friend Murphy, who was back home north when Morgan returned to action down south. One of Morgan's troops was a fella you may *think* you've heard of, namely Sam Houston.

No, not *that* Sam Houston—this was his dad. Major Samuel Houston Sr. was an officer in Morgan's rifle brigade.

He was also my seventh great-grandfather on my mom's side. My dad's ancestors served in the Revolutionary and Civil Wars. They were rebels in the first, but picked the wrong side in the second.

By the winter of 1780–81, Dan Morgan had amassed a force of at least 1,900 Continental regulars, state troops, and militiamen, plus a small cavalry unit. His men hailed from South Carolina, Virginia, North Carolina, Maryland, Georgia, and Delaware. They had been given a simple task: raise as much hell among the British as they could in the Carolinas.

British Lieutenant General Charles Cornwallis had invaded the states in 1780 in an attempt to crush the rebellion in the South with the help of friendly American Tories and Native Americans. He did well at first, trouncing a rebel force under Horatio Gates and taking effective control of South Carolina. But as he expanded his campaign into North Carolina, the Revolutionary Army was able to regroup and slow his progress. In the meantime, small groups of rebels bit away at his supply lines, continually harassing him. The war behind the lines was ferocious in the South, just as it was in parts of the North; American Tories and American patriots massacred each other in small hand-to-hand encounters. Gruesome atrocities were the order of the day: scalping, hatcheting, spontaneous summary hangings, the slaughter of prisoners, you name it. It was a no–holds–barred kind of war.

As dirty and bloody as it may have been, the actions of one British commander in the south stood out as truly outrageous. Colonel Banastre Tarleton led the elite British Green Dragoons cavalry force, a small but highly effective unit of horsemen who moved with explosive speed and struck terror in American soldiers and civilians alike. By 1781, he was arguably the most hated man in America, a cold-blooded killer rebels called "the Butcher." The title wasn't propaganda. In his most notorious and controversial act, he had either ordered or stood by as his men slayed Americans attempting to surrender at Waxhaw Creek on the border of the Carolinas. Word of the massacre spread throughout the states; ironically, it helped turn the tides against the British, outraging many who'd been neutral in the war.

Whatever his morals, Tarleton was bold and audacious—and effective. At one point, in a daring raid deep behind American lines, he came within a whisker of capturing Thomas Jefferson and the entire Virginia legislature.

All this made him the perfect opponent for Morgan. Occupied in an ill-fated attempt to extend the Southern campaign to Virginia, Lord Cornwallis tasked Tarleton to find and destroy Dan Morgan and his unit operating in South Carolina.

For his part, Morgan was under orders only to harass the British with hit-and-run tactics, and to avoid the risks of an open battlefield confrontation. But Morgan knew the Butcher was hot on his trail, thirsting for blood, and about to catch up with him. So on January 16, 1781, with Tarleton closing in a few miles away, Dan Morgan decided to dig in to stand and fight in a field (or "cowpens") near Burr's Mill in South Carolina. That night, Morgan cooked up one of the most brilliant battle plans in American history, a masterpiece of combined arms, fire, and movement that featured the American long rifle in a starring role. It would go down in history as the Battle of Cowpens.

Dan Morgan's men likely were armed with a mix of muskets and frontier rifles, personal guns the militiamen would have used in their regular jobs as hunters, trappers, and farmers. That night, Morgan delivered an inspiring speech to his troops. One soldier recalled, "It was upon this occasion I was more perfectly convinced of Gen. Morgan's qualifications to command militia, than I had ever before been. He went among the volunteers, helped them fix their swords, joked with them about their sweet-hearts, told them to keep in good spirits, and the day would be ours. And long after I laid down, he was going about among the soldiers encouraging them, and telling them that [he] would crack his whip over [Tarleton] in the morning, as sure as they lived."

Folklore paints a rosy picture of the American militia, the part-time army of local farmers and the like. But truth be told, the militia's record through the Revolution was, to be polite, mixed. The majority of the American militia troops were ragtag, volunteer part-time soldiers who might panic, break, and run at the sight of a thousand enemy troops charging them with muskets, bayonets, and cavalry. Few had been trained to any degree of professionalism. Many didn't necessarily want to be on the battlefield in the first place, only answering the summons to serve out of a sense of duty, pride, and in a few cases, fear. Their time in the field was generally supposed to be measured in months, and even if they stayed on, their homes, farms, and families were never far from their minds.

Morgan told them their part in the battle would be short and sweet. All he needed them to do was hold formation for three volleys. Then, battle over, they would be released from service—and be called heroes, even.

"Just hold up your heads, boys, three fires," he said, "and you are free, and then when you return to your homes, how the old folks will bless you, and the girls kiss you, for your gallant conduct!"

Just three shots and you are free.

Nostalgic Currier & Ives prints depicting American militia men setting off for the Revolution.

Morgan's men chowed down on a hearty meal of butchered beef fresh from the pasture, stacked their guns, and tried to grab some shut-eye. Just before sunrise on January 17, Tarleton the Butcher and his 300 cavalry and 950 infantry troops fell into Morgan's trap.

Morgan knew of Tarleton's hair-trigger lust for the lightning-fast combat strike, so he constructed a plan that exploited the strengths and weaknesses of his own men, and the peculiar dynamics of the terrain at Cowpens. It all hinged on an elaborate trick, a stunning deception that required split-second timing by the Americans.

At dawn Tarleton emerged from the woods, saw the Americans, and quickly formed up his troops. Just as Morgan hoped, he lunged like a hound after a thick steak, barely waiting for all his men to arrive. The British were cold, dehydrated, and exhausted from a long, fast march, and they hadn't eaten or slept properly for days. But Banastre Tarleton saw his chance for a grand victory, one that would annihilate a good portion of the American southern army. His men played drums and fifes and cheered as they covered the length of three football fields in three minutes.

The British were, Morgan wrote a few days later, "running at us as if they intended to eat us up."

Morgan had laid his pieces on the battlefield like a chess master. He deployed his troops in three main formations—the first line made up of riflemen-sharpshooters, the second line of militia armed with rifles and muskets, then musket-armed regulars. They created what you could call "a defense-in-depth on high ground," or a "reverse slope defensive strategy." The idea was to goad Tarleton into a premature victory rush up a broadly sloping hill, where Morgan would snap the trap shut.

Morgan put his long-rifle snipers at the tip of the spear. Some one hundred and fifty sharpshooting riflemen from Georgia and the Carolinas scattered in swamps and behind trees, guerrilla-style. Following Morgan's plan, they opened fire individually at the advancing British from close range, with special attention given to the officers. Then, having blooded the enemy, they broke off and ran uphill toward the American lines, re-forming to commence long-range fire. With their slow reloading time and lack of bayonets, these soldiers had a special incentive to try to avoid close contact with the British regulars toting bayonet-tipped muskets.

The American second line, theoretically the riskiest bunch and the most likely to break, consisted of roughly 1,000 North and South Carolina militia troops.

They opened fire, as Morgan ordered, inflicting major damage on the royal troops who were less than forty yards away. Most of the Americans couldn't manage to pull off the three shots Morgan hoped for, and some could only manage one, but no matter. As a group, they turned their backs to the charging British and high-tailed up the hill, simulating a panicked retreat.

As intended, the sight of a broadly collapsing American line cheered Tarleton's remaining troops, who charged forward uphill—bloodied, weakened, and disorganized, not realizing that the third and final line was made up of five hundred battle-hardened regular American troops. These were General Dan Morgan's best men, the Maryland, Delaware, and Virginia continentals. These seasoned vets acted as a screen for the fleeing militia troops, who ran behind and through them, then about-faced and started re-forming into a new unseen fourth line preparing to face the British. Meanwhile a reserve American cavalry force of light dragoons under Colonel William Washington (second cousin of George) stood ready to pounce at the right moment.

The American third line opened fire in good order, leading one militia man to report, "When the regulars fired, it seemed like one sheet of flame from right to left. Oh! It was beautiful."

But suddenly, disaster appeared for the Americans.

In the chaos of combat, an order by American Lieutenant Colonel John Howard to his Virginia regulars to adjust their line to face the onrushing Scottish Highlanders of the 71st Regiment was misinterpreted as an order to retreat. Instead of wheeling to form a new line perpendicular to their unit, portions of the line withdrew, triggering a domino effect, and most of the American regulars started withdrawing. Colonel Howard later explained the catastrophe-in-progress: "Seeing my right flank was exposed to the enemy, I attempted to change the front of Wallace's company. In doing this, some confusion ensued, and first a part and then the whole of the company commenced a retreat. The officers along the line seeing this and supposing that orders had been given for a retreat, faced their men about and moved off."

To the British, it looked like yet another collapse of the American lines was under way, and they rushed forward, now in badly disconnected fragments.

This was not, however, part of the American plan, and it threatened to doom them on the battlefield.

But Morgan and two of his officers reacted instantly to the sudden crisis and created a new plan on the spot: stop the retreat, spin the whole line of five hundred Virginia regulars around, and blast the British from inside fifteen yards away, shooting muskets virtually from hip level.

"They are coming on like a mob!" declared cavalry leader Colonel Washington, sensing an opportunity to strike the British with a final blow. "Give them a fire," he called to Lieutenant Colonel Howard of the Virginia militia, "and I will charge them!"

Howard yelled for his troops to stop and about-face. They did exactly that. "In a minute we had a perfect line," recalled Howard. "The enemy were now very near us. Our men commenced a very destructive fire, which they little expected, and a few rounds occasioned great disorder in the ranks. While in this confusion, I ordered a charge with the bayonet, which order was obeyed with great alacrity." As Dan Morgan later explained, "We retired in good Order about 50 Paces, formed, advanced on the Enemy & gave them a fortunate Volley which threw them into Disorder."

At the same moment the Continentals fired, the American cavalry, until now held in reserve, appeared from behind the hill. They raced around the British and struck into their ranks. Simultaneously, the militia troops, having re-formed behind the screen of the regulars, jumped back into the fight, ripping away with musket and rifle fire into the British left flank. The exhausted British troops, stunned by the abrupt volley of fire and with their officer ranks withered by constant pressure from American long-rifle fire on their flanks, couldn't take the punishment.

Now it was the Brits' turn to panic and haul ass in the opposite direction. British Legion infantrymen fled. The Highlanders tried to form pockets in a doomed attempt to defend themselves, but their commander quickly ordered them to drop their guns in the dirt. Tarleton galloped onto the field and tried to rally his fleeing troops, briefly engaging in a mounted saber duel with the American cavalry. He soon realized it was hopeless and fled himself, barely escaping with his life. When he got back to British lines, he recommended that his boss court-martial him.

Dan Morgan had manipulated the enemy into a battlefield commander's dream of maneuver warfare: the double envelopment, first perfected by Hannibal against the Romans at the Battle of Cannae two thousand years earlier. As the chief of the nineteenth-century German General Staff Alfred von Schlieffen wrote, the "Cannae model" was a sure recipe for victory in battle: "The enemy front is not the goal of the principal attack. The mass of the troops and the reserves should not be concentrated against the enemy front; the essential is that the flanks be crushed. . . . To bring about a decisive and annihilating victory requires an attack against the front and against one or both flanks." At Cowpens, ol' Dan Morgan slammed the British in their left flank, their right flank, and their rear. It was a complete victory.

In the twenty-minute battle, Tarleton lost roughly a hundred men, about a third of them officers. Over eight hundred were taken prisoner. Less than fifty Americans were killed. The Americans captured Tarleton's cannon, supplies, and equipment, even his personal slaves. It was the worst psychological defeat for the British since Saratoga. Chief Justice John Marshall later wrote, "seldom has a battle, in which greater numbers were not engaged, been so important in its consequences as that of Cowpens." The Battle of Cowpens, wrote British historian Sir George Otto Trevelyan, led to "an unbroken chain of consequences to the catastrophe at Yorktown which finally separated America from the British crown."

Tarleton escaped, but neither he nor his commander were loose in America for much longer. In October 1781, sealed off from reinforcements by George Washington's army and the French navy, Cornwallis surrendered at Yorktown, Virginia. Benny the Butcher Tarleton escaped, returned to England, wrote a book, served in Parliament, and enjoyed a comfortable estate in retirement. Dan Morgan was awarded a special medal by the new U.S. Congress.

Original battle flag from the Battle of Cowpens.

I like to think of my ancestor Major Houston Sr. standing beside Dan Morgan as the redcoats surrendered. It's recorded that the Americans graciously treated the defeated British officers to a delicious feast to show their honor. If Major Houston was anything like me, he introduced those tea drinkers to venison steaks and American whiskey. Now, that's honorable.

Remember Tim Murphy, the sniper who killed General Fraser at Saratoga with a shot from his long rifle?

He was reported to be in the crowd of American soldiers who witnessed the surrender ceremony at Yorktown, when eight thousand British troops stacked their guns and a military band played "The World Turned Upside Down."

I bet he had a fat grin on his face.

When I was growing up, I heard a lot of different stories about Sam Houston Junior. Some of them weren't too good—you see, he earned a reputation among some folks as a general who ran away from the action during the Texas Revolution.

My ancestor, a coward?

Damn.

But if you check deeper into the story, you'll see that Sam—founding father of Texas—wasn't a coward at all, far from it. He was a hell of a crafty tactician and a master strategist. Though sometimes, as Dan Morgan proved at the Battle of Cowpens, running away from your enemy can turn out to be a good way to smash him right in the jaw.

Samuel Houston Sr. died when his son was fourteen years old. But I think it's entirely possible that father and son might have talked about what happened at Cowpens, and maybe—just maybe—that served as inspiration for what became Sam Houston's biggest moment on the battlefield in the spring of 1836.

In the decades after the Revolution, Americans kept pushing west—and took their long rifles with them every step of the way. They proved themselves on the frontier, and even did service in the War of 1812—not a particularly fun war for the U.S., though it at least showed Britain we wouldn't let them push us around without fighting back. Then between October 1835 and April 1836, long rifles and a host of other firearms starred in Texas settlers' bid to shake free from Mexico. In fact, the Texas Revolution was like a big gun show, showcasing the grab-bag assortment of weapons available on the open market at the time. It also offered a last snapshot of the old firearms designs that were soon to give way to new technologies. There is no good inventory of the guns used at these battles, but experts make educated guesses.

When Mexican dictator and president-general Antonio López de Santa Anna and his troops marched up to the Alamo in late February 1836 and began their epic thirteen-day siege, they outnumbered the fewer than two hundred rebellious Texas volunteers inside the fort by 10 to 1. Here and at the later Battle of San Jacinto, both sides would have been armed with European-patterned, muzzle-loading, single-shot, flintlock muskets like the English Brown Bess and some French models, too, plus Spanish-style *escopeta* short muskets and Spanish *pistolas* that would have featured the classic Miquelet lock.

The Texans would have had American long rifles, but also "blunderbuss" short-range muskets, carbines (a shorter version of the musket or rifle, often preferred by cavalry), bird guns, and some pistols here and there. The Texans may even have had a few guns featuring the new "caplock" or percussion-cap firing mechanism, which was a big improvement on the flintlock because it replaced the troublesome flash pan and flint with a sturdy, waterproof copper cap that triggered a spark when it was struck. Toss in some Bowie knives, tomahawks, and Belduques (a long fighting knife similar to the Bowie), and you've got yourself a gang that can really do some damage.

During the Battle of the Alamo, one legendary American long-rifleman was spotted on the wall by Captain Rafael Soldana of the Mexican Army. The "tall man with flowing hair" on the wall wore "a buckskin suit with a cap all of a pattern entirely different from those worn by his comrades. This man would rest his long gun and fire, and we all learned to keep a good distance when he was seen to make ready to shoot. He rarely missed his mark, and when he fired, he always rose to his feet and calmly reloaded his gun, seemingly indifferent to the shots fired at him by our men. He had a strong, resonant voice and often railed at us."

Soldana later learned the man was known as "Kwockey"—the national celebrity frontiersman and former congressman Davy Crockett.

After almost two weeks of siege, Mexicans punched through the Alamo's flimsy defenses and killed or massacred all but two of the Texan defenders of the Alamo, including Crockett. A month later, when General Santa Anna ordered the cold-blooded bayonet-and-bullet massacre of 353 more Texan prisoners near Goliad on Palm Sunday, March 27, terrified Texas civilians started fleeing eastward.

The panicked exodus was called the Runaway Scrape, and Texas General Sam Houston assumed the role of Skedaddler-in-Chief. Day after day, Sam led his troops eastward, away from Santa Anna, moving as fast as he could in the direction of Louisiana. Texas politicians were appalled, as were some of Sam's own troops. They publicly wondered if he was a coward.

But Houston was just biding his time, looking for an opening to turn around and strike. The deeper Santa Anna marched into Texas, the more worn out his troops and equipment got. Camped near the meeting of the San Jacinto River and the Buffalo Bayou, Santa Anna decided it was time for a siesta on the afternoon of April 21, 1836. He forgot to post sentries. His men lay snoozing as a burly, mangy-looking Sam Houston

"The King of the Wild Frontier": Born in
Tennessee, Davy Crockett died, long rifle in hand,
defending the Alamo in 1836.

and his more than eight hundred Texans and their allies snuck up through the cover of a forested hill, led by a contingent of uniformed Kentucky riflemen. "Now hold your fire, men," Houston cautioned, "until you get the order!"

It was time for payback, Texas-style.

Screaming "Remember the Alamo!" and "Remember Goliad!" the Texans overwhelmed the Mexicans in a mere eighteen minutes, enough time for Sam Houston to lose two horses—both shot out from under him—and sustain a bad gunshot wound to the ankle.

The Texans were in no mood for mercy and unleashed a full-scale slaughter. No one was spared, not even the wounded or soldiers trying to surrender. "Take prisoners like the Meskins do!" shouted one Texan, and scores of Mexicans were shot to pieces after surrendering, or hunted down in the river and clubbed to death while pleading "Me no Alamo!" or "Me no Goliad!" A horrified Sam Houston tried to stop the massacre, shouting "Parade! Parade!" in a vain attempt to call his men back to form a dress formation and leave off killing. By the time the butchery stopped, a total of 630 Mexicans died that day, versus nine Texans.

The people of Texas were jubilant, grasping that independence was theirs. A messenger raced into one refugee camp on the Sabine River waving his hat and

Sam Houston—and his long rifle—
accept Santa Anna's surrender.

shouting, "San Jacinto! San Jacinto! The Mexicans are whipped and Santa Anna a prisoner!" A lady named Kate Scurry Terrell witnessed the reaction and wrote: "The scene that followed beggars description. People embraced, laughed and wept and prayed, all in one breath. As the moon rose over the vast flower-decked prairie, the soft southern wind carried peace to tired hearts and grateful slumber."

When Santa Anna was captured, he asked Sam Houston to "be generous to the vanquished."

Houston told the prisoner curtly, "You should have remembered that, sir, at the Alamo." Santa Anna would eventually be shipped off to Washington; he later returned to Mexico and in fact would go to war twice more, against France and finally against the U.S.

The epic revenge-victory at the Battle of San Jacinto marked the birth of a free American Texas, and it altered the fate of three republics: Mexico, Texas, and the United States, then a country barely fifty years old. Mexico was forced to sign a withdrawal and peace treaty three weeks later that conferred legitimacy on the new Republic of Texas. Mexico never ruled Texas again, despite periodic raids in the 1840s. The United States absorbed the Republic of Texas in 1845, plus more Mexican land after the Mexican War in 1848.

If you drive about twenty-five miles southeast of downtown Houston today, you'll come across the 570-foot-tall San Jacinto Monument, the world's tallest memorial column. (Everything's bigger in Texas, right?) The inscription reads, in part: "Measured by its results, San Jacinto was one of the decisive battles of the world. The freedom of Texas from Mexico won here led to annexation and to the Mexican-American War, resulting in the acquisition by the United States of the states of Texas, New Mexico, Arizona, Nevada, California, Utah and parts of Colorado, Wyoming, Kansas and Oklahoma. Almost one-third of the present area of the American Nation, nearly a million square miles of territory, changed sovereignty."

Not a bad day's work for Sam Houston and his riflemen.

The battles of the Alamo and San Jacinto were crossroads battles, fought on the edges of several great eras of gun technology, when the flintlock was destined to give way to the caplock, the single-shot to revolving and repeating guns, and the muzzle-loader to the breechloader.

By the time it left the stage, the American long rifle helped give birth to a new nation. Generations of men and guns would now rise to save the United States from tearing itself apart, and raise it to a place of glory.

2

The Spencer Repeater

"What kind of Hell-fired guns have your men got?"

—*Anonymous Confederate prisoner, 1863*

braham Lincoln was thinking about guns.

It was a clear, beautiful morning in the spring of 1861, and the recently elected President had two things on his mind—firearms, and the survival of the United States of America. So he left the hubbub of the White House, with its long line of petitioners and politicians, and went out to do some target shooting. Walking into a weed-and-garbage-strewn field east of the White House that served as his personal gun-testing range, he took stock of his weapons, a pair of new-fangled long guns. Both purported to let a man fire several shots before he had to stop and reload. That was a powerful promise under any circumstances, but especially on the field of battle. It was a promise that, if kept, could determine the course of the Civil War and help preserve the Union.

The weapons of war had evolved in the four score and odd years since independence had been won, but they would have still been recognizable to anyone who'd marched at Yorktown. The primary weapon of the U.S. Army and the recently formed Confederacy were smooth-bore muskets like the Springfield Model 1842. Unlike their Revolutionary War forebears, these modern muskets used percussion locks. In a flintlock, as you may recall, a piece of flint held in the hammer is struck to make a spark, creating a fire in a pan of fine priming powder, which in turn ignites the gunpowder charge and sends the bullet flying. Anyone who's tried to light a match in the middle of a rainstorm knows the downside to that. Damp primer, wet powder, a worn flint—so many steps almost guarantee complications.

It might not have been foolproof, but the percussion cap simplified the process, making the gun less vulnerable to bad weather and random voodoo. A hammer hit a small cap, causing the material it held to explode.

(That mercury fulminate your chemistry teacher warned you about was used as a primer at the time.) The explosion ignites the gunpowder charge, and off we go.

Increasing the dependability and simplicity of infantry weapons was an important step in the evolution of firearms, but other improvements were needed. The most obvious was accuracy. Bullets fired from smoothbore muskets were notoriously fickle. To have any chance at all of striking his opponent, a soldier had to get pretty close to him. That's not a popular activity on a battlefield.

Rifles were a solution. Loading bullets into a rifled barrel became much easier with the invention of the Minié-ball. Named after its inventor, the French gunmaker Claude-Étienne Minié, the cone-shaped projectile fit loosely enough to be easily inserted down a rifled muzzle. Its hollowed lead base expanded once the gun was fired, snugging it up against the barrel. The bullets had a side benefit—or a side horror, depending on whether you were on the receiving end of one or not. The .58-caliber projectile common at the time flattened and deformed on impact, shredding organs and bones and tearing out gaping exit wounds. Given the state of battlefield medicine at the time, the Minié-ball was truly an angel of death.

Muzzle-loading Springfield and British-made Enfield muskets were the dominant infantry weapons during the Civil War. Above: "20 Enfield Muskets" reads the writing on the crates in this Confederate arsenal. Below, Union troops pose with identical weapons.

Rifle-muskets such as the Springfield 1861 and the 1853 Enfield quickly became the mass-produced standard infantry gun as the conflict revved up. By the time Lincoln went out that fine morning, both North and South were trying to get as many of them as they could. But there's one thing every soldier knows: the quicker your reload time, the better your odds of living to fight another day. Ol' Abe had spent a bit of time in the militia during the Black Hawk War, and I suspect that lesson was still fresh in his mind some thirty years later out on the White House lawn. The weapons he was testing were capable of firing several rounds before a soldier had to stop and reload.

The first gun Lincoln picked up was believed to be a Henry Repeater. It was a lever-action rifle that could reliably fire sixteen shots in stunning succession using a tube magazine that ran down beneath the barrel of the gun to the breech. It could be loaded relatively fast through an opening at the end of the tube.

The weapon had been manufactured by the New Haven Arms Company. New Haven had been purchased by a man named Oliver Winchester a few years before. Winchester was pretty wily for a Yankee; he'd bought the company for a song from two guys named

Smith & Wesson when they hit financial problems in 1857. We'll come back to Misters Smith & Wesson later.

Oliver Winchester had made his money manufacturing shirts. It's said that he didn't know all that much about guns, but he certainly understood a lot about manufacturing, which in mid-eighteenth-century America was more important. And he also must have been a good judge of talent, because he quickly entrusted a man named Benjamin Tyler Henry with improving the factory's most promising but tempermental product, the Volcanic repeating rifle.

Henry made a host of improvements to the design, but the most important was arguably in the type of ammo it packed. The Volcanic repeater fired a Rocket ball. The bullet was similar to a Minié-ball, except that the hollow base was filled with powder, then sealed with a primer cap. The closed metallic cartridge gave the gun a complete piece of ammunition. Unfortunately, the small size of the bullet limited the size of the charge; the bullet didn't have quite enough pop for the bloody but necessary business of killing an enemy on the battlefield.

Henry changed that by providing his repeater with a hefty rim-fire cartridge. His copper cartridge fit some twenty-five grains of powder behind a 216 grain, .44-caliber bullet. It had pop to spare.

Back at the target range near the White House, Lincoln was impressed by the Henry. The multi-shot, fast-loading rifle was a potential game-changer for the Union army. It took about half a minute to reload; a soldier could then squeeze off another sixteen shots as fast as he could jerk the lever back and forth. There were downsides—among others, you had to move your hand out of the way of the cartridge follower after a few shots, and the barrel got awful hot if you shot fast and long enough. Still, it was an exciting weapon with a lot of potential.

After firing the Henry, Lincoln gazed at the plank of wood he'd perforated with a contented smile. The repeater concept was sound, the execution good. Lincoln's aide, William O. Stoddard, handed him a second weapon. This was a modified Springfield smoothbore musket that used a screw-on adapter to feed nine high-powered rounds into a breech, rather than a single round rammed down the muzzle. It was called a Marsh rifle, after its inventor, Samuel Marsh.

As the president was kneeling down to line up a shot, a voice began cursing loudly behind them. "Stop that firing!" bellowed a pissed off man in uniform. Trailed by four enlisted soldiers, the captain marched toward the two amateur civilian marksmen who were not only interrupting the peaceful Washington, D.C., morning, but were violating a presidential order forbidding shooting in the capital city. Swearing up a storm—cussin' like some Navy SEALs I know—the captain reached his hand out as if to confiscate the guns and arrest the shooters. It looked like the Second Amendment was about to face its very first challenge in Washington, D.C.

Lincoln peered down the barrel and squeezed the trigger. Then, smiling shyly, he rose from the ground.

"Here comes the fun!" thought Stoddard, watching his boss get up. Or as Stoddard put it later, "Lincoln's tall, gaunt form shoots up, up, up, uncoiling to its full height, and his smiling face looks down upon the explosive volunteers.

"Their faces, especially that of the sergeant . . . look up at his, and all their jaws seem to drop in unison. No word of command is uttered, but they 'right about face' in a second of time. Now it is a double-quick, quicker, quicker, as they race back toward the avenue, leaving behind them only a confused, suppressed breath about having 'cussed Old Abe himself.' His own laugh, in his semi-silent, peculiar way, is long and hearty, but his only remark is:

"Well, they might [have] stayed to see the shooting. . . ."

Abe Lincoln was a gun buff and a technology whiz. Other presidents before him—including George Washington, Thomas Jefferson, and Andrew Jackson—were highly gun-savvy, as were most Americans at a time when the nation was primarily rural. But Lincoln took presidential involvement with gun technology to a new level. Fiddling with another experimental repeating gun on his firing range one day, he shot off a few rounds, then announced, "I believe I can make this gun shoot better." He produced a hand-whittled wooden sight from his vest pocket, clamped it on the rifle, and let loose at a piece of congressional stationery pinned more than eighty yards away. He hit the paper almost a dozen times out of fourteen.

Another time, Lincoln showed up at a target practice for the 2nd U.S. Sharpshooters, one of the few specialized Union marksmen units. He borrowed a rifle from one of the surprised soldiers in Company F and scored three good shots as the men whooped and hollered. A witness reported that Lincoln "handled the rifle like a veteran marksman, in a highly successful manner, to the great delight of the many soldiers and civilians surrounding."

"Boys," said the President to the cheering troops, "this reminds me of old-time shooting!" Now, that's a

President Abraham Lincoln (directly below flag) observes
Union troops in front of the White House.

commander in chief any combat vet would be proud to
serve.

Lincoln was also a man who loved machines of all
kinds. Abe liked to roll up his sleeves, get dirty, and
take contraptions apart. He scoured magazines like
Scientific American for the latest technology. He was
the first chief executive to embrace telegraph communication. He personally heard pitches from gun inventors and entrepreneurs, tested products, reviewed plans
and machinery, and battled bureaucrats. Abe pushed
his underlings for research and development, threw his
weight and opinions around like a seasoned CEO, and

managed the equivalent of a multimillion-dollar fire-arms investment fund through the U.S. military. He was a venture capitalist of weaponry.

Lincoln seems to have admired the Henry Repeater he fired that spring morning, putting him in line with a lot of soldiers. As the war progressed, many would dig into the patched pockets of their woolen pants to purchase a Henry for themselves. Officers would outfit whole units with them, raiding the family treasury in hopes of giving their men an edge in combat. But Lincoln eventually turned his favor to a rival model—the Spencer Repeater. He did this even though his own experiment with the gun was something of a failure: Testing two models supplied by the Navy, he had one misfeed and the other lock up after a double feed. Reports by others who raved about the gun apparently convinced Lincoln that his experiences were just flukes, and so it was the Spencer's manufacturer, Sharps, that got the prized Union contract to supply 10,000 repeat-ers later in 1861.

Named after its inventor, Christopher Spencer, the repeater was a marvel of both advanced design and (comparative) simplicity. Handling this weapon or even a replica today, you can sense the careful smithing as soon as you pick it up. It has weight to it, and when you move the trigger guard down, the smooth action of

Cavalry Carbines
1: Model 1865 .52 Spencer carbine
2a: Sprung loading tube
2b: Blakeslee cartridge box

the metal components, all expertly fitted, reminds you of a fine watch.

The Spencer fired a .52-caliber metallic rimfire cartridge. Seven cartridges fit into its magazine, which loaded through the back of the weapon's stock. Using an innovative dropping-block design and lever action, all seven rounds could be quickly and accurately fired. When you pulled down on the trigger guard, the breech opened and the spent cartridge was ejected. Push the guard back on up and the new cartridge slipped into place, ready to fly. Spare magazines could be kept ready for speedy loading in combat. Sharing parts with the single-fire Sharps rifle—another classic American gun—it was easy to manufacture, and proved very reliable in field tests and in combat.

But like presidents before and after him, Lincoln would soon find that executive power was often more theory than promise. Even though his War Department placed initial orders of 25,000 of the Marsh guns and 10,000 seven-shot Spencer Repeaters before the end of 1861, they didn't reach Union troops. Or anyone else.

If I were writing this up as fiction, I might spin a yarn about a daring Confederate attack against the factory, complete with 1860s-style special ops work, fine explosions, and general pandemonium. But the Rebs had nothing to do with it.

No, a Yankee was responsible for sabotaging Lincoln's plans to get modern technology into the hands of his men. And not only was he on the Union's side, he was one of its highest ranking officers.

Head shed'll get you every time.

James Ripley was an ultrapowerful bureaucratic monster, a cantankerous, backward-looking, sixty-seven-year-old Northern Army general. He was the chief of Army procurement, and he was a wizard of red tape, delay, and obfuscation. Truth be told, he was also a master at supply logistics and standardizing artillery ammunition, but he was an idiot when it came to guns. He hated breech-loading weapons, even the superb Sharps rifle, considering them "newfangled gimcracks." And he absolutely detested repeating rifles like the Spencer Repeater. By his convoluted logic, soldiers would only waste ammunition with a multi-shot gun. He wasn't crazy about the prices, either: he could buy good muskets for $18 each from multiple vendors, but a Spencer Repeater was $40.

Through the end of 1861 and much of 1862, General Ripley conducted a one-man mutiny of disobedience and delay against President Lincoln, General-in-Chief George McClellan, and many other officers and regular troops who were begging for breechloaders and repeaters. He refused to approve production orders, threw

Ambrose Burnside leads Union forces at Bull Run, 1861.
The blinding layer of smoke was typical of Civil War
battles fought with black-powder muskets.

gun inventors out of his office, and repeatedly slow-tracked Lincoln's orders. Lincoln couldn't fire him, because Ripley had powerful friends on Capitol Hill. The delays and the threat of a patent suit sunk Marsh's gun and his company, rendering him and his weapon a footnote to history. And what would have been the largest order for breech-loading rifles to that point was never fulfilled.

Some historians accuse Ripley of dooming many thousands of American troops to unnecessary carnage and death by prolonging the war. I'm inclined to agree. Thanks to the untalented Mr. Ripley, hardly any breechloaders or repeaters were in the hands of Union forces by the end of 1862, a full year and a half after the President's early tests. Pretty much the only repeaters in Unions hands at all came from a small order for Spencers by the Navy, which was out of Ripley's reach, and the guns soldiers bought themselves.

I suppose you could take Ripley's side by saying he had no way of knowing how long the war would go, or what gun platforms would gain traction. Besides worrying about paying for everything— a unique and unusual concern for a government official, in my experience—he was also trying to avoid the headache of figuring out new supply pipelines to feed multiple forms of ammunition to the far-flung troops.

But let's face it: the guy was a threat to national security.

Luckily for America, Lincoln eventually managed to fire him, aided in part by an anti-Ripley revolt that erupted in 1862 as some units demanded to be armed with the latest guns, especially the Sharps rifle.

The Sharps was a breech-loading, single-shot, percussion-cap rifle that a trained soldier could load and fire up to ten times a minute, or three times faster

CALIFORNIA JOE, OF THE BERDAN SHARP-SHOOTERS.—[From a Photograph.]

The most celebrated member of Berdan's Sharpshooters, "California Joe" (aka Truman Head), and his 1859 Sharps rifle. Below: A Union recruiting poster seeking "the best rifle shots."

than a Springfield. A sleek forty-seven inches long, a trained marksman could reliably hit targets at six hundred yards or more with it. The gun was easy to handle and reliable, and it became a favorite of civilians as well as professionals heading toward the frontier. "The Sharps mechanism made the gun so easy to use, anyone could fire it and stand a fairly good chance of hitting something—or someone," wrote historian Alexander Rose.

Even more popular in the Army was a carbine version, which featured a shorter barrel—which is, after all, the main difference between a "rifle" and a "carbine." The highly accurate and easy-to-carry weapon was a favorite with mounted cavalry, both North and South. It should be said that one of the reasons the Sharps was liked by soldiers was its reliability. The gun was well-designed and well-made. The quality of manufacturing was one reason for the higher price; you get what you pay for. Ripley might not have thought so, but the less-well-produced Southern clones proved the point. They didn't hold up nearly as well.

That's one of the things historians are talking about when they write that the North's manufacturing abilities won the war. The days of hand-built guns were past. Armies were now too big to be supplied by a handful of craftsmen toiling away in local workshops.

An industrial base and skilled factory workers were nearly as important to winning a battle as great generals were.

The precision of the Sharps meant that marksmen could play an important role in the battle. Special units were created. Among the most effective were Colonel Hiram Berdan's 1st and 2nd U.S. Sharpshooters regiments, whose weapons of choice were the Sharps rifles. These specialized, highly trained marksmen, skirmishers, and long-range snipers wore green camouflage, and, thanks to the easy-loading Sharps design, shot safely from concealed positions, such as flat on the ground or from behind trees. They also carried rifles equipped with the earliest telescopic sights.

To qualify to join the elite unit, you had to be able to put ten shots inside a ten-inch-wide circle from two hundred yards. The Sharpshooters gave the Union army a powerful combat edge and fought effectively in many major battles of the Civil War, including Mechanicsville, Gaines's Mill, the Second Battle of Bull Run, Shepherdstown, Antietam, Gettysburg, Yorktown, Vicksburg, Chattanooga, Atlanta, Spotsylvania, and Petersburg.

But as fine a weapon as the Sharps and other breechloaders from the period may have been, in my opinion the real badass infantry weapon of the Civil War was the Spencer Repeater. And in early 1863, it made its first big appearance on the battlefield. It was a shocking debut.

By now, small batches of at least 7,500 Spencers had made it into the regular Army pipeline, and some commanders were even shelling out their own money to equip their units with the gun. One Colonel John T. Wilder of Indiana was so impressed by a field demonstration of Spencers that he lined up a loan from his neighborhood bank to buy more than a thousand Spencer repeating rifles for his "Lightning Brigade" of mounted infantry.

Colonel Wilder's commander was Major General William S. Rosecrans, whose Army of the Cumberland was tasked to rout the Rebs from Middle Tennessee. Though slow to move against Confederate General Braxton Bragg and his Army of Tennessee, once Rosecrans got moving he did so with style. In the last days of spring 1863, Rosecrans began a series of maneuvers that are still studied today for their near flawless execution. Wilder and his men, now armed with those Spencers he financed, were smack in the middle.

The brigade was a one-off outfit, a hybrid of cavalry and infantry at a time when those two forces were very

Possibly a member of Colonel Wilder's "Lightning Brigade" of mounted infantry—armed with a Spencer rifle.

separate animals. Colonel Wilder was a bit of a different beast himself. Hailing from New York's Catskill Mountains, he commanded a collection of infantry units totaling some fifteen hundred foot soldiers, along with a detachment of artillery. His first assignment was to run down a rebel cavalry unit that had made mincemeat of Rosecrans' supply line. You don't need to know much about combat to guess how that went; pretty much every horse I've seen is faster than any man I've met. Wilder came away from the assignment a wee bit frustrated.

But from that setback came a solution—he asked permission to mount his infantry. Wilder wasn't transforming his brigade into horse soldiers. He wanted a force that could move at lightning speed, then dismount and fight. And when he said fight, he meant *fight*. Besides the repeaters, he armed his men with long-handled axes for hand-to-hand combat. Here was an officer who fully understood the phrase *violence of action*.

Colonel Wilder also appreciated the meaning of the word *charge*, which is what he did on June 24, 1863, when tasked to take Hoover's Gap, a key pass Rosecrans needed to outmaneuver his enemy. Wilder's men slammed through the gap like a bronc busting out of its gate. They routed the 1st Kentucky Cavalry, then pushed well ahead of the main body of infantry they were spearheading.

The Rebs counterattacked ferociously, sending two infantry brigades and artillery against the Northerners. Though badly outnumbered, Wilder's men held their ground. The volume of fire poured out by the Spencers—nearly 142 rounds per man—was so large that the Confederates thought they were facing an entire army corps. The rebel lines collapsed into retreat.

"Hoover's Gap was the first battle where the Spencer Repeating Rifle had ever been used," Wilder later wrote, "and in my estimation they were better weapons than has yet taken their place, being strong and not easily injured by the rough usage of army movements, and carrying a projectile that disabled any man who was unlucky enough to be hit by it." He added, "No line of men, who come within fifty yards of another armed with Spencer Repeating Rifles can either get away alive, or reach them with a charge, as in either case they are certain to be destroyed by the terrible fire poured into their ranks by cool men thus armed. My men feel as if it is impossible to be whipped, and the confidence inspired by these arms added to their terribly destructive capacity, fully quadruples the effectiveness of my command."

One of Wilder's soldiers wrote of the Spencer that it "never got out of repair. It would shoot a mile just as accurately as the finest rifle in the world. It was the easiest gun to handle in the manual of arms drill I have ever seen. It could be taken all to pieces to clean, and hence was little trouble to keep in order—quite an item to lazy soldiers."

"Those Yankees have got rifles that won't quit shootin' and we can't load fast enough to keep up," said a Confederate soldier who was on the losing end of the Battle of Hoover's Gap. After another Tennessee battle, a Confederate prisoner asked his captors, "What kind of Hell-fired guns have your men got?"

The performance of the Spencer Repeater that June day in Tennessee marked the true dawn of the multiple-shot infantry gun, an era that would dominate the battlefield of the twentieth and twenty-first centuries.

A week after Hoover's Gap, North and South faced off in an epic battle destined to be remembered for centuries. It was the Battle of Gettysburg, and while the vast majority of guns fired there were rifle-muskets, breechloaders and repeaters appeared at critical moments to help tip the scales in favor of the North.

Fighting was reaching its climax on the third day of the battle, July 3, 1863, when Confederate General James Ewell Brown "Jeb" Stuart and his legendary cavalry force prepared to smash deep into the rear of the Union forces guarding Cemetery Ridge. Stuart's maneuver was intended to support the Rebs' frontal assault on the Ridge, flanking the Northerners and cutting their supply lines. If Stuart's cavalry managed to penetrate the Union rear, there was a good chance that Union General George Meade would be forced to siphon off troops and leave the main force disastrously exposed to what is now known as Pickett's Charge.

The only thing between Stuart and the vulnerable Union rear was a cavalry division commanded by General David McMurtrie Gregg. His forces included

An artist's depiction of the vast Gettysburg battle scene.
Union troops armed with the newly adopted Spencer
Repeaters held their own against the Rebel flank, helping
keep the main force intact to repel Pickett's Charge.

a brigade of cavalry temporarily attached to his command and led by the Union Army's newest and youngest general, twenty-four-year-old George Armstrong
Custer. Custer has gone down in history as a peacock
of a leader, a commander who dressed so flamboyantly
that one observer compared him to "a circus rider gone
mad." He's also considered a ridiculously bold general,
rash or daring depending on your point of view. But no

matter how you look at it, he had courage and guts in spades.

Even more important than courage and guts on that day were the Spencer repeating rifles in the hands of the dismounted 5th and 6th Michigan Cavalry brigades that were part of Custer's command. They bore the brunt of Stuart's attack at Rummel Farm. Stuart's idea was to plow through the skirmishers and plunge into the weak underbelly of the left side of the Union line. He might have done it, too, had the Michigan men not been equipped with Spencers. Their ferocious fire turned the Confederates back. Finally Stuart decided to send the 1st Virginia Cavalry down their necks. Exhausted by nearly two hours of fighting, the Blues buckled and were overwhelmed. The thin skirmish line broke.

Gregg ordered a counterattack to turn back the Rebel swarm. Shouting, "Come on, you Wolverines!," Custer personally led the 7th Michigan Cavalry against the Rebs. Horse flew at horse, man at man. Bullets were followed by sabers, then knives, then fists. Men fought with every breath and heartbeat they had. Custer's horse was shot out from under him. He grabbed another. As one historian noted, it was "the most dramatic, largest man-to-man, horse-to-horse, saber-to-saber galloping cavalry engagement ever fought in the Western

Hemisphere and the final horse battle fought on a scale of this magnitude in the entire world."

It was also the end of Stuart's assault; his goal of out-flanking the Union lines had failed. Pickett's Charge collapsed later that afternoon.

Gettysburg, like many large battles, was a series of turning points, decisions, and movements made and not made. Any one of them might have changed the course of history. Take away the Union Spencers and maybe Jeb Stuart gets far enough to ruin the Yankee defense. Then maybe Pickett's charge gets through . . .

Any way you think about it, those Spencer Repeaters proved that volume of fire was one important key to winning a battle that's been called a turning point of the Civil War.

Back in the White House, President Lincoln learned of the superb performance of the Spencers in combat, and decided he wanted to take another crack at shooting the gun himself.

Christopher M. Spencer arrived at the White House on August 18, 1863, bearing a new rifle as a gift. Take it apart, Lincoln suggested, and show me the "inwardness of the thing."

Spencer complied. The next day, the two men went out to Lincoln's target range to do some shooting. With the inventor personally demonstrating the mechanism and the four basic movements to load and fire, the Spencer performed beautifully for the president.

Lincoln cradled the rifle, lined up his shot, and fired from forty yards away. He hit the bull's-eye on his second try, and, rapidly cranking the lever, placed four more shots close by. The inventor shot even better.

"Well," said Lincoln good-naturedly, "you are younger than I am, have a better eye and a steadier nerve."

Lincoln's secretary wrote in his diary, "This evening and yesterday evening an hour was spent by the President in shooting with Spencer's new repeating rifle. A wonderful gun, loading with absolutely contemptible simplicity and ease with seven balls & firing the whole readily & deliberately in less than half a minute. The President made some pretty good shots."

Lincoln and the inventor parted with hearty handshakes. Now that Lincoln was personally convinced of their effectiveness, the Union military put through purchase orders that would eventually bring nearly 100,000 Spencer carbines and rifles into the Union armories and onto the shoulders of its troops. Don't be too impressed by that number, though. It's a tiny thing compared to the roughly two million total Union muzzle-loading rifle-muskets in the field.

Late in the war, Major General James H. Wilson led an audacious raid through Alabama and Georgia to defeat the infamous— though innovative—General Nathan Bedford Forrest at Selma, Alabama. Forrest was a scourge of the Union. He took mobile warfare to new heights and is reputed to have even killed one of his own officers following a "discussion" over orders. To beat Forrest, Wilson relied not just on superior numbers but a large number of Spencers. Using the rifle as an early "force multiplier" and employing tactics nearly as aggressive as Forrest's, the Northern general managed to break the Confederate defenses at Selma, sending the better part of the militia there running. That forced Forrest to sue for surrender, and in effect ended the war in that section of the Deep South. Wilson gave full credit to the gun that got him there.

"There is no doubt that the Spencer carbine is the best fire-arm yet put into the hands of the soldier," wrote the Northern general, "both for economy of ammunition and maximum effect, physical and moral. Our best officers estimate one man armed with it [is] equivalent to three with any other arm. I have never seen anything else like the confidence inspired by it in the regiments or brigades which have it. A common belief amongst them is if their flanks are covered they can go anywhere. I have seen a large number of dismounted charges made with them against cavalry, infantry, and breast-works, and never knew one to fail."

Historians have argued that without the Union's Spencers, the war would have gone on another six months more, with tens of thousands of additional fatalities on both sides. That point puts me in mind of a simple but I think obvious question: What would have happened if more advanced weapons like the Spencer and Sharps had been adopted earlier in the war? If our friend General Ripley had not been around to delay and doom Abe Lincoln's early wishes, would the bloodiest war in our nation's history have ended sooner?

I'm not the only one who's given that some thought. A number of soldiers on both sides expressed the opinion that the Spencer or another multiple-shot, easy-firing gun would have turned the tide earlier on. Some of their comments are the sort of exaggeration you hear about Texas weather—for instance, a Michigan cavalry officer who served under Custer at Gettysburg was said to claim that Spencers would have ended the war in ninety days. But even a respected Civil War scholar like Robert Bruce thinks that advanced rifle technology would have had a huge impact on the war.

This assumes (maybe overoptimistically) that the Northern generals could have adapted their tactics to the new weapons fairly quickly. The rifle-musket was an improvement over the Revolutionary War–era musket, but both firearms led generals to mass their troops in tight lines where their inaccurate fire could be effective. That in turn dictated a series of other decisions and tactics.

You can criticize the generals for being stuck in old and inefficient ways of thinking, but step back in their boots and you start to see the world from a whole different perspective.

The average soldier in the Civil War had scant firearms training. A good number probably never even knew that their rifled weapons sent their bullets in a parabolic arc, often over their target. Then again, individual targets were often impossible to pick out through the smoke-curtained battlefield. Most of the infantrymen on both sides simply pointed their gun in the general direction of the enemy and prayed they hit something when they fired.

Change the technology and you have to change the training that goes along with it. Or more correctly, initiate some, since weapons training at the time was poor to nonexistent. A few weeks of basic work with the weapons would have done it, so long as General

Ripley or one of his minions wasn't standing by *tsk-tsk*ing about the number of bullets being "wasted" in practice.

The end result would have been an army of men who could hit what they were firing at, more or less, from a greater distance at a much faster rate of speed than the enemy. Given that, you could alter your tactics appropriately. The possibilities are endless with that sort of advantage. Small, mobile forces emphasizing speed like the cavalry or mounted infantry would have played an even bigger role in the fight. I know I'm expressing my prejudices as a SEAL—what are special-operations forces but mobile and fast? Still, the success of such units throughout the war practically makes the argument for me. Spencer Repeaters would have shortened the war, maybe by a lot.

But there is an old saying that's worth remembering: Be careful what you wish for. Meaning, there's no way to tell what the future will bring. Alter one thing, and a host of others will change. Good, bad, somewhere in the middle.

Mr. Bruce, who won the Pulitzer Prize for history, put it this way: "If a large part of the Union Army had been given breech-loaders by the end of 1862," he speculated, "Gettysburg would certainly have ended the war. More likely, Chancellorsville, or even

Fredericksburg would have done it, and history would record no Gettysburg address, no President Grant, perhaps no carpetbag reconstruction or Solid South. Instead, it might have had the memoirs of ex-President Lincoln, perhaps written in retirement during the administration of President Burnside or Hooker." So who knows?

A friend of a good friend of mine by the name of John Navaro has shot any number of weapons from the period. Mr. Navaro is your basic weapons expert. He's worked for movies, television shows, and the like. If you've watched *Walker, Texas Ranger,* and paid any attention to the weapons the characters are packing, you've seen his work—he's the prop and weapons master responsible for getting it right. He also does a fair amount of historical reenacting as a hobby.

John really likes the Spencer, calling it a "gun before its time." But he pointed out that maybe, just maybe, its real advantage was psychological. The way he puts it, knowing that the gun gave you more shots than your opponent couldn't help but boost your morale. "Stronger, bolder—you just felt like you were going to come out on top," he says. That edge is important to a fighter, especially someone in the cavalry where the tactics demand that the troopers be aggressive and hard-charging.

You can't win a war in your head, but if your head ain't right, you've got no chance at all.

The Civil War was the world's last muzzleloader war. By its end, breechloaders increasingly dominated the battlefield. The potential of multiple-shot rifles was also clear. The Spencer Repeater anticipated some of the watershed gun platforms that would arrive in the future, like the automatic rifle, magazine-feeders, self-loading rifles, and the Tommy gun.

But while it helped end the Civil War, the Spencer would not have a major role in the next great American challenge, the winning of the great frontier. Two other revolutionary firearms stepped up to meet the challenges posed by the wild American West.

3

The Colt Single-Action Army Revolver

"The good people of this world are very far from being satisfied with each other and my arms are the best peacemakers."

—*Samuel Colt, 1852*

O n the morning of June 8, 1844, a Texas Ranger spotted a beehive up in a tree near a creek in the Hill Country of central Texas. With the scent of honey tempting his taste buds, the young lawman climbed the branches halfway up to inspect the bounty. Then he froze.

"Captain," shouted the Ranger to his commander on the ground, the legendary Texas Ranger Captain John Coffee Hays, "yonder comes a thousand Indians!"

The hour-long firefight that followed became known as the Battle of Walker Creek, or "Hays' Big Fight." The tussle marked a new era of American history and westward expansion, one where the balance of power shifted decisively to the white settlers moving into the western expanse. It was also part product and part symbol of a vast awakening of American industry, which would eventually see factories producing millions of guns. This boom would continue through the Civil War and beyond, reaching its peak in 1873 with a masterpiece of design and performance, the Colt Single Action Army revolver, aka Model P, M1873, Single-Action Army, SAA, Colt .45, and my favorite tag of all, Peacemaker. Just the fact that it has this many nicknames tells you it's a hell of a gun.

But the Colt 1873 did not spring up from dust, whole-formed as a sidearm so perfectly suited to its needs and surroundings that you can't picture the West without it. In a way, it all began back in the summer of 1844 with those sixteen Texas Rangers, each armed with two copies of a fragile-but-revolutionary .36-caliber pistol called the Colt Paterson revolver, the grandfather of the Peacemaker.

To that date, most successful handguns were one-shot models. Horse pistols, meant to be used by cavalry and others on horseback, were single-shot pistols too long and awkward to hang from your hip or properly strap to your leg. Often sold as a pair, a man would holster them on either side of his saddle, giving himself two shots before having to reload. When Meriwether Lewis went exploring the continent on President Jefferson's dime, he most likely chose the military standard Model 1799 North & Cheneys. Like the muskets and rifles of the time, these guns used a flintlock mechanism and were loaded from the front of the barrel. The North & Cheneys fired the same-sized ball as the Army's musket, which made for convenience all the way around.

Compare that to the Colt Paterson the Rangers were carrying. These early Colts featured a nine-inch barrel and a revolving cylinder that enabled the shooter to let loose with five rounds before reloading. The design seemed to hold promise, and the weapons had done well in testing. The only problem was, they had yet to see action.

The Indians were about to correct that. With an exclamation mark and a good bit of underlining. Some eighty warriors rode toward Hays' Rangers. Most of the Indians were Comanche, with a few Waco Indian and Mexican allies sprinkled in. Eighty is a lot less than a

Frederic Remington's depiction of a mounted
assault by Plains Indian warriors.

thousand, but we can forgive the young lawman's exaggeration given the reputation of the Comanche—each
brave may have fought like ten ordinary men. Armed
with lances, war clubs, spare horses, and bows and
arrows, the Comanches were the most highly skilled
light cavalry troops in the world. In 1844, the nomadic
Comanche were the undisputed rulers of a vast swath
of the country's interior named the "Comancheria,"
almost a quarter-billion square miles that centered on
the southern Great Plains.

Each of the sixteen Texas Rangers was armed with
two copies of the Colt.

Sketch of an early Texas Ranger. First organized by
Stephen F. Austin, the Rangers protected settlers
from bandits and hostile Native Americans.

The Colt Paterson revolver, the weapon Texas Rangers
used against Comanches in 1844. The publicity would
make Samuel Colt famous—and launch an American icon.

A typical Comanche tactic was to send scouts ahead to taunt their enemy, then fall back and lure their opponents into a trap where they would be showered by arrows. Another was simply to provoke an initial volley of fire and then rush their opponents before they had time to reload. Before this day, when the Texas Rangers were mainly stuck with single-shot, slow-reloading pistols and rifles, those tactics were deadly effective. In the time it took to reload, a Comanche could serve up a half-dozen arrows, launch a spear, or pick a prime spot of flesh to test the weight and edge of his tomahawk.

When Captain Hays saw the Comanches trying their usual tactics, he knew exactly what was going on. Rather than taking the bait, he took his fifteen mounted men and circled around the Indians' position, galloping up a hill behind them.

"They are fixin' to charge us, boys," Hays yelled, "and we must charge them!"

The Rangers readied their long guns. Hays told them to hold off firing until their foes were close—damn close.

"Crowd them!" he ordered, "Powder-burn them!"

The Rangers set off. The Comanches, confident in their superior numbers, met the charge. All hell broke loose as the rifles cracked. Then, instead of pulling off to reload, the Rangers drew their pistols and commenced to give the Comanches a whoopin'.

In the running, three-mile battle, the highly disciplined Rangers thinned the Indian ranks with a vengeance. Fighting on horseback and hand to hand, the Texans whipped the much larger force from one end of the scrub to the other. The Colt Paterson was a cap and ball pistol, which meant that the powder, ball, and cap were loaded separately. To get this done, you had to take a fair amount of the gun apart. If you've ever been to a black powder meet, you know this can be a daunting task to perform under pressure, let alone on a horse. But the Rangers likely had come prepared with preloaded cylinders, and worked themselves in relays, with one group firing away while the other swapped out their empties. Even this would have been a trial in combat, but however they managed it, they kept firing away at those Comanches.

Finally, a stunned Chief Yellow Wolf tried to rally the remaining warriors for a counterattack. With his Rangers running down on ammo, Hays called out to his troops, "Any man who has a load, kill that chief!" A Ranger named Robert Gillespie came forward, took aim, and struck the Comanche leader in the head. The Indians fled.

The Comanches had suffered twenty-three fatalities; the Rangers lost only one man. It was a triumph for both the Colts and the Rangers. One Indian who survived the battle said later it seemed like the Rangers "had a shot for every finger on the hand." Hays, who would head out to California and a political career a couple years after the battle, credited the pistols with the victory. "Had it not been for them," he wrote later, "I doubt what the consequences would have been. I cannot recommend these arms too highly."

The legend of the Colt revolvers quickly spread. From that day forward, the Texas Rangers had a proven "equalizing" force for mounted and close-quarter combat with the once-invincible Plains Indians. The frontier was a far sight from tamed, but Walker's Creek was a crucial turning point in the American settlement of the West. Hearty ranchers and homesteaders began establishing (in some cases, reestablishing) claims not only in the western half of Texas, but also across the great southern Plains. You could say the year 1844 marked the dawn of the Wild West, an era in which generations of Colt revolvers would play a starring role in the hands of legendary lawmen and outlaws who roamed America's rugged, half-settled landscape.

Now, you'd figure the company that made Colt revolvers would take off in a blaze because of all the good publicity.

There was, however, one small problem—the manufacturer had gone bankrupt a few years earlier.

Sam Colt, the firm's owner and namesake, got a patent on his revolver design from the British government in 1835; two from the U.S. followed the next year. The idea of a revolving magazine wasn't new, but Colt's improvements and the availability of ammunition based on percussion cap technology made his gun a technological leap. And you could build a good argument that the gun's success was due not just to its design but the ability to manufacture it using the most advanced techniques of the day. The Colt-Paterson was a mass-produced marvel.

Or it would have been if Colt had been able to work out all the early problems. The pistols that came from Colt's Patent Arms Manufacturing Company of Paterson, N.J., were a mixed bag. Some were excellent; some not. Standardizing production so parts could be used interchangeably was still more art than science. Hampered by the Panic of 1837, Colt had trouble both selling weapons and raising money to continue doing so. Adding to the problems, a promising debut of the company's prototype revolving rifles in the Seminole War in Florida in 1838 didn't pan out. The rifles were just not rugged and reliable enough for combat, let alone curious soldiers who took them apart to examine their workings. Sometimes they jammed, sometimes they blew up from "chain-fire" malfunctions. The factory closed in 1843, and its assets sold.

Samuel Colt had a restless mind. Busy on other inventions, including a naval mine, he kept thinking of ways to improve his revolver and resurrect his manufacturing company.

Meanwhile, the Colt Paterson revolver did so well for the Texas Rangers that one of the veterans of the fracas at Walker Creek, a young captain named Samuel Walker, set out from Texas to New York to personally suggest some improvements to Sam Colt. Together in 1847 they cooked up a design for a new, nearly five-pound behemoth trail gun called the Walker Colt, a weapon that soon became the most powerful handgun on the market. In fact, it stayed so until the introduction of the .357 Magnum in 1935. The Walker Colt fired .44-caliber rounds in a gun not with five chambers, but six. The "six-shooter" was born. It was so big and heavy you could use it as a club if you had to. And many did.

COLONEL COLT.

Colonel Sam Colt and his handiwork. After partnering with industrial genius Eli Whitney, Colt set up his operations in Hartford, Connecticut.

Colt's Manufacturing Company, Inc.

Sam Colt struck a deal with industrial wizard Eli Whitney in Connecticut to crank out the new model. The U.S. Army soon picked up the Walker Colt with an initial order of 1,000 guns. It performed well in the Mexican War (1846–48). But in shades of things to come, the real boost came from publicity following a wild shootout that came to be known as the Jonathan Davis Incident.

As the story goes, Davis, a skilled marksman and combat veteran of the Mexican War, was prospecting for gold along the river near present-day Sacramento, California, with two friends. A gang of between eleven and fourteen cutthroat killers shot down Davis's companions and then moved in to finish him off. Armed with a pair of Colt percussion revolvers, Davis took out the thieves one by one, finishing off seven before he ran out of ammo.

Four surviving outlaws then tried to rush him with knives and a short sword or cutlass. Unfortunately for them, Davis was an artist with a Bowie knife. He carved up all four, quite fatally. Captain Davis survived with flesh wounds and a shredded set of clothes. The early accounts of the episode were so unbelievable that Davis had to produce witness affidavits to verify his tale. That apparently satisfied the journalists of the time, and the story gained wide circulation.

The U.S. Army ordered thousands of the Colt Model 1860 revolvers as its basic sidearm during the Civil War. Explorers John Frémont and Kit Carson carried Colt revolvers during their epic surveys of the West. Riders and guards of the Pony Express relied on them to guard the dangerous mail run from Santa Fe to Missouri. The Colt revolver, in all its many forms, helped make Samuel one of the richest men in America before dying at age forty-seven in 1862.

But it wasn't until a decade later that his company perfected its greatest product, the Single Action Army Revolver.

It's hard to find the right words to describe the Peacemaker. Somehow, there's no way to set down on paper why this gun had such an impact without sounding a little soft in the head. You really have to hold the weapon, load it, fire it, and load it again if you want to understand it.

Fire, load. Fire. Half-cock, then eject your spent cartridges one at a time with the ejection rod. Load one bullet, skip a chamber, go four bullets, drop the hammer on an empty chamber. Set it in the holster and draw. Single-action means the gun is not going to fire until you cock the hammer back. Pull on the trigger all you want until then, and it's not going off.

You will, however, be dang impressed at the gun's balance and smooth action. The recoil is sweet, the weapon moving up easy in your hand. If you're using black powder, you'll be surrounded by a thick wreath of smoke after shooting your load. But that's part of the fun.

The Colt is one of the most powerful guns I've ever fired. It is quite literally a man-stopper. They used to say you can knock down a grizzly bear with one, though I've never tried.

Probably just as important on the frontier and range, the weapon could take a beatin' and still kick ass. "Sometimes a bad horse would blow up and send my Colt doing fart-knockers across the prairie," said one old-time cowboy from Montana. "I'd just blow the dust off of it and shove it back in the holster. It was the only handgun you could trust that way."

Push away all the legend attached to the gun, the tales of shootouts and ne'er-do-wells, sheriffs, and bandits—get all of that romantic stuff out of your head. When you pick up the gun and handle it on its own terms, you can't help but admire it and know that the hype was well deserved. The Colts were as accurate as your hands made them; effective range depended a lot on the operator, but a decent shooter with a steady hand could expect to hit his target at twenty-five

A Confederate soldier wielding an 1851 Colt Navy and an equally impressive Bowie knife. Civil War vets on both sides were allowed to keep their weapons after the war, leading to a spike in civilian gun ownership.

yards. A practiced, steady gunman could do it at fifty and more.

The Colt Single-Action Army Revolver was the first Colt pistol to accept center-fire cartridges. To this point, most Colt revolvers used percussion caps; powder and ball would be loaded down the front of the cylinder, with the percussion cap set on the other end. But the Smith & Wesson Model 3 started a revolution when it was introduced in 1869. The S & W revolver fired .44-caliber metal cartridges, greatly simplifying loading. All three parts of the ammunition—bullet, powder, primer—were married together in a container that could be easily carried and inserted into the weapon under even the worst conditions. Smith & Wesson wasn't the first to use metal cartridges, and paper cartridges had been around since the beginning of time, or at least the early days of guns. But their system was reliable and efficient. It worked better than many of their predecessors. Just as important, it came at a time when people needed weapons that could fire multiple shots and be quickly reloaded. The U.S. Army put in an order, and the future of handguns was set.

The Russians had actually gotten their hands on the S & W Model 1 first, and in fact the Russian Imperial Government made several suggestions that improved the weapon. Their involvement almost ended up being a financial disaster for Smith & Wesson when disputes rose over payments due. The company persevered, and its handguns remained the chief American alternative to Colts for going on one hundred years. Times have changed, but in a lot of ways they're still the Ford and Chevy of handheld armament.

There's nothing like a little competition to spur the creative juices. Colt's weapon was a definite improvement on its own earlier designs, and the new ammo made it easier to use. The pistol was an immediate best-seller. As you can tell from the name, the weapon was designed for the Army, which was holding trials for a new sidearm contract. The government put in a large order, and the gun continued to be a military standard for two decades. Civilian models and a host of variations quickly followed. While the Army's Colts were chambered for .45 caliber, the Colt Frontier used .44–40.

Lawmen loved the Single-Action Army. Cowboys and ranchers did, too. But it was the heroes and desperadoes who made the gun not just a legend, but part of the American identity. Buffalo Bill Cody, John Wesley Hardin, Judge Roy Bean, Wild Bill Hickok, Doc Holliday, Wyatt Earp, Pat Garrett, Billy the Kid, the Dalton Boys . . . you can't hardly mention one of those names and not see a Colt in their hand.

And I don't suppose you can talk about the Peacemaker without throwing at least one story of ne'er-do-wells and bank robbers into the mix.

I've always been partial to the tales surrounding Butch and Sundance myself. The outlaws Butch Cassidy (legal name: Robert LeRoy Parker) and the Sundance Kid (legal name: Harry Longbaugh) were big fans of the Colt Single-Action Army. Though they were both highly skilled shooters, they claimed to take great pains not to kill people during their legendary bank and train heists in the 1890s with their Wild Bunch Gang, also known as the Hole-in-the-Wall Gang.

According to one account, during their final exile in Bolivia, they put on an exhibition of fast drawing and fast shooting for a friend visiting from the States.

"Let's show him, Kid," said Butch.

"Let's go, Butch," said the Sundance Kid, who spun the cylinder of his six-shooter and jumped up.

The pair grabbed some empty bottles, went outside, and started throwing them high in the air, firing from a crouch.

"I never saw anything like it," said their friend. "I never saw two guns drawn faster and I was with men skilled in firearms all my life. Before I knew it the Colts were in their hands and they were shooting. The four bottles crashed in splinters. They repeated this trick

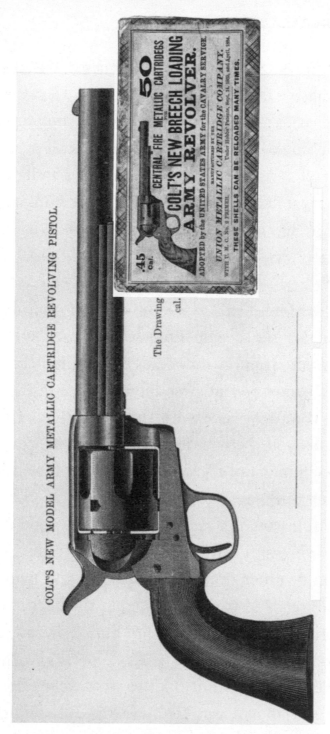

An American icon: the 1873 Colt Army .45 revolver.

several times. Sometimes Butch missed but the Kid always hit the falling targets."

Another time, Butch explained his preference for the Colt Single-Action Army: "It has a long and heavy barrel and can be used as a weapon. I'd rather crack a messenger across the nose than kill him. All the messenger has is a bump on the head. Hell, it isn't his money anyway."

In the second half of the nineteenth century, the Western frontier began filling up with a motley cast of characters: miners, trappers, buffalo hunters, cattle rustlers, gamblers, outlaws, opportunists. In the midst of such company—and with the law still an irregular presence—you were well served to know your way around a gun. Clint Eastwood–style, one-on-one, fast-draw gun duels weren't that common in the Old West, though you wouldn't know it from Hollywood movies and TV shows. There were plenty of drunken shoot-outs, lots of which occurred in saloons, plus many ambush killings and cowardly shots in the back, but the number of classic "High Noon" gun showdowns was surprisingly few.

The exceptions to this rule are what we're after. One of the best-known was the "Hickok-Tutt Gunfight," which took place on the town square of Springfield,

Missouri, on July 21, 1865, between Wild Bill Hickok and Davis Tutt. They're still talking about it in Springfield, and quite a few other places as well.

This was the Super Bowl of shoot-outs, featuring a man who would become the dominant "gun celebrity" of his era, and an angry contender who'd once been his friend and business partner. The cause was a highly personal dispute over money and women. It featured a long buildup, hot emotions, and a crowd of spectators on the town square. All that was missing were hot dog vendors, sponsorship deals, and a halftime show.

The star of the showdown was Wild Bill. Not yet famous as the most skilled gunman of his time, Hickok had been a frontier scout and courier during the Indian and Civil Wars, a town marshal, U.S. deputy marshal, and a county sheriff. George Armstrong Custer said Hickok was a "strange character, just the one which a novelist might gloat over."

And he looked the part. "He was a broad-shouldered, deep-chested, narrow-waisted fellow, over 6 feet tall, with broad features, high cheekbones and forehead, firm chin and aquiline nose," wrote author Joseph G. Rosa, a Western historian and modern-day authority on Hickok. "His sensuous-looking mouth was surmounted by a straw-colored moustache, and his auburn hair was worn shoulder length, Plains style. But

"Inseparable companions": from hardworking ranchers (above) to outlaws (below right), Colt revolvers defined the Wild West.

THE COWBOY AND THE COLT

are inseparable companions. The COWBOY sticks to the COLT REVOLVER because it never fails him in the hour of need. He may neglect or misuse it, but it is always ready for instant action.

Catalog Mailed On Request

Colt's Patent Fire Arms Manufacturing Co.
HARTFORD CONN. U.S.A.

it was his blue-gray eyes that dominated his features. Normally friendly and expressive, his eyes, old-timers recalled, became hypnotically cold and bored into one when he was angry."

The tussle was still a few years before the Peacemaker was invented, and Hickok wore an ivory-handled version of Colt's 1851 Navy revolver, a cap and ball weapon that fired five .36-caliber rounds. It's called Navy because of the size of the bullets, but don't let that fool you. While the caliber was specified by the Navy and there was a Navy contract to make the original purchase, the primary customers were landlubbers, civilian and military. The smaller caliber made the gun a bit lighter and easier to carry and work in a fight.

Hickok's prowess with handguns became legendary on the American Plains after a *Harper's* magazine article published in 1867 made him a national celebrity. While a great deal of mythology surrounds Will Bill, he was a hell of a shot, no doubt about it.

What were Wild Bill's secrets? Another famous cowboy who knew him well and carefully studied his gun-handling technique was Buffalo Bill Cody. Cody employed Hickok, briefly, in his traveling show. To Cody, Hickok's main assets were decisiveness and a thorough understanding of the science of shooting and the weapon he carried. Not to mention the ability to conjure a calm in the heat of the moment.

"Bill beat them to it," declared Cody, summing up the gunman's method. "He made up his mind to kill the other man before the other man had finished thinking, and so Bill would just quietly pull his gun and give it to him. That was all there was to it. It is easy enough to beat the other man if you start first. Bill always shot as he raised the gun. That is, he was never in a hurry about it; he just pulled the gun from his hip and let it go as he was raising it; shoot on the up-raise, you might call it. Most men lifted the gun higher, then threw it down to cock it before firing. Bill cocked it with his thumb, I guess, as it was coming into line with his man. . . . But he was not the quickest man by any means. He was just cool and quiet, and started first. Bill was not a bad man, as is often pictured. But he was a bad man to tackle. Always cool, kind, and cheerful, almost, about it. And he never killed a man unless that man was trying to kill him."

Hickok was often armed with two pistols, and according to eyewitness accounts, he used both simultaneously when the situation called for it. Years after the Hickok-Tutt shoot-out, the August 25, 1876, edition of the *Chicago Tribune* carried the account of an unnamed observer who believed, "The secret of Bill's success was his ability to draw and discharge his pistols, with a rapidity that was truly wonderful, and a peculiarity of his was that the two were presented and discharged simultaneously, being 'out and off' before the average man had time to think about it. He never seemed to take any aim, yet he never missed. Bill never did things by halves. When he drew his pistols it was always to shoot, and it was a theory of his that every man did the same."

Hickok himself explained that he wouldn't shoot an innocent man, but he was willing to kill men in the line of duty or in self-defense. He offered helpful tips on how to properly shoot someone, like "Whenever you get into a row, be sure and not shoot too quick. Take time. I've known many a feller to slip up for shooting in a hurry." Another time, he told a friend, "Charlie, I hope you never have to shoot any man, but if you do, shoot him in the guts, near the navel. You may not make a fatal shot, but he will get a shock that will paralyze his brain and arm so much that the fight is all over." Good advice, in my experience.

Hickok's opponent that hot summer day in Springfield was a man who until recently had been his friend and gambling partner, Davis K. Tutt. Legend has it that women caused them to fall out, though which women exactly is a matter of speculation.

Hickok was rumored to be the daddy of Tutt's sister's child. Tutt reportedly had the hots for Hickok's girlfriend.

Whatever the reason, Hickok decided to stop playing cards with Tutt, who retaliated by staking other card players in a public effort to embarrass and bankrupt Hickok. Either Tutt backed the wrong players or they ran into a cold streak wider than Alaska, because Hickok raked in the winnings. Tutt became infuriated, to use a fancy word for pissed off. On an impulse, he grabbed Wild Bill's gold Waltham pocket watch as collateral for a separate, disputed debt. It was a public insult that branded Hickok as a mooch and a welsher. These were labels that would have ruined Hickok as a professional gambler, and were more than enough to provoke a fight. But Hickok, outnumbered in the saloon, kept his cool. Tutt grinned and made off with the watch.

Tutt's supporters mocked Hickok relentlessly about the confiscation, trying to goad him into a situation where they could, as a group, safely gun him down. Their antics strained Wild Bill's patience to the breaking point. When they told him that Tutt was planning to parade across the town square the next day wearing the watch for all to see, Hickok decided enough was enough. "He shouldn't come across that square unless dead men can walk," he growled, and went home to polish up his pistol.

The next day, the two former friends sat down over a drink and discussed the terms of a truce, but negotiations broke down. At 6 p.m., Tutt began his march across the town square, wearing the watch. Hickok coolly strode onto the square holding his Colt Navy. He cocked it and placed it in his hip holster. The crowd scattered.

"Dave, here I am," called out Hickok from a distance of seventy-five yards away as a rush-hour crowd of spectators gathered around the square. "Don't you come across here with that watch."

Tutt, who was standing sideways in the style of a formal duelist, pulled his gun to fire. Hickok drew his revolver and braced it on his other arm. Two shots rang out almost simultaneously. Tutt missed. Hickok didn't. His bullet traveled right through Tutt's chest.

Tutt's last words were "Boys, I'm killed." Hickok, meanwhile, had pivoted to wave his gun at Tutt's flabbergasted cronies. He let his pistol do the talking. "Do you want some of this?" the weapon asked. They didn't.

A jury cleared Wild Bill of manslaughter, deciding he'd acted in self-defense. He had many more adventures before being fatally shot in the back by a coward named Jack McCall in a saloon in Deadwood, South Dakota, in August 1876.

We can't leave the Wild West or Colt pistols without mentioning what has to be the most famous shootout in American history. It happened on the cold afternoon of October 26, 1881, when four lawmen faced off against four cowboys in a vacant lot in Tombstone, Arizona. Of course I'm talking about the Gunfight at the O.K. Corral.

On the one side were two sets of brothers, Tom and Frank McLaury and Ike and Billy Clanton. These cowboys were not what you might call model citizens. All four were regularly suspected of rustling cattle, but the crime that seems to have really stirred things up was their alleged connection to a string of stagecoach robberies outside the town.

The law, in the person of Marshal and Chief of Police Virgil Earp and Deputy Marshals Wyatt and Morgan Earp, pursued the robbery investigations with a zeal unusual at the time, especially considering that a good number of lawmen had night jobs as thieves themselves. Ike Clanton complained that the Earps were picking on the cowboys unfairly. Then he supposedly ratted out some of the robbers to the Earps. Ike got angered when the confidential information started leaking out, identifying him as the source. One of the Earps' friends, a sometime dentist, gambler, and occasional hothead known as Doc Holliday, figured into the argument when friends of the cowboys tried to frame him for the robberies. It was all a twisted, vicious mess.

Tempers escalated, liquor flowed, and reason fled. Threats and harsh words were exchanged on October 25. By the next afternoon, both Ike and Tom were sporting fresh head wounds from where the Earps had pistol-whipped them with their mammoth Colts in separate encounters.

There was a gun-confiscation law on the books that made carrying a firearm illegal inside the crime-infested silver-mining boomtown. If you ventured into Tombstone you had to check your weapon behind the counter of a designated retail location like a saloon. But on October 26, at least two of the cowboys, Billy Clanton and Frank McLaury, appeared to be defying the gun ban by wearing holstered Colt .44 revolver pistols in plain view.

Virgil, Wyatt, Morgan, and Doc headed to the O.K. Corral to arrest the Clantons before they could leave. Virgil, Morgan, and Wyatt all had six-shooters. Wyatt had on either a Colt Single Action Army or a .44-caliber Smith & Wesson. (Nobody's quite sure, and

Wyatt never clarified the point.) In an expert gunfighter's touch, Wyatt lined the inside of his coat with wax to facilitate a smooth gun draw. Morgan was probably packing a Colt .45, and Virgil Earp was carrying either a Colt or a Smith & Wesson, caliber unknown. Doc Holliday had a short-barreled 10-gauge shotgun under his coat, as well as a nickel-plated Colt Single-Action Army or a smaller Colt model.

"You sons of bitches," yelled one of the lawmen at the cowboys as the two groups met. "You've been looking for a fight, and you can have it!"

They were a few yards away from each other. They were all good shots, but at least one of the cowboys was drunk. The Clantons were also tired from all their drinking, and seemed to have left some of their orneriness in the dust of the nearby streets.

"Don't shoot me," declared Billy Clanton. "I don't want to fight!"

Tom McLaury opened his coat to show he was unarmed and announced, "I have got nothing."

But then both Billy Clanton and Frank McLaury, maybe sensing that the Earps and Holliday were in no mood for negotiation, reached for their Colt Single-Action Army six-shooters. Tom McLaury moved toward his horse and a Winchester lever-action rifle in a scabbard in the saddle.

"Hold, I don't mean that!" shouted Virgil Earp. "I have come to disarm you!"

In the next thirty seconds, somewhere between seventeen and thirty shots were fired, one of the cowboys ran away, and an episode of American history was written that would fascinate and confuse people for generations to come. As the prominent gun historian Massad Ayoob wrote, "Seven men shoot at each other. Six get shot. Three die. And a century and a quarter later, people are still trying to figure out what the hell happened."

Black smoke from the gunfire lingered in the cramped lot, and it obscured details of the shoot-\out. "The gunfight came in bursts, snippets and spurts so rapid that witnesses and participants never agreed on an order of events," wrote author Casey Tefertiller. "Gunfire exploded in the cold afternoon air; cowboys struggled to control their twisting, bounding horses. It was a scene of disarray, where impressions were left frozen in time." What follows is an approximation of what happened, based on legal testimony and press accounts.

Doc Holliday drew his pistol, shoved it into Frank McLaury's belly, and moved a few steps back.

Wyatt Earp later testified that he didn't draw his pistol until after he saw cowboys Billy Clanton and

Frank McLaury draw their pistols. But an analysis done in the 1930s by trick-shooting expert Ed McGivern demonstrated that to "beat the drop" on someone who has already started to draw on you would require a nearly impossible degree of speed. So it's likely Wyatt had the gun out before them, though he hadn't fired.

Ike Clanton, who was unarmed, lunged at Wyatt to plead for mercy. Wyatt, according to Clanton, stuck his gun in his belly and said, "You son of a bitch, you can have a fight!" Ike tried to grab Wyatt's gun hand, but Wyatt shoved him away. "The fight has commenced," Wyatt reported telling Ike. "Go to fighting or get away." Ike ran to safety at high speed.

Gunfire erupted from several guns almost simultaneously, probably first from Doc Holliday and Morgan Earp.

Holliday switched from his revolver to his double-barreled shotgun. He swung around Tom McLaury's horse, and shot McLaury in the chest at close range as he was trying to grab his Winchester rifle out of the saddle scabbard. Tom staggered out of the alley into Fremont Street, then fell down permanently, the twenty-eight-year-old victim of a tight-patterned, 12-pellet buckshot blast through the rib cage.

Holliday chucked away the shotgun and switched back to his revolver, no doubt to save critical reloading time in such a close-quarter, rapid-fire environment. He fired his revolver at Frank McLaury and Billy Clanton, both of whom were hit. Despite their wounds, Billy Clanton and Frank McLaury kept on shooting.

Morgan Earp caught a round across his shoulder blades and vertebrae, fell down, then managed to get up. Virgil was flattened by a bullet in his calf muscle, but he, too, popped up shooting.

Hit in the gut, Frank McLaury pulled his horse by the reins into Fremont Street, where the horse wisely decided to run off, taking Frank's protective cover away with him, not to mention his Winchester rifle. Doc Holliday ran up, and the wounded McLaury took aim and growled at him. "I've got you now!"

"Blaze away!" snapped Holliday.

This is not always the smartest thing to say during a gunfight, as it might serve to focus your opponent's intentions. In this case, Frank obliged by firing a round at Holliday, clipping the dentist's pistol pocket and grazing his skin.

"The son of a bitch has shot me," yapped Holliday, "and I mean to kill him!"

A bullet found its way into Frank's head moments later, though it was probably fired by Morgan Earp. In any event, the thirty-three-year-old Frank hit the ground. For good.

"They have murdered me," gasped Billy Clanton nearby. "I have been murdered. Chase the crowd away and from the door and give me air." Shot in both the chest and belly, he asked for a doctor and some morphine, and some more cartridges for his pistol. His last request wasn't honored, as he quickly died on the spot. He was nineteen years old.

Three cowboys dead, three lawmen wounded. Ike Clanton fled unharmed. Wyatt had come through without a scratch.

Ike filed murder charges against the lawmen, claiming that his brother and friends had been killed in cold blood. In Tombstone, the event was initially praised by much of the local populace, who were grateful that the Earps and Holliday had cleared the town of four dangerous cowboys. But opinion started shifting when word spread that Tom McLaury appeared to have been unarmed, and that he and Billy Clanton made peace gestures at the start of the gunfight. Worse still, a credible court witness quoted Virgil Earp saying before the fight, "Those men have made their threats; I will not arrest them but will kill them on sight."

It started looking like premeditated murder might well be a viable charge. But evidence was missing and many questions stayed unanswered, details unknown or in conflict. The lawmen were eventually cleared by both a local judge and a grand jury.

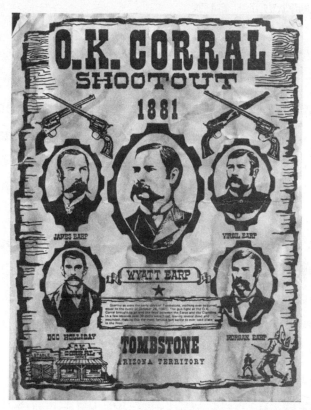

A souvenir poster and tourist marker cashing in on the
events of October 1881 in Tombstone, Arizona.

Vendetta killings of friends on both sides ensued. Morgan Earp was slain by a bullet in his back while he was playing pool, less than five months after the fracas in the corral. He was thirty years old. Billy Claiborne was killed in a gunfight in Tombstone, and Ike Clanton was shot to death by a lawman who caught him stealing cattle.

Doc Holliday died of tuberculosis at age thirty-six. Virgil Earp survived an assassination attempt in Tombstone and became a lawman in California, where he died at age sixty-two in 1905, still on the job as a peace officer.

Wyatt Earp took a lady friend and wandered around the American West with her for decades, squeaking out a living as a professional gambler. He died in Los Angeles at the ripe age of eighty, the last survivor of the Gunfight at the O.K. Corral.

None of the guns used in the shoot-out has ever been found.

The gunfight triggered press coverage across the United States, and inspired movies, articles, and reenactments all the way into the twenty-first century. As the *Tombstone Nugget* wrote of the triple killing: "The 26th of October, 1881, will always be marked as one of the crimson days in the annals of Tombstone, a day when blood flowed as water, and human life was held as a shuttle cock, a day to be remembered as witnessing the bloodiest and deadliest street fight that has ever occurred in this place, or probably in the Territory."

The era of the gunfighter soon died off, but their weapons, most especially the Colt Single-Action Army, endures to this day. Prized by historians and collectors for its simplicity, power, and beautiful design, it is truly an American classic.

Colt revolvers had been instrumental in opening up the American West. Still, the region remained dangerous, largely unconquered land through much of the late nineteenth century.

To finally "win" the West, the United States needed an even bigger gun. As it happened, that weapon made its debut the same year the Colt Single-Action Army did.

4

The Winchester 1873 Rifle

"The Winchester stocked and sighted to suit myself is by all odds the best weapon I ever had, and I now use it almost exclusively."

—*Theodore Roosevelt,* Hunting Trips of a Ranchman

On the morning of October 5, 1892, two hardware stores in Coffeyville, Kansas, conducted the first and maybe only mass gun giveaway in the history of the United States.

Any adult was free to grab a firearm and a couple of boxes of ammo off the shelf, no paperwork or money required. Word spread in a lightning flash, drawing a crowd of people who reached behind the counters

Jesse James's Winchester.

and helped themselves to rifles and shotguns. The big prizes were the lever-action Winchester rifles, elegant weapons that had proven themselves both dependable and deadly since their introduction some nineteen years before.

This wasn't a sales promotion. In fact, the reason for the giveaway was clear to anyone brave enough to peek in the window next door: The bank was being robbed. Actually, two banks were being taken simultaneously. Five fully armed men were pointing their guns at terrified bank customers and employees inside the First National Bank and the Condon Bank, both right in the middle of town. The infamous Dalton Gang had come to town for an unauthorized withdrawal.

The Dalton Gang was on a bit of a roll. They'd just pulled off a string of successful train robberies in Indian Territory, robbin', thievin', and killin' at a pace few had matched before. Not content to rest on their laurels, they had decided to top themselves with a brazen stunt in their old hometown—take two banks at the same time in broad daylight. As far as they knew, it had never been done. And that was the main point— cement their cred as the baddest crew of cutthroat thieves who'd ever ridden in the West.

Emmett, Bob, and Gratton "Grat" Dalton were related to members of the James-Younger Gang (led by Frank and Jesse James), which partly explained their competitiveness. A little harder to explain was the fact that both Bob and Grat were former lawmen. Their older brother Frank, a deputy U.S. marshal, was killed in the line of duty by a horse thief. But in the West allegiances shifted fast. Frustrated by irregular pay, the Dalton boys decided to apply their talents to crime.

The C.M. Condon Bank was located at the center of the town plaza, a wide, open space in the middle of Coffeyville. The First National Bank was across the way. The Daltons had fixed on a particular strategic point as the lynchpin of their plan—a hitching post next to the First National where they could park their horses for a convenient getaway.

What they hadn't counted on was something that was becoming as American as, well, Winchesters and apple pie—road repairs. When the five desperados rode into town, they found the hitching post had been removed. This led them to leave their horses in a side alley several hundred feet away from their targets. More importantly, it complicated their escape route, hemming them into a spot where they could be easily ambushed.

They were a bit too full of themselves to think of that when they tied up their horses. Wearing fake beards and wigs, they strode across the town plaza, focused on their mission. The disguises were meant to keep anyone who saw them from realizing who they were and what they were up to. That didn't work. A shopkeeper sweeping his sidewalk looked up as they passed, realized something was up, and discreetly trailed them as they split up and entered the banks.

I suspect the rifles they were packin' gave them away.

"God damn you! Hold up your hands!" ordered Grat Dalton as he pointed his Winchester inside Condon Bank. With his confederates Bill Power and Dick Broadwell spreading out behind him, Grat told bank employees to fill up a grain sack with cash and silver dollars. Then he went over to the main vault and told one of the bankers to open the inner doors.

Which prompted bank cashier Charles Ball to utter the most famous lie in the Old West.

"It's not time for that to open," he told the outlaw, explaining that the burglarproof money chest was on a time lock that wouldn't open for ten minutes. Another employee helpfully turned the handle, but did not pull it.

Time locks had been around in the West for a while, and Grat was familiar enough with them to recognize that the contraption on the door was indeed such a lock. What he didn't know was that it had gone off earlier that morning; if he'd've simply pulled the handle himself, it would have swung open free and easy. But he fell for the bluff.

"We can wait ten minutes," he announced.

But patience wasn't his strong suit. Soon he began to fidget, then stalk back and forth. Finally he exploded. "God damn you! I believe you are lying to me. I've a mind to put a bullet through you! Open it up or I will shoot you!"

Ball stuck to his story.

"Where is your gold?" demanded Grat finally.

"We haven't any," said the banker. Ball then evaded Grat's questioning with a stream of unintelligible banking lingo, explaining why this was the case.

Meanwhile, inside the First National Bank around the corner, Bob and Emmett Dalton were also being bluffed by bank employees, including one who insisted he didn't know the combination to the safe. Finally deciding that time was wastin', they filled up a bag with what they could find from the teller stations and patrons. This wasn't chicken feed: a total of twenty thousand dollars went into the sacks. But the Daltons felt like they'd been gypped anyway. Swearing and shouting, they took three civilians hostage as human shields, and moved to the door.

The delay at both banks had been long enough for the good citizens of Coffeyville to arm themselves, courtesy of the gun dealers at the hardware stores. The decision to go to war against the Daltons seems to have been spontaneous, but sometimes spur of the moment is the best way to do things. Volunteers sprinted to the scene from all over town, many of them gathering at Isham Brothers hardware store, right next to the First National Bank. The staff at Isham's, along with their rivals at A. P. Boswell's hardware store a short distance away, gave guns and ammo away to all comers as fast as they could grab them from the display.

The civilian gunmen scrambled into positions around the two banks. Several men hauled wagons together to create cover. One store owner grabbed a Colt .44 from his basement and ducked behind a wooden sign. A wagon driver pulled a double-barreled shotgun off the shelf at Isham's and hid behind a post that gave him a point-blank view of the First National Bank. The proprietor of Isham's ducked behind a big iron stove in the front of the store, backed up by two of his clerks, one with a revolver and the other with a Winchester.

"Look out there at the left!" Emmett yelled to Bob as he cleared the doorway to the sidewalk. Two citizens blasted the robbers with a Winchester and Colt .44 from the doorway of the Rammel Brothers' drugstore. They missed, but the Daltons were driven back into the bank, frantically searching for a back exit. One hostage broke free and scrambled across the street, where he grabbed a Winchester of his own to join the opposition. A firestorm of lead sailed into the First National.

Over at the Condon bank, Grat and his men gave up waiting for the lock to open, deciding to settle for the silver and cash they'd grabbed and head out. But before they could leave, townspeople began raining fire into the building. As some eighty rounds of rifle and shotgun slugs poured in, a witness spotted Grat and the others "running back and forth" inside. It reminded her of "rats in a trap." She described the firing as "continuous like bunches of firecrackers exploding, both shotguns and rifles." Anyone not firing at the Daltons was busy running for cover wherever it could be found.

You don't have to be particularly bright to be a bank robber, but it's probably helpful not to be so gullible you'll believe anything you're told. When Grat asked a Condon Bank employee if there was a back door, the banker lied and claimed there was only one exit.

"Let's get out of here!" Grat shouted, heading to the front. Realizing he couldn't drag a two-hundred-pound sack of silver in the middle of a firefight, he abandoned the bag and stuffed paper money into his clothes.

Grat and his two fellow bandits dashed out the southwest entrance of the bank into the street. Braving a blizzard of gunfire, they ran in the direction of the alley and their horses, periodically stopping to return fire. They ran, according to one account, "with heads down, like facing a strong wind."

Grat hadn't gotten too far before City Marshal Charles T. Connelly appeared in his way. They traded gunfire; while most sources believe that Connelly wounded Grat, the outlaw got the best of the marshal, killing him in the exchange. But the robbers were still a long way from their horses.

"The moment that Grat Dalton and his companions, Dick Broadwell and Bill Power, left the [C. M. Condon] bank that they had just looted, they came under the guns of the men in Isham's store," wrote newspaper editor David Elliott. "Grat Dalton and Bill Power each received mortal wounds before they had retreated twenty steps. The dust was seen to fly from their clothes, and Power in his desperation attempted to take refuge in the rear doorway of an adjoining store, but the door was locked and no one answered his request to be let in. He kept his feet and clung to his Winchester until he reached his horse, when another ball struck him in the back and he fell dead at the feet of the animal that had carried him on his errand of robbery."

At First National, Bob and Emmett grabbed a hostage and escaped through a back door. They promptly shot and killed a man who happened to be passing by.

"You hold the bag, I'll do the fighting," Bob told his brother as they headed around the corner back toward the horses. "Go slow. I can whip the whole damn town!"

For a few dozen paces, it looked like he could. Bob walked along calmly, snapping his fingers and whistling. Gunfire began dropping civilians. The injured were pulled into Isham's hardware shop, and soon the store resembled a blood-soaked hospital emergency room.

An unsuspecting boy wandered into the path of the robbers, one of whom shoved him aside with the warning, "Keep away from here, bud, or you'll get hurt."

Grat, Broadwell, and Power were now dead. The two other Daltons made it to the alley where their horses were, and if luck or maybe a convenient road detour were on their side, they might just have made it out. But luck wasn't something they had much of that day, and the citizens' superior numbers began to tell.

Depending on the model and caliber, the Winchesters the town was armed with fed as many as fifteen bullets through a round tube magazine into the breech. Pull down on the trigger guard, come back up with it, fire—even if most of these folks hadn't grown up around guns all their lives, they still would have had no trouble learning how to fire the rifle in the heat of the battle. The front sight was fixed, and while the rear could be adjusted, my suspicion is that at close range the good citizens of Coffeyville didn't have to do much messing around with the sight.

One by one, the Dalton boys were shot to pieces. Emmett made it to his horse, but Bob staggered and fell, finally perforated to the point where he couldn't go on.

"Good-bye," Bob told his brother as Emmett tried to pull him to safety. "Don't surrender, die game."

Emmett might have obliged, but he was hit several times and settled to the dust. There he was grabbed and dragged into the office of a local Dr. Welles. The doctor had taken an oath to preserve life, but as a good part of the town crowded in, he realized they were fixin' to apply their own medicine to his patient with the short end of a rope.

"No use, boys. He will die anyway," he told the crowd.

"Doc, Doc, are you certain?" someone asked.

"Hell, yes, he'll die," said the doctor. "Did you ever hear of a patient of mine getting well?"

The mob laughed, then ran off to gawk at the four robbers who hadn't the luck to make it to Doc Wells' office alive.

The four were about as dead as men can get. One was said to have "as many holes in him as a colander," and another report estimated twenty-three pieces of lead in

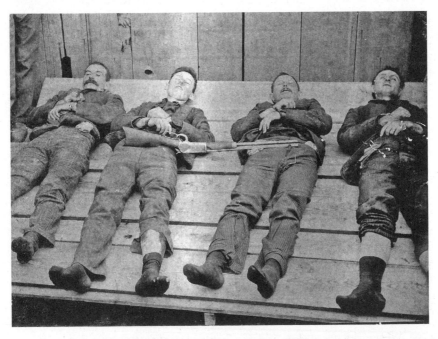

The Dalton Gang pose with a Winchester.

one of the bodies. The town had saved its money and earned a place in history, though it had paid a steep price: Four civilians were dead.

The deceased robbers were propped up for a picture, with a Winchester draped across them. Some dumb ass figured out that if you moved the dead Grat Dalton's arm up and down, blood flowed out of a prominent hole in his throat; quite a number of people amused themselves trying it.

Contrary to the doctor's assessments of his skills, Emmett survived almost two dozen gunshot wounds and wound up in jail. Sentenced to life, he turned over a new leaf and was freed after serving some fourteen and a half years. Freed, he became an actor and a writer, somewhat less dangerous activities than robbing banks, though in some eyes nearly as dubious.

The Coffeyville battle is a great action story, probably as exciting to hear and tell today as it was a hundred-some years ago. But it wasn't just the bullet slinging that makes it stand out from a historical point of view. In deciding to stop the robbery, the citizens had drawn a big red line not in the sand, but across the West. The country was to be wild no more. Law and order would prevail. Not only were Americans taming the West, they were taming themselves.

And if the people in the West had evolved, so had the guns they used to instill order on the chaos of nature and themselves. The Winchesters used in the Coffeyville battle represented a climactic moment in the century-long evolution of American frontier rifles.

The Winchesters were never commonly used as combat weapons by American military forces. There were a bunch of reasons, from head-shed (aka top brass) prejudice against repeaters to the difficulty of cycling rounds while lying flat behind thin cover. Instead, the repeater became the all-purpose working rifle for countless thousands of cowboys, ranchers, lawmen, and homesteaders for the last quarter of the nineteenth century.

I love lever-action rifles. I have since I was old enough to chase my little brother, Jeff, around the family house playing cowboys and lawmen. As a matter of fact, I lusted after his Marlin .30-30 when we were kids. I had a fine bolt-action .30-06, but his lever-action Marlin looked to me like a cowboy gun, and in my mind that made it the best.

The whole idea of a lever-action rifle is to slip a cartridge into the breech quickly and easily, so it can then be put to good use by pulling the trigger. The trigger-guard mechanism on the outside of the gun works a lever that pushes the spent cartridge out of the breech

Protecting the Herd, by Frederic Remington. Winchesters were standard issue for cowboys and ranchers.

when it's pulled down. Sliding the lever back up snugs a fresh one into place. The inside cogs and springs of the action that get this done are tucked out of sight, of course; all the operator sees and feels is a very satisfying click-click that shouts WILD WEST in capital letters.

The Spencer had been the most successful repeater of the Civil War era, but even so, it did have limitations. The operation came to a full stop after the cartridge was chambered. Before the bullet could fly, the shooter had to pull back the hammer manually, usually with his thumb. Only then was the gun ready to fire.

Wouldn't it be easier, someone thought, if you could use the same lever that was getting the bullet in place to ready the hammer as well?

Actually, you could. And while it may not seem like that big a deal to someone used to a Spencer, or other weapons of the day, that little touch of simplicity made for a much smoother and quicker shooting process.

As it happens, someone had thought of this setup well before the Spencer reached Gettysburg. The Henry Repeater, such as the model Lincoln tested in 1861, used just such an arrangement. The weapon had other shortcomings, but the ideas behind its action were solid.

In the late 1860s, Oliver Winchester purchased the remains of the company that created the Spencer Repeater. One of the reasons he had the cash to do so was the success of his firm, now known as Winchester Repeating Arms Company. Winchester and company had stayed with the basic design of the Henry, but made so many improvements that the Winchester Model 1866 was really a very different animal. True, it had a bronze-alloy frame like the Henry, and it still used the same rim-fire cartridge. But where the Henry had been more than a tad on the temperamental side, the 1866 was a robust shooting iron. Its red brass or gunmetal receiver had a yellowish tint to it, earning it the nickname "Yellow Boy." But there wasn't anything yellow about it. The magazine was sealed. You could load the weapon at the side thanks to a loading gate. There were a bunch of other little improvements that helped the gun stand up to the strains of the frontier.

But it was the company's next rifle, Model 1873, that earned Winchester its everlasting fame. Again, this was a sturdy weapon, even more so than the 1866. It also used a .44–40 cartridge. This gave the gun more stopping power, while not being so large that it made the rifle hard to handle. It also meant you could use the same ammo in your rifle and Colt Frontier revolver. The Winchester found a sweet spot where power, convenience, and versatility were in perfect balance.

The search for a perfect weapon had been a long, dusty trail, with a number of detours and missteps. It produced some mighty fine weapons, even if none were "perfect." The ideal weapon depends on the circumstances you find yourself in. Sometimes you want a lot of bullets. Sometimes you want just one big one.

Size did matter on the Plains. American settlers surged westward from the eastern forests and quickly discovered that the original flintlock American long rifles with a .32-caliber ball weren't powerful and fast-loading enough for the larger game out West. Buffalo, elk, bighorn sheep, grizzly bear, and mountain lion all required guns with bigger loads. And unless you were a skilled contortionist, the American long rifle was pretty awkward to carry and use from the saddle.

So new single-shot, muzzle-loading hunting rifles came on the scene. The most famous Plains rifle was a model made by the Hawken brothers, gunsmiths in St. Louis, Missouri. The Hawkens cut the barrel down to thirty inches, and boosted the projectile to at least .50 caliber. That gave their weapons the power to knock down big animals at long range. On the wide-open plains, accuracy at distance was essential, due to the fact that it was difficult to sneak up on anything. The weapon became a favorite among hunters, trappers, mountain men, traders, and explorers, first as a flint-lock and then as a percussion cap gun after 1835. The Hawkens called them "Rocky Mountain Rifles."

But the big daddy of all Plains rifles was the post–Civil War "Sharps Big 50," the quintessential power-house buffalo gun. This piece contributed directly to the shaping of America by powering the final expansion of European settlers across the continent. Its bullets slaughtered millions of buffalo. The consequences were complex and, for Indians as well as the animals, not very pleasant, but the weapon itself was a fine piece of work.

Above: An 1879 broadside boasting its advertiser's stock of Winchesters to settlers and travelers headed into Indian country. Below: A later Sears and Roebuck ad hawking the latest models.

The large-caliber Sharps built on the design and reputation of the single-shot, breech-loading, falling-block Sharps rifle, which had done so well on the field of battle during the Civil War. The new model had center-fire metallic cartridges and a half-inch-diameter projectile. It retained its vertical dropping-block action, which was operated by the trigger guard. The action was not only strong but limited the release of gases when the gun was discharged. The thirty-inch barrel had eight sides, which was not uncommon at the time. I don't know if that made it stronger or just easier to build, but it did give the weapon a special feel.

The big Sharps had the power to drop a distant buffalo or stop a charging grizzly. It was also highly accurate. The kick was strong, or as the National Firearms Museum in Virginia puts it, the rifle had "knockdown power at both ends." Elmer Keith, writing about the gun in 1940 after conducting a number of experiments with it, pronounced its recoil "darn heavy" and its report "something to remember," which I suppose you'd expect from a cartridge two and a half inches long.

The .50 Sharps' main target was the American bison. Before 1800, much of middle American grassland was a paradise for vast herds of grazing buffalo. Twelve feet long and weighing up to two thousand pounds each, the buffalo were self-service supermarkets for the several hundred thousand Native Americans. Their carcasses provided not only food, but also clothing and shelter. They even served up raw materials for war shields, boats, fuel, and glue. As many as 50 million buffalo remained on the Plains in 1830, split into northern and southern groups. A single herd of roughly 4 million was spotted as late as 1871.

For the arriving white settlers, the buffalo were a cash machine: hides fetched a hundred dollars each. Among other things, the leather from the animals was being used to make belts for commercial sewing machines and other equipment as the Industrial Revolution expanded. The animals were just one more raw material. But as they vanished, so would the people who depended on them.

The big Sharps was capable of bringing down bison at distances approaching half a mile. It "shoots today and kills tomorrow," Native Americans said of the Sharps. "The Sharps was a different kind of gun," wrote Keith McCafferty in *Field & Stream* in 1997. "Originally a target rifle of great accuracy and crushing power, Sharps rifles became the tools of choice for those who came to slaughter the great buffalo herds. There was no nobility in what the hide hunters did. It was wretched, fast-money work that they themselves despised, and it represents a dark page in our history."

The orgy of wholesale buffalo slaughter surged after the Civil War and peaked in the 1870s and 1880s, powered by the Sharps and other accurate, high-powered long-range hunting rifles firing big metallic cartridges. A single "Big Fifty" Sharps .50–90 rifle owned by legendary buffalo hunter J. Wright Mooar was believed to have dispatched more than 22,000 buffalo.

Bison weren't the only things you could take with a Big Fifty. A legendary sniper named Billy Dixon made what came to be known as "the Shot of the Century" with a Sharps. He was at a trading outpost in Texas named Adobe Walls, on June 27, 1874, when the settlement came under fierce attack by as many as a thousand Indian warriors. One woman and twenty-eight white men—including a young Bat Masterson—huddled inside the fort walls and five buildings, fending off the attack. Indians pounded on doors and windows with their clubs and rifle butts as defenders held them off with Winchesters and pistols.

Finally repulsed, the Indians were gathering for a fresh round of attacks on the second day of the siege when Dixon borrowed a Sharps buffalo gun from the post's well-stocked arsenal. He squeezed off a shot that killed a mounted Indian warrior from a distance measured two weeks later by a team of U.S. Army surveyors at 1,538 yards. The shot apparently broke the morale of the Native American strike force. They abandoned the siege two days later in a major psychological defeat. Worse, the failed attack convinced the military to step up their campaign against the natives. The Red River War followed in 1874–75; at the end of the conflict, the survivors of the defeated tribes were relocated to Oklahoma reservations.

The other big buffalo gun in the West was the classic Remington Rolling Block rifle, a single-shot breech-loader with a simple but extremely strong mechanism. On a gun with a rolling block, the breach is sealed by a lock or breechblock that rotates backwards for loading. To load, the hammer is pulled back to full cock. The breechblock is then pulled back, opening the chamber so the cartridge can be put in. Push the breechblock back into place, and you're ready to fire.

The extremely durable weapon could handle the large charges and calibers needed to knock down buffalo and other large game. The range and accuracy of both the Remington and the Sharps were an important asset, since they allowed hunters to shoot from a good distance. The idea was to get precision kills without alerting the rest of the herd to what was going on. It

A buffalo hunter and his Winchester Model 1895.

was an idea that applies with some modifications to all long-range shooting, not just buffalo hunting.

By 1875, the southern buffalo herd had been all but exterminated—and in that year, partly as a consequence, the mighty Comanche surrendered at last. America's surviving buffalo now roamed only over the Dakotas, Montana, and Wyoming, where they helped the northern Plains Indians resist the onrush of whites and their ways. These last great buffalo-hunting grounds would host the final acts of the Indian Wars. Ironically, it was the native tribes who reaped the advantage of American firearm innovation in the most famous confrontation in that end game: Custer's Last Stand.

When the Battle of Little Bighorn began on June 25, 1876, at 4:15 p.m. near a riverside Indian settlement in eastern Montana, George Armstrong Custer had 210 mounted troops and scouts of the U.S. Army Seventh Cavalry under his command. They were largely armed with single-shot 1873 "Trapdoor" Springfield carbines.

Less than sixty minutes later, Custer and all of his men were gone. Their deaths were serenaded by the staccato crackle of gunfire from Winchester repeating rifles—in the hands of Lakota, Cheyenne, and Arapaho warriors.

Guided by poor intel and his own bad judgment, Custer's plan was to attack the Indian settlement quickly. A separate force under his command would engage from another direction while a third detachment blocked the escape route through a nearby valley. Custer apparently aimed to induce the Indian warriors to sue for peace by taking their women and children as hostages and human shields. He figured, according to author Evan S. Connell, that the Indians "would be obliged to surrender, because if they started to fight, they would be shooting their own families."

But Custer never got his hostages. Instead, he was cut off by a multi-tribal strike force of perhaps 1,500 combat-seasoned Indian fighters. He was hugely outnumbered, and, just as importantly, outgunned.

The "Trapdoor" Springfield carbines in the hands and saddles of Custer's men were recycled weapons from the Civil War. Faced with tons of surplus muzzle-loading rifle-muskets when the Civil War ended, the Army decided to modify the guns by cutting into the rear of the barrel and installing a breechblock, chamber, and "trapdoor" bolt, a system into which metal cartridges could be loaded fairly quickly. Under perfect conditions, a trooper might get twelve to fifteen shots off in a minute.

Under perfect conditions.

The U.S. Army continued to use the single-shot Trapdoor Springfield well into the Spanish American War, despite all evidence of their shortcomings. Army planners were not only cheap, but stuck in the past.

To be fair, the Springfields did have some upsides. The carbines were fairly rugged, fired a good-sized bullet, and were accurate at long range. They could throw a .45-caliber, 405-grain bullet as far as 600 yards or more with fine results. But as it happened, the battle climax at Little Bighorn was fought at relatively close range. Like most U.S. Army troops in those days,

Custer's men were not intensively drilled in marksmanship, and were prone to shoot high, especially when aiming downhill. They had trouble reloading quickly under pressure. The guns themselves suffered a kind of combat fatigue: the Springfields were known to jam, overheat, and get fouled with residue during fighting.

Custer's problems were magnified by his tactics and the terrain. The brushy landscape hid the size of the Indian force. His impulsive race to attack the huge Indian village took him out of range of reinforcements. He split up his command repeatedly on the battlefield, and launched his attack without much in the way of reconnaissance.

According to Indians who fought in the battle, Custer's "last stand" was actually a series of five individual stands made by groups of cavalrymen, as Custer's lines repeatedly collapsed up the hill in ten-minute stages. At one point the dismounted Army troops held a fairly continuous line along a half-mile backbone in the hill. But everything changed when the Lakota's warrior chief, Crazy Horse, led a sudden, surprise mounted charge through their ranks.

"Right among them we rode," said a Little Bighorn vet named Thunder Bear, "shooting them down as in a buffalo drive." Daniel White Thunder remembered,

An artist's depiction of the Battle of Little Bighorn. The Native American force employed more repeaters—such as the Winchester held by the Indian warrior at front—than Custer's U.S. Army troops.

"As soon as the soldiers on foot had marched over the ridge," he and his fellow warriors stampeded Custer's horses "by waving their blankets and making a terrible noise." The horses carried away most of the cavalry's reserve ammunition. Red Hawk described a scene of mass confusion: "The dust was thick and we could hardly see. We got right among the soldiers and killed a lot with our bows and arrows and tomahawks. Crazy Horse was ahead of all, and he killed a lot of them with his war club." Cheyenne Two Moons recalled the chaos as "all mixed up, Sioux, then soldiers, then more Sioux, and all shooting."

As the Indians' momentum increased, they used "battlefield pickups" and corpse-stripping of U.S. Army weapons and ammo to boost their firepower. "By this time," said Red Hawk, "the Indians were taking the guns and cartridges of the dead soldiers and putting these to use."

The Indians had begun the day armed with a plethora of weapons, including a favorite Native American rifle, the Winchester. The repeater gave them a powerful edge when the fighting got closer. "The Indians at the Little Bighorn used at least 47 different types of firearms against the 7th Cavalry," reports Doug Scott, a prominent historian of the battle who has studied its archaeology. "The Henry, Winchester Model 1866, and [Winchester] Model 1873 were used in abundance." Archeological analyses performed by Scott and others in recent decades has estimated that roughly 25 percent of the Indian warriors were armed with repeating Henrys or Winchester 1866 or 1873 models; another 25 percent were armed with single-shot rifles and muzzleloaders of various types, and the remaining half used traditional war implements like clubs, lances, and bows and arrows. The Indians had obtained the repeaters through trade,

U.S. government clearance sales, raids, and battle-field pickups.

The complete annihilation of Custer and his troops at Little Bighorn was the biggest victory ever achieved by Native Americans against the U.S. Army. It also marked a milestone in the long climax of the Indian Wars, which finally ended at Wounded Knee in 1890. There, troops of the same Seventh Cavalry massacred one hundred and fifty or more Indian men, women, and children.

Debates have raged among historians and firearms buffs for decades around Custer's mistakes, over alternative histories of the Bighorn battle, and about what difference various guns might have made. It's possible Custer wouldn't have stood much of a chance no matter what weapons he had, given the overwhelming number of Indian warriors he faced.

At the risk of armchair quarterbacking, let's suggest one gun that Custer should have taken along, a revolutionary weapon that might have saved him and his troops.

It was the Gatling gun, a two-man, hand-cranked, rapid-fire "machine gun" that could fire hundreds of bullet rounds a minute. First used during the Civil War, the weapon could spit bullets out at a furious pace. Custer had access to a battery of six Gatlings.

Though heavy, the guns could be broken down, packed onto mules or horses, and hauled, with some difficulty, over the rough terrain. The downside was they had a tendency to jam and otherwise malfunction, and they could roll over and shatter to pieces while being handled on hilly inclines.

But it wasn't the Gatling's awesome firepower that would have saved Custer. It was the fact that the bulky Gatlings, even when disassembled for portability, would have slowed his march to Little Bighorn long enough for his forces to consolidate. Reinforcements would have arrived in time. Custer would have hours to spare to formulate a coherent plan of action.

But time was the reason Custer left them behind in the first place. He figured they'd slow him down.

On second thought, maybe there was no hope for Custer at all. He was in too much of a hurry to meet his fate.

Dubbed "the gun that won the West," the Winchester Model 1873 was an instant hit, destined to be a long-running best-seller for the company. The first cartridge it fired was a .44–40 Winchester center fire round, which proved particularly popular with people who owned revolvers in the same caliber. Winchester soon produced rifles in other calibers, making it possible for more gun owners to use the same bullets for their long gun and their pistol.

Other models followed. Winchester developed the 1876 with an enlarged and strengthened receiver, which allowed for larger and more powerful cartridges. Eventually available in a series of calibers ranging from .40–60 on up to .50–95 Express, the gun packed enough wallop to make it suitable for buffalo hunting. The 1876 and the 1886 that followed were versatile and powerful rifles, and straddled the transition from black powder to smokeless.

Winchester lever-action rifles became the prized possession of ranchers, movie stars, and presidents alike. The Winchester Model 1892 Lever-Action Repeater was the favorite of sharpshooter Annie Oakley and tagged along in Admiral Robert Peary's baggage on a trek to the North Pole. Winchester sold a million of those guns. The Model 1894 was an even hotter seller, with more than 7 million produced in its different forms, making it the number one sporting rifle in history. Though it was first built to fire black powder rounds, it switched easily to new smokeless cartridges. In the United States, the Winchester 94 .30–30 combo became synonymous with "deer rifle." You can still buy one new, fresh from the factory.

But my all-time favorite Winchester repeater has to be the Model 1892. If you've watched only John Wayne movies, you've probably seen the gun. It has an over-sized loop trigger guard that looks like a miniature metal lasso under the stock. Unlike the 1876 and 1886 models, the 1892 was made to handle shorter rounds, again allowing a frontiersman to carry the same bullets for pistol and rifle.

For years, a friend of mine had a fine example of an 1892 sitting in his weapons vault. This particular version was a specially made Winchester John Wayne Commemorative edition. It had special engraving on the metal and a silver indicia on the stock showing the Duke's profile. Any time I'd go over to the vault, just about my favorite thing would be to take that rifle and rack it. I'd work the action like I was riding with the Duke himself.

One day, we were in there talking, and I went over to the gun. My friend looked at me a little funny, so I stopped and backed away.

"Take it," he told me. "It's yours."

"Huh?"

"You like that gun so much," he insisted. "Take it."

"Really?"

"Really."

I did. And I've enjoyed it ever since.

You can't make a Western without a Winchester.
Above, John Wayne takes aim in *El Dorado;* below,
in the hands of Jimmy Stewart in *Winchester '73.*

In the early morning hours of Valentine's Day, 1884, a young politician sat at the bedside of his dying wife, trying to make sense of the way joy had suddenly turned to tragedy over the past twenty-four hours. He had returned home to New York City through a terrible fog and storm after receiving a wire that his wife had given birth to their first child. Now he was shocked to find his wife dying of kidney failure, then known as Bright's Disease. Downstairs, his mother was in the final stages of typhoid fever.

His daughter was healthy, but both his mother and wife would die that same day.

Devastated and utterly alone, the young man left politics and New York. Wandering the American West in search of a new life, he settled into the life of a rancher and outdoorsman in the badlands of Dakota Territory.

The man was Theodore Roosevelt. TR went on to become America's youngest president and a Nobel Peace Prize winner—as well as a lifetime National Rifle Association member, world-famous big-game hunter, gun collector, and the biggest celebrity endorser that the Winchester firearms brand ever had. "The Winchester," he wrote, "is by all odds the best weapon I ever had, and I now use it almost exclusively."

As a hunter out West, Roosevelt liked not only the punch but the utility of the 1876 Model. "It is as handy to carry, whether on foot or on horseback, and comes up to the shoulder as readily as a shotgun," he declared. "It is absolutely sure, and there is no recoil to jar and disturb the aim, while it carries accurately quite as far as a man can aim with any degree of certainty." The .40–60 Winchester, he noted, "carries far and straight and hits hard, and is a first-rate weapon for deer and antelope, and can also be used with effect against sheep, elk, and even bear."

In the West, Roosevelt found his reason to go on living. Hunting inspired him. He was a cowboy poet when it came to guns. "No one but he who has partaken thereof can understand the keen delight of hunting in lonely lands," Roosevelt wrote. "For him is the joy of the horse well ridden and the rifle well held; for him the long days of toil and hardship, resolutely endured, and crowned at the end with triumph. In after years there shall come forever to his mind the memory of endless prairies shimmering in the bright sun; of vast snow-clad wastes lying desolate under gray skies; of the melancholy marshes; of the rush of mighty rivers; of the breath of the evergreen forest in summer; of the crooning of ice-armored pines at the touch of the winds of winter; of cataracts roaring

Teddy Roosevelt photographed in 1895 with his
favorite gun, a Winchester 1876 Deluxe.

between hoary mountain masses; of all the innumerable sights and sounds of the wilderness; of its immensity and mystery; and of the silences that brood in its still depths."

In a few short years living in the West, Roosevelt became an authentic cowboy-rancher. He tamed bucking broncos, drove a thousand head of cattle on a six-day trail ride, punched out a cowboy in a saloon fight, and faced down Indian warriors. In 1886, with an 1876 Winchester in hand, he tracked and captured three desperadoes in the wilderness and marched them forty miles to face justice.

TR was witnessing the end of the American frontier. By 1890, fewer than a thousand American bison remained. Most of the available land claims had been staked. Countless lives had been claimed by nature, and by man. Yet for many settlers, and for millions more who would follow, the opening of the West offered opportunity and freedom. That frontier spirit is still branded into our national character.

As for Teddy Roosevelt, the West eventually repaired his spirit. He found his bearings again, returned to politics, and started a new family. He worked to clean up the New York City police department, then became an assistant secretary of the Navy. Wanting to see more action, he quit that job when war came, rounding up a group of volunteers to form one of the most famous cavalry units of all time. .

And it was in a single hour in 1898, in the thick of combat, when Teddy Roosevelt would discover the key to the White House—while ducking bullets from a gun design that would help shape America into a world power.

5

The M1903 Springfield

"The French told us that they had never seen such marksmanship practiced in the heat of battle."

—*Marine Colonel Albertus Catlin, 1918*

"I am the ranking officer here," yelled Colonel Theodore Roosevelt, "and I give the order to charge!"

It was July 1, 1898. America was a few hours away from becoming a world power.

But it sure didn't look it. Thousands of American troops were roasting in the hot sun below the hills guarding the eastern approaches to Santiago, Cuba. Palms and the nearby mountains made the place look like a picture postcard paradise. But the whizzing bullets and heat made it feel like hell.

The Americans were bunched up, clogged and trapped by their sheer numbers.

Bullets shredded the tall grass around them. "The situation was desperate," wrote Richard Harding Davis, a reporter on the scene. "Our troops could not retreat, as the trail for two miles behind them was wedged with men. They could not remain where they were, for they were being shot to pieces. There was only one thing they could do—go forward and take the San Juan hills by assault."

Roosevelt's thick glasses fogged in the boiling humidity. He was leading a force of nearly one thousand "Rough Riders," officially named the First United States Volunteer Cavalry. The handpicked, motley-crew cavalry regiment took Texas Rangers and Western cowboys and mixed them with East Coast Ivy Leaguers, polo players, and tennis stars. Not only were they a varied unit, they were on foot, except for Roosevelt. The rest of the unit's horses were still back in Florida.

Mounted or not, they'd just be targets if they stayed where they were. But the American infantry officer at the head of the mass formation didn't want to command his troops to move without orders from his superior. And his unit was in Roosevelt's way.

Cuba, 1898: a sensationalized depiction of Teddy Roosevelt leading the Rough Riders up the San Juan Heights.

Screw that, said TR. *Move or get your butt out of the way.*

Not in those exact words. But he did pull rank.

"Charge!" barked TR.

Roosevelt galloped around the field cursing and cheering his cavalry forward. The infantry troops around and in front of them realized it was their best option, too. Soon they were all rushing up Kettle Hill.

"The entire command moved forward as coolly as though the buzzing of bullets was the humming of bees," recalled Lieutenant John J. Pershing, who would lead the American Army in World War I and the years that followed. "White regiments, black regiments, regulars and Rough Riders, representing the young manhood of the North and the South, fought shoulder to shoulder, unmindful of race or color, unmindful of whether commanded by ex-Confederate or not, and mindful of only their common duty as Americans."

But as the Americans advanced, the gunfire intensified, both on Kettle Hill and the nearby San Juan Heights, where the main American assault was focused. Soldiers dropped in bunches. Not only did the enemy have artillery pieces in position, they had better rifles. Though the Spanish were vastly outnumbered, they commanded the high ground, and had a serious edge in firearms.

The main Spanish infantry rifle, the German-made Spanish Model 1893 Mauser rifle, was a fast-firing, speed-loading, repeating firearm of excellent reliability and smooth, safe, and effective performance. It was close to a masterpiece of a gun. It fired a high-velocity 7 × 57mm full-metal jacket cartridge with a spitzer—or pointed—bullet at its tip. The ammo fed smoothly from an integrated five-round staggered box magazine that could be loaded via stripper clips. The bullets were nicknamed "Spanish Hornets" by

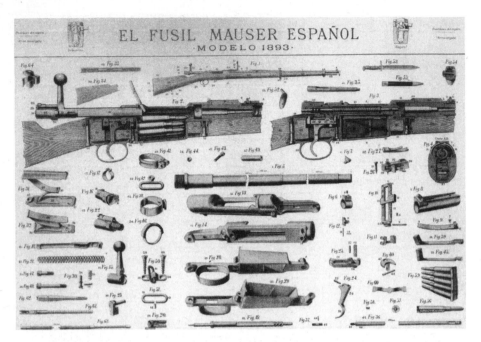

"The Spanish Hornet": the Spanish Mauser, Model 1893,
which bedeviled American troops in Cuba.

American troops who heard the supersonic rounds
zipping by their ears. The weapon was so efficient
that it served as the starting blueprint for many of the
world's infantry rifles for the next fifty years.

The Americans had their own bolt-action weapon,
the magazine-fed Krag-Jorgensen, officially named
"U.S. magazine Rifle (or Carbine), .30 caliber, Model
1896." While the Krag was a step up from the past,
the Norwegian-designed gun wasn't in the same
league as the Mauser. Worse, most of the regular U.S.
Army troops on the battlefield were carrying the 1873

"In the trenches on San Juan Hill, Cuba."
American Krag rifles (shown here) proved inferior,
launching the quest that lead to the M1903.

Trapdoor Springfields, which fired dangerously obsolete, shorter-range .45–70 black powder cartridges. Yes, those are the same rifles Custer's men used at Little Bighorn. The clouds of smoke they shed were "bullet magnets" letting the enemy know where they were. Let me tell you, I don't recommend announcing your position like that when there are snipers around.

Before arriving in Cuba, Roosevelt had decided the trapdoor Springfield was "antiquated" and "almost useless in the battle." He wasn't too sure about the Krags, either. He had shelled out money from his own pocket to buy his officers some of his favorite Winchester repeaters, but his force was still hopelessly outgunned.

And stuck, with only one way to go—up the hill, toward the bullets.

"Spanish fire," remembered Roosevelt later, "swept the whole field of battle up to the edge of the river, and man after man in our ranks fell dead or wounded." The Mauser's smokeless powder made it harder for the Americans to find targets. "The Mauser bullets drove in sheets through the trees and the tall jungle grass, making a peculiar whirring or rustling sound," said Roosevelt. "Some of the bullets seemed to pop in the air, so that we thought they were explosive; and, indeed, many of those which were coated with brass did explode, in the sense that the brass coat was ripped off, making a thin plate of hard metal with a jagged edge, which inflicted a ghastly wound."

Lines of American soldiers, led by Roosevelt, climbed the hills like streams of ants into the carpets of Spanish bullets. It was a slow-motion charge, with the Americans fighting not just the Spanish bullets and the slope, but also the intense heat. Some fell; others dropped for cover. The assault crawled along.

With his men hugging the ground, an American officer stood up and paced in the open to inspire his troops. "Captain, a bullet is sure to hit you," protested one of his men. The officer took his cigarette out of his mouth, blew out a smoke cloud, and laughed. "Sergeant, the Spanish bullet isn't made that will kill me!"

Roosevelt witnessed what happened next: "As he turned on his heel, a bullet struck him in the mouth and came out at the back of his head; so that even before he fell his wild and gallant soul had gone out into the darkness."

Reporter Richard Harding Davis recalled, "They walked to greet death at every step, many of them, as they advanced, sinking suddenly or pitching forward and disappearing in the high grass, but the others waded on, stubbornly, forming a thin blue line that kept creeping higher and higher up the hill. It was as inevitable as the rising tide. It was a miracle of self-sacrifice, a triumph of bulldog courage, which one watched breathless with wonder."

For all their bravery, the assault might have failed except for an ace of a weapon. A battery of three hand-cranked Colt M-1895 Gatling guns swept the Spanish-held heights with sheets of .30-caliber gunfire, covering the advance and clearing paths for the American assault.

The drum of the guns was like no other sound on the battlefield. The sound cheered the Americans even as it mowed down the Spanish. The Gatlings would lay down an impressive 18,000 rounds in support of the U.S. troops that day.

The assault picked up steam. Roosevelt was grazed by bullets twice. He waved his bloody hand in the air to rally his troops forward. Finally the Spanish, realizing they were about to be overrun, retreated from their Kettle Hill fortifications.

Forty yards from the crest, a wire barrier blocked Teddy's stallion. Roosevelt spun out of the saddle like the rancher he once was, climbed over the wire, and dashed to the top. For a moment, he stood atop Kettle Hill nearly alone, his troops climbing to meet him.

Over on San Juan Heights, the main force sent the Spanish reeling. Roosevelt reinforced Kettle Hill, surveying a horrible sight.

The Spanish fortifications, Roosevelt recalled, were "filled with dead bodies in the light blue and white uniform of the Spanish regular army." He came across very few wounded, as "most of the fallen had little holes in their heads from which their brains were oozing."

Suddenly, two Spanish soldiers popped up from the piles of bodies, leveled their Mausers at Roosevelt, and fired from ten yards away.

Colonel Roosevelt and the Rough Riders at the top of
San Juan Heights, after weathering the storm of Spanish
Mauser fire. TR's holster contains a Colt revolver that was
recovered from the wreck of the *Maine*.

They missed. Roosevelt jerked his Colt revolver and
held it at hip level as they turned to run. He fired twice,
missing the first and killing the second.

A reporter watching the Americans consolidate
their positions atop San Juan Heights at about 2 p.m.
remembered the scene: "They drove the yellow silk
flags of the cavalry and the Stars and Stripes of their
country into the soft earth of the trenches, and then
sank down and looked back at the road they had
climbed and swung their hats in the air." The reporter

heard a faint, tired cheer. The battle was won, and over.

American losses were immense: over two hundred dead and nearly another twelve hundred wounded. The Spanish lost 215 dead and another 376 wounded. The real story of the numbers, though, is this: the American force was 15,000; the Spanish started with 750. The fact that the Spanish could hold off such a large force at all is a testament not only to their weapons but their courage and skill as warriors.

The charges up Kettle Hill and San Juan Heights alone did not win the Spanish-American War. But it had numerous effects. With the hills taken, Santiago could not be held. The admiral who headed the Spanish fleet had been sitting on his ass for days, debating whether to go out and face the American fleet or not. Now he had no choice. His ships sailed out to their destruction in Santiago Bay July 3. The city of Santiago surrendered July 17; game over.

The Spanish sued for peace. The Treaty of Paris was signed on August 12, and the Americans were granted authority over the Spanish colonies of Philippines, Guam, Puerto Rico, and Cuba. Just like that, the United States was an international power. The epic images of Roosevelt and the Rough Riders' actions that day were celebrated by the press. His fame propelled him into the governorship of New York State in a few short months. Then came the vice presidency, and after William McKinley's assassination in September 1901, the presidency itself, at the tender age of forty-two.

The episode also marked a turning point in American guns: the shift from antiquated military rifles to cutting-edge, modern weapons that could dominate the battlefield. The road ahead would continue to be filled with curves and detours, but change would no longer be resisted on the grounds that proven technology was still too new.

And one of the prime movers of the new direction was Teddy Roosevelt, who as president helped push the American military to adopt what was essentially a bootleg copy of the gun that had done so much damage to his forces on Kettle Hill.

For more than sixty years, America had been cursed by bad decisions coming out of one office in Washington, D.C.: the U.S. Army Ordnance Corps. The head shed there controlled the nation's weapons arsenals, including the biggest ones at Springfield, Massachusetts, and Harpers Ferry, Virginia.

The men in charge were the bureaucrats and generals who were supposed to equip our fighting men with the latest firearms and the top technology. Instead, as we've seen, they managed to do their best to condemn American soldiers to failure and death. They pissed away opportunities to get superior weapons and consistently chose clunkers, again and again.

When George Washington ordered his artillery chief Henry Knox to start an American weapons arsenal in Springfield in 1776, he helped spark the stirrings of the American Industrial Revolution. But by the Civil War, the arsenal was stuck in the past. The arteries were so clogged it affected the Army's brain. Bad weapons mandated bad tactics; bad tactics encouraged bad training; bad training justified bad weapons.

"The armory also spawned a culture of obdurate bureaucracy that has afflicted parts of the U.S. military establishment down to the present day," wrote John Lehman, who served as secretary of the Navy during the Reagan administration. "Having made a vital contribution to winning independence, the Springfield armory had great prestige in the new republic. Unfortunately, the armory and the Ordnance Corps developed an autonomy within the new War Department that rapidly hardened into orthodoxy and an aversion to new weapons technology."

After the Revolution, the ordnance bureaucrats ignored the obvious promise of the breech-loading rifle and percussion cap and forced the military to cling to outdated muzzleloaders and flintlocks into the Mexican War era and beyond. During the Civil War, breechloaders, repeaters, and Gatling Guns were available for mass production and might have won the war for the Union much more quickly, but officials stubbornly sidetracked each breakthrough.

In the Indian Wars, they kept Winchester repeaters out of our troops' hands. Incredibly, after the Little Bighorn disaster, Army Chief of Ordnance Stephen Vincent Benét insisted that the totally obsolete single-shot Trapdoor Springfield would remain in service as the regulation infantry shoulder weapon from 1874 to 1891. His successor, Daniel Webster Flagler, chose the Krag-Jorgensen to replace the Springfield Trapdoor over the Mauser. Why? Partly because the boob-ureaucracy thought the Krag would use less ammunition and so reduce costs. These guys had a fatal fetish for conserving ammo. I'm all for cutting back on government waste, but there's a point where saving money ends up costing a heck of a lot more in people's lives. The Ordnance officers flew past that point time and again.

Privately, many U.S. Army officials were horrified by the carnage wreaked by the superior firepower of the Mauser rifles at the Battle of San Juan Heights. They were determined to get their soldiers a much better gun than the Krag. Captured Spanish Mausers were carefully analyzed, and gradually an idea began to spread:

"Why not just copy the Mauser?"

And so they did.

Developed from earlier Mauser designs, the Mauser M93 used on Cuba stands at the head of a family of weapons that saw rapid improvement in the years around the turn of the century. As you'd expect, the rifle's development and innovations in ammunition went hand in hand. Advances in the science of alloys led to stronger steel and more powerful and lighter weapons. That meant that other improvements in powder could be put to work. Cartridges could be more powerful without damaging the weapon. Bullets could go faster and farther.

The Mausers used what is known as "bolt action" to handle the complicated business of putting the ammo in place and then sending it on its way. The breech of a bolt-action rifle is opened by a handle at the side of weapon. When that handle is drawn back, the spent cartridge is ejected. The handle is then pushed forward, stripping the cartridge from the magazine and placing it into the chamber. The bolt is locked in position, and the gun is ready to fire. It's tough to improve on this system—most of my sniper rifles were bolt-action.

Going from black to smokeless powder didn't just make it easier to see on the battlefield. Rifle bullets could now move faster and go farther with the same or even less volume of powder. The design of the bullets and their cartridge evolved hand in glove with the powder and the rifles, becoming more efficient and cleaner in the gun.

Not to mention deadlier.

Four years after the charges at San Juan Hill, following extensive testing, experimentation, and input from veterans including Roosevelt, the Springfield Armory unveiled the five-round-magazine, stripper-clip-fed, bolt-action M1903 Springfield. Officially called the "U.S. Rifle, Caliber .30, Model of 1903," it was known by troops as the "aught three," or, in later years, simply "the Springfield." There were a few key differences and improvements, most notably in the firing pin, but the aught-three was pretty much a Mauser. In fact, the Americans plagiarized so badly that the U.S. government lost a lawsuit brought by Mauser and was forced to pay the foreign company hundreds of thousands of dollars in royalties. Still, the United States had its gun.

Teddy loved the new Springfield 1903 so much he put in an order for his own custom-made hunting model. For the next twelve years he used the rifle to bag more than three hundred animals on three continents, including lions, hyenas, rhinoceros, giraffes, zebras,

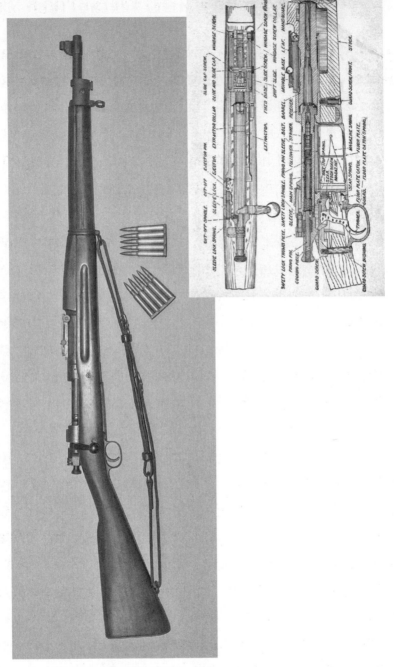

The M1903 Springfield. It so closely "borrowed" from the Mauser design that the U.S. government was forced to pay royalties to the German company.

gazelles, warthogs, hippopotamuses, monkeys, jaguars, giant anteaters, black bears, crocodiles, and pythons.

But there was one thing Roosevelt hated about the rifle's original design. He thought the weapon's slim, rod-type bayonet was a piece of junk. He wanted it changed, so he halted production.

"I must say," he fumed in a memo to Secretary of War William Howard Taft, "I think that ramrod bayonet about as poor an invention as I ever saw." The point of the slim bayonet was to serve as an emergency ramrod in case the rifle jammed. Roosevelt as well as countless Army men realized it was too fragile to do its main job. So in 1905 a sixteen-inch knife-style blade bayonet was added. The bayonet was a real beast; the devil himself wouldn't have wanted to pick his teeth with it.

Even better was the improved ammo, which was introduced in 1906. The new cartridge was based on the old one, but had a lighter, 150-grain pointed "boat tail" bullet at its head. It became the classic American military round for decades, and remains probably the most popular civilian hunting round today. Known as the .30-06, the "aught-six" refers to the year it was introduced rather than the size of the ammo. The new ammunition made the 1903 Springfield rifle a superstar, conferring the advantages of greater speed, force, and accuracy than a round-tipped projectile. Along with the new ammo the barrel was shortened, making it a bit easier to handle.

You may have noticed that the size of rifle bullets has started coming down. Throughout history, there was a tradeoff between speed and size, weight of the gun, and ease of use. It's tough to make a blanket statement about what ammo or bullet is better without viewing the entire system or the job that needs to get done. The rifles the Americans had in Cuba fired bigger bullets than the Spaniards; obviously that wasn't an advantage there. But here's an interesting observation from that war, made by Roosevelt himself:

"The Mauser bullets themselves made a small clean hole, with the result that the wound healed in a most astonishing manner. One or two of our men who were shot in the head had the skull blown open, but elsewhere the wounds from the minute steel-coated bullet, with its very high velocity, were certainly nothing like as serious as those made by the old large-caliber, low-power rifle. If a man was shot through the heart, spine, or brain he was, of course, killed instantly; but very few of the wounded died—even under the appalling conditions which prevailed, owing to the lack of attendance and supplies in the field-hospitals with the army."

That's an observation that would be made again, though in different words and context, when rifle technology took another step forward (and half-step back) with the birth of the M16 family and its 5.56 × 45mm rounds.

With the new .30-06 cartridge giving the gun serious stopping power, the 1903 Springfield became one of the best infantry rifles in the world. The Germans had a decent weapon themselves in the Gewehr 98, another improved Mauser. I've heard it contended that the Springfield's manufacturing was more consistent, but on the other side of that people say its firing pin is weaker than the Mauser's.

Take your pick. I'd happily shoot either or both any day of the week.

The Springfield 1903 first saw action in the U.S. military operations in the Philippines, Nicaragua, Dominican Republic, and in General John "Black Jack" Pershing's deep penetration raids into Mexico, in pursuit of Pancho Villa. When World War I started, it was ready for war before the Doughboys were.

On June 2, 1918, it looked like the Germans were about to win World War I.

The Russian army had collapsed and a peace treaty between the two countries was signed in February.

"A quiet moment in the German trenches."
Various Mauser rifles lay in position on top of the trench.

That set nearly fifty German divisions loose. They were switched to the Western Front, and the German General Staff got ready to push the Allies to the sea. German planes bombed Paris; their long-range guns lobbed shells in the direction of the Eiffel Tower. The British high command started planning how to get its troops back to England without having them swim. The German army had seized the initiative and shattered the spirit of the Allies. Oh, and they had Mausers, too.

The imminent capture of Paris was likely to deliver a psychological blow the French would never recover from. The Germans pressed on, sure that the Allies would soon be forced to sue for peace. Just forty-five miles northeast of Paris, near a patch of forest called Belleau Wood and the town of Chateau-Thierry, U.S. Marine Corps Colonel Albertus Wright Catlin saw the leading edge of the methodical German advance as it steamrollered through the French lines. "The Germans swept down an open slope in platoon waves," he recalled, "across wide wheat-fields bright with poppies that gleamed like splashes of blood in the afternoon sun."

It was a thing of beauty, unless you were tasked to stop it. The French troops fell back, fighting as they retreated across the wheat field. "Then the Germans, in two columns, steady as machines," wrote Colonel Catlin. "To me as a military man it was a beautiful sight. I could not but admire the precision and steadiness of those waves of men in gray with the sun glinting on their helmets. On they came, never wavering, never faltering, apparently irresistible."

What the Germans didn't know was that a force of thousands of tough young U.S. Marines was lying in wait for them, supported by thousands more U.S. Army troops nearby. In a desperate, last-second move, they had been rushed to the scene as a blocking force to stop the German advance.

It had been more than a year since America declared war on Germany, but its troops had yet to play a major role in any battle. That was because the Allied high command didn't think the American forces were ready to fight. They thought them soft and unprepared. Before they arrived in 1917, one British general even proposed that American recruits be used directly as replacements in British divisions, entirely under British command.

The Americans told them what they could do with that.

Even so, General Pershing, the commander in chief of the American Expeditionary Force, knew there was a lot of truth in the harsh assessment of his troops. He spent the better part of 1917 and the first half of 1918 training them up.

Now they were ready. Black Jack, who we saw in Cuba as a lieutenant, had been urging the reluctant allies to get his Marines and soldiers into real action for months. The German offensive made the French so desperate they had no choice. The U.S. Second Division, which included a brigade of Marines, and the Third Division were moved into positions along the line of the expected German advance.

Every one of the Marines lying in ambush was a highly skilled, long-range rifleman. The Marines were supported with some artillery and machine guns, but

World War I recruitment poster featuring
a Marine and his trusted M1903.

their main instrument of battle was the light, accurate, bayonet-tipped M1903 Springfield rifle. Each Marine had endured eight weeks of brutally intense training at Parris Island, South Carolina, drills that included extensive practice in the care and feeding of his rifle. Besides long-distance marksmanship, there was also close-quarter bayonet and hand-to-hand combat training. Unlike the Army, which assumed mass firepower from large units and didn't pay too much attention to marksmanship, the Marines started from the idea that they'd be fighting in small units that had to make every shot count.

As they arrived in the fields near Belleau Wood that early morning, one of the Marines asked, "Where's this here line we're supposed to hold, Sarge?"

The reply: "We're gonna *make* a line, sonny."

The French had a line, but it was moving the wrong way. Now the Germans were aiming to blow a gap in it that would take them from Belleau Wood, across the Marne river and on to Paris. The Americans were between them and the best road to Paris for miles. As the Americans marched in, Captain Lloyd Williams of 2nd Battalion, 5th Marines Regiment, was advised by withdrawing French army troops that his best bet for survival was to fall back.

"Retreat, hell!" he said. "We just got here!"

All the Marines felt that way. As one commander explained to a French general, "We will dig no trenches to fall back into. The Marines will hold where they stand."

The Germans who came through the wheat field that afternoon had little or no idea they were about to stumble on American Marines. Their intel had them facing the crumbling French army, and their eyes told them no different. The Americans waited until the right moment, then unleashed a barrage of rifle and machine gun fire on the German spearhead. Marines methodically picked off individual targets with their Springfield 1903s from hundreds of yards away.

"The French told us that they had never seen such marksmanship practiced in the heat of battle," recalled Colonel Catlin. "If the German advance looked beautiful to me, that metal curtain that our Marines rang down on the scene was even more so. The German lines did not break; they were broken. The Boches [Germans] fell by the scores there among the wheat and the poppies. They hesitated, they halted, they withdrew a space. Then they came on again. They were brave men; we must grant them that. Three times they tried to reform and break through that barrage, but they had to stop at last. The United States Marines had stopped them."

The remains of the German force retreated into the thick cover of Belleau Wood. A delighted French pilot swooped low over the scene and signaled "Bravo!" to the Marines.

A savage back and forth bloodbath followed over the next three weeks, as the two sides fought for control of Belleau Wood. The terrain was straight out of a nightmare, a barely-penetrable two-hundred-acre tangle of thick vegetation stocked with German mustard-gas mortars and machine-gun nests. In the words of one Marine commander, it was "like entering a dark room filled with assassins." Plagued by confusing orders and bad maps, scanty food, little intelligence, and poor communications, the American Marines and soldiers launched five failed attempts to sweep the forest, coming up short each time.

On June 6, at 5 p.m., clutching his bayonet-tipped M1903 rifle, Sergeant Major Dan Daly rose from the wheat and yelled to his marines the order to advance on the German machine-gun positions bracketing the edge of the forest.

"Come on, you sons of bitches!" yelled Daly, who at a five-foot-six weighed all of 132 pounds. "Do you want to live forever?"

The only thing small about the sergeant was height. He'd already received two Medals of Honor for conspicuous bravery under fire, one in Haiti and the other in China. A thousand Marines stood up and ran forward when he yelled. The Germans unleashed a fierce barrage of rifle, machine gun, and artillery fire. "The losses were terrific," said Colonel Catlin. "Men fell on every hand there in the open, leaving great gaps in the line. [3rd Battalion commander Major Ben] Berry was wounded in the arm, but pressed on with the blood running down his sleeve. Into a veritable hell of hissing bullets, into that death-dealing torrent, with heads bent as though facing a March gale, the shattered lines of Marines pushed on. The headed wheat bowed and waved in that metal cloud-burst like meadow grass in a summer breeze."

When they reached the trees, Private W. H. Smith and his squad put their Springfield 1903 rifles to good use against lingering German troops: "There were about sixty of us who got ahead of the rest of the company. We just couldn't stop despite the orders of our leaders. We reached the edge of the small wooded area and there encountered some of the Hun [German] infantry. Then it became a matter of shooting at mere human targets. We fixed our rifle sights at 300 yards and aiming through the peep kept picking off the Germans. And a man went down at nearly every shot."

German officers and soldiers were stunned at both the tactics and the appearance of the attacking Americans. The Marines used "knives, revolvers, rifle butts and bayonets," complained one German. "All were big fellows, powerful, rowdies." The Marines were so fierce, the Germans were convinced they were drunk and oblivious to pain. My guess is that they were just being badass Marines. Or as a German military report put it, "vigorous, self-confident, and remarkable marksmen."

A letter was found on the battlefield in which a German soldier despaired, "They kill everything that moves."

Yes to that. And they still do.

Captain John W. Thomason wrote that the Marines' rifles let them carry the day. "All [the German] batteries were in action, and always his machine-guns scourged the place, but he could not make head against the rifles. Guns he could understand; he knew all about bombs and auto-rifles and machine-guns and trench-mortars, but aimed, sustained rifle-fire, that comes from nowhere in particular and picks off men—it brought the war home to the individual and demoralized him. And trained Americans fight best with rifles.

Men get tired of carrying grenades and *chaut-chaut* [French-made machine gun] clips; the guns cannot, even under most favorable conditions, keep pace with the advancing infantry. Machine-gun crews have a way of getting killed at the start; trench-mortars and one-pounders are not always possible. But the rifle and bayonet goes anywhere a man can go, and the rifle and the bayonet win battles."

By midday, the Marines had settled things. They owned the woods. The Germans weren't getting to Paris, except maybe as tourists after the war.

It was the bloodiest day in U.S. Marine Corps history to that point, with 1,087 casualties, more than the Marines had suffered in the Corps' whole previous history. But they died heroes and helped save the war. It would be nearly three weeks before the sector was completely secured, but the last great German offensive of the war was pretty much history.

"The effect [of the Marine action at Belleau Wood] on the French has been many times out of all proportion to the size of our brigade or the front on which it has operated," American General James Harbord wrote in his war diary. "They say a Marine can't venture down the boulevards of Paris without risk of being kissed by some casual passerby or some *boulevardiere*. Frenchmen say that the stand of the Marine Brigade in

The site of the Marines' greatest victory during World War I.

Copyr. by Over There Review, Inc.
52 — Belleau Woods
Americans and their Captives—
A few who escaped the
bayonnettes.

"American cemetery—Belleau Woods, France. Where
over 2,000 regulars and Marines who gave their
lives . . . sleep their last sleep."

its far-reaching effects marks one of the great crises of history, and there is no doubt they feel it." Years later, the commander of the 1st Infantry Division, General Robert Lee Bullard, concluded that the Marines "didn't 'win the war' here, but they saved the Allies from defeat. Had they arrived a few hours later I think that would have been the beginning of the end."

The grateful French renamed the forest "Bois de la Brigade de Marine," or "Wood of the Marine Brigade," and awarded the 4th Marine brigade the Croix de Guerre.

The Springfield 1903 remained in service through World War II and was even used in Korea and Vietnam. At least one World War II general is known to have carried and used his with great relish. Omar Bradley, at the time an Army corps commander, habitually kept his in his Jeep in Africa and on Sicily. General Bradley often used the gun to take potshots at attacking German planes.

Though an excellent shot, Bradley is not known to have brought down a plane.

Then again, the German pilots missed him as well.

Much of the Springfield's service in World War II was as a sniper weapon. Army sergeant William E. Jones used it in Normandy with great success. So did many others. While not initially designed as a sniper weapon, its inherent abilities of sure fire and long range made it a good one. Jones credited much of his success to his scope, which provided 2–5× magnification. It was a huge advantage over iron sights, even though it's a far cry from even the less expensive civilian hunting sights we use today.

Inevitably, improvements in technology made the Springfield obsolete as a sniping weapon. Still, its influence lived on, as did its ammunition. Legendary Vietnam-era sniper Carlos Hathcock—the greatest American combat sniper ever—shot a .30–06 from his Winchester Model 70. Even today, the longer range weapons preferred by most snipers can trace their roots back in some way to the bolt-action long gun and its ammo.

Most of my sniper kills in Iraq were made with weapons chambering a .300 Win Mag. The Winchester Magnum round was developed after the 30-06, and in fact the round was first wildcatted, or made privately, after Winchester introduced the cartridges in three other sizes. The new ammo gave more punch to the Model 70 rifle, letting it reach out and touch someone just a little farther than before.

Over the course of my career, I used a number of different bolt-action weapons chambering that particular ammo. Early on, my best combo was probably a gun that used McMillan stocks, customized barrels, and a Remington 700 action. Later on, I shot a weapon from Accuracy International that had a slightly shorter barrel and a folding stock.

I would imagine that most serious hunters are familiar with the Remington 700 rifle and its bolt-action. Running through all the possible variations would take the better part of a day; that's how popular this particular platform has been. Another measure of its success is its adoption by many military forces, police departments, and SWAT teams as the weapon of choice for their long-range shooters. Most famously, the Army's M24 Sniper Weapon System is made by Remington and based on the Remington 700 rifle. The Navy's MK13 sniper weapon is also based on the Remington action, though it uses a different chasis.

The Remington family is so popular that many manufacturers make a ton of accessories, add-ons, and replacements for it. From the days of the Revolution and our friend Tim Murphy, shooters have always wanted to have a little personal touch on their weapon, with customized triggers, stocks, cheekpieces; you name it. You've got to constantly look for an edge anywhere you can find it.

Remington's recent ad campaign puts this gun's popularity in perspective. Above a photo of a modern stainless sporting version of the Model 700 the headline reads, "Over 5,000,000 sold. The world's largest army ain't in China."

One of my favorite personal sniper weapons was a highly customized Mk 13 put together just for me by a friend and fellow SEAL named Monty LeClair. I met Monty when he was a sniper instructor. I'd already seen some of the work he'd done on guns for himself when I picked up a rifle of his one day. As soon as I held it, I knew I had to have one for myself.

We ordered a bunch of parts and went to work. Monty started by taking a Remington 700 action and truing it. This meant going over the workings until they were to exact specifications, removing what for most people wouldn't even be considered blemishes. He put a Rock Creek barrel on it, and then added a number of other high-tech, top-shelf parts. One of Monty's little personal touches had to do with the way he bedded it into the Accuracy International chassis he used. There'd been the tiniest external warp to the action, and he cured any flaw that might have caused.

When he was done, the weapon was a sub-half MOA gun, or accurate to within a half-minute of angle when fired at a target at one hundred yards away. It's a standard snipers and marksmen use to gauge a gun's accuracy without interference from the shooter. In this case, it meant that five military spec bullets hit less than a half-inch apart when fired. Rifles have been improving steadily over the past few years, but that's a damn good grouping by any measure.

Monty's been building guns since he was a teenager, and taking them apart before that. He probably hasn't met a weapon he doesn't think he can improve on. Chief LeClair is still in the Navy, but he ought to eye a career as a gunmaker if he ever retires.

Toward the end of my service as a SEAL, we started working with guns that fired the .338 cartridge, a larger round that in the right weapon has tremendous power and range. The .338 Lapua Magnum round is a great option; in fact, it's the ammunition I was shooting when I got my longest kill, at some 2,100 meters outside Baghdad. I was able to use both a McMillan and an Accuracy International version of the 338; I was on the McMillan when I made that shot. The bullet shoots farther and flatter than a .50 caliber, weighs less, costs less, and will do just as much damage. While the guns are heavier than those designed to fire a WinMag, they're a good sight lighter than a .50. They're awesome weapons.

In case you're wondering, the round is named Lapua after the Finnish company that developed it in the 1980s. The bullet was first intended for a gun being developed by Research Armament Industries in Arkansas to meet a Marine Corps requirement for a new long-range sniper weapon to replace .50 caliber sniper guns. The gun, known as the Haskins rifle after its designer Jerry Haskins, influenced a new generation of designs.

To stand up to the round, the gun required a thick bolt and a wider frame for the action; one of the first companies to produce such a weapon was Mauser, which came out with a .338 Magnum SR93. A lot had changed in a hundred and twenty years since their rifles buzzed past TR's ears, but the company, now a subsidiary of Sig-Sauer, still aimed for the cutting edge of gun design.

Since we're talking about sniper weapons and the cutting edge, I should mention that some of the most important developments in the technology have come in the area of optics. There's no sense having a gun that will shoot 2,000 meters if you can't see what you're aiming at. Improvements in scopes and guns are being made every day. And then there's this: One system I looked at recently allowed the gun—or more specifically its computer—to decide when to take the shot.

Here I am with my Lapua .338, a distant
relative of the bolt-action M1903.

With that system, say its developers, anyone can be a
sniper.

I don't know about that.

The sighting system sure is sweet, and the gun definitely packs a wallop. Is it the future? I guess we'll
find out.

The Springfield M1903 enjoyed a long run. It lives
on today not only in the hands of collectors and shooters who like its solid feel, but in movies and classic
novels. Steve McQueen handled a Springfield in *The
Sand Pebbles,* and an M1903 with a telescopic sight

was used by the sniper played by Barry Pepper in *Saving Private Ryan*. Ernest Hemingway and Kurt Vonnegut wrote Springfields into their stories, and in James Jones's *From Here to Eternity*, soldiers drilled with Springfields and fire them at Japanese aircraft on December 7, 1941.

But another gun developed in the pre–World War I era had an even greater role in movies and popular culture.

I'm talking about the M1911 pistol, standard side-arm for the U.S. military from 1911 to 1985, and the gun that defined semi-automatic pistol for several generations of Americans.

6

The M1911 Pistol

"Beyond a doubt, there is no other service handgun made in the lifespan of the Colt .45 that can equal—or even approach—that of the M1911 Government Model when it comes to resolving conflicts, stopping fights, and keeping Americans alive and fighting."

—*Wiley Clapp,* American Rifleman

On October 18, 1918, a tall, red-haired American Army corporal found himself behind enemy lines in the Argonne Forest in France.

German machine gunners on a nearby ridge were sweeping the bushes around him with bullets. A slug slapped a hole in his helmet, though it somehow left his skull intact.

The corporal had two weapons: a rifle and a hand-gun. The first was an M1917 Enfield bolt-action rifle, a British rival to the Mauser and Springfield that was a little cheaper to make. The second was a .45-caliber, semiautomatic Colt service revolver with the official name of "Automatic Pistol, Caliber .45, Model 1911." It was a weapon that in the right hands could turn bad luck good. It simply kicked ass.

Just like the guy holding it.

The trapped U.S. Army corporal's name was Alvin Cullum York, and the pickle he found himself in had materialized quicker than a New York minute. Bare moments before, the soldier and sixteen other men from Company G, 328th Infantry, 82nd Division, had surprised a group of German troops and taken them prisoner behind the lines. But before they could organize the POWs, the Americans came under concentrated machine gun fire. Nine, including the sergeant leading the three squads on patrol, fell to the ground, all dead or severely wounded.

They were spotted and pinned down by a force that outnumbered them by 20 to 1. Six Americans were shot dead.

"The Germans got us, and they got us right smart," remembered York. "They just stopped us dead in our tracks. Their machine guns were up there on the heights overlooking us and well hidden, and we couldn't tell for certain where the terrible heavy fire was coming from. . . . And I'm telling you they were shooting straight. Our boys just went down like the long grass before the mowing machine at home."

York grew up in the mountains near the Tennessee-Kentucky border. Before the Army, he'd been a hard drinker, a brawler, and a bit of a redneck goof-off. Somehow, he'd grown into a gentle, God-fearing Christian. He'd also become a pacifist, and tried for conscientious-objector status. In fact, it had taken a long talk with his unit commander before he decided his duty as a soldier didn't conflict with his beliefs.

Crouched on the ground, York held his bolt-action Enfield with one hand as bullets flew over his head. He waited for the machine gunner above to stop firing and look down. York was between the prisoners and the machine-gun nest, so close to the enemy that the German had to pitch the barrel down sharply to get at him. The nearby POWs made things tougher for the gunner; he had to get a good fix on his target before firing or risk killing his own people.

Sure enough, a head popped up. York squeezed the trigger.

The German disappeared, dropped by a .30-06 round from York's rifle. York waited. Up came another head, York fired, and the enemy vanished.

"That's enough now!" he yelled out in his hillbilly drawl."You boys quit and come on down!"

The Germans didn't take his advice. They'd been in the war long enough to know that his Enfield had only five rounds in the magazine, so maybe when a lieutenant and five men jumped out to take him with bayonets, they figured they had numbers on their side.

Problem was, York didn't use his rifle next. He switched to his M1911 pistol. And instead of taking down the first man in line, which might've sent the others scurrying to the ground, he worked from back to front, popping them one at a time until finally it was the lieutenant's turn. The German officer fell with a scream, gut-shot.

"You never heard such a racket in all of your life," said York, talking about the battle after it was done. "I didn't have time to dodge behind a tree or dive into the brush. . . . There were over thirty of them in continuous action, and all I could do was touch the Germans off [shoot them down] just as fast as I could. I was sharp shooting. . . . All the time I kept yelling at them to come down. I didn't want to kill any more than I had to. But it was they or I. And I was giving them the best I had."

Finally, York sensed someone behind him. He spun around to see a German officer in the woods with an

Above: Sgt. Alvin York after receiving the Medal of Honor. Below: Sgt. York in winter 1919, "standing in front of hill where 132 German prisoners were taken in Oct. 1918."

empty Luger pistol. The German had been trying to shoot him, but missed every time. Spooked and sure that York would kill every last member of his unit, the man offered a deal; *If you don't shoot anymore, I'll make them surrender.*

Covering the officer with his M1911, York told him to go ahead. The lieutenant blew a whistle, and fifty Germans emerged with their hands up. More followed.

One die-hard threw a grenade at York and the six other Americans who'd survived. The grenade missed. York didn't. Another German stalled when told to leave his machine gun. York shot him, too.

"I hated to do it," he said later. "He was probably a brave soldier boy. But I couldn't afford to take any chance so I let him have it."

York ordered the officer to guide them toward American lines. The mass formation marched off, with the seven Americans using the Germans as human shields. They gathered more prisoners as they went.

After they reached safety, York reported to battalion headquarters. "Well, York, I hear you captured the whole damned German army," said his brigade commander, General Julian R. Lindsey.

"No sir," said York. "I only have one hundred and thirty-two."

When someone asked the corporal how he did it, he gave them a Tennessee smile. "I surrounded 'em."

York's shooting had been honed through thousands of hours of practice in the mountains where he'd grown up. There he'd hunted with a muzzle-loading Kentucky rifle his granddad had used. The gun was an authentic American long rifle—ball, black powder, and all. He also had an old-fashioned cap-and-ball revolver he shot for target practice while riding a mule. Like many guys from backwoods, rural America, he was a crack shot. But probably the high point of his unofficial training had to be the hidden-turkey shoot.

It went like this: York and friends would tie a turkey behind a distant log. The shooter would have to knock it down with the first shot as the bird poked its head up. That itself was pretty hard—turkey heads aren't too big. But just to make it interesting, his friends could do anything they imagined to distract him in the act of shooting, short of actually touching him. Crack jokes, holler, whistle—it all taught York to shoot with supreme focus and aim.

A day after his tromp through the enemy lines, York went back to the scene of the battle. He was shocked by the corpses still lying there. He stopped and said a prayer for his dead friends, then thanked God for letting him live.

"I prayed for the Germans, too," he admitted later. "They were all brother men of mine."

As word spread, York's actions seemed just too incredible. A thorough military investigation was launched. But eyewitnesses and German reports largely confirmed the events. York's division commander, Major General George B. Duncan, said "the more we investigated the exploit, the more remarkable it appeared."

A legend was born. York was soon promoted to sergeant and awarded the Congressional Medal of Honor, the Distinguished Service Cross, the Croix de Guerre, and the Legion of Honor.

"What you did was the greatest thing accomplished by any private soldier of all the armies of Europe," declared French Commanding General Ferdinand Foch. Before returning to Tennessee, York received a ticker-tape parade in New York City and was carried on the shoulders of Wall Street stockbrokers. Offers from Hollywood, publishers, and companies seeking his endorsement streamed in.

Sergeant York lives on in American mythology as one of the toughest soldiers who ever lived. The "Government Model" 1911 pistol he used to pop those Germans has a place right next to him too. The M1911 is a true warrior's tool. It figures into quite a number of war stories, and for its time and place was probably the greatest handgun ever made. We're a hundred years from its birth, but it's still going strong. It's the basis for any number of customized models, including a SEAL commemorative by Para-Ordnance that's one of several M1911s in my personal collection. Even when gun makers don't use it as their model, it's the design they're looking to beat.

Many gun experts agree it rules the roost. When *American Rifleman* recently named their top ten guns of all time, they practically gushed over the weapon. "It fits the hand like a trusted tool," wrote Brian Sheetz. "It functions without fail. It has proved itself in brutal service throughout two world wars. It works just as well on the firing line and on the front lines of combat today as it did the day it was adopted." Editor Wiley Clapp added, "I cannot name a handgun that delivers more mud-and-sand reliability than the Government Model."

The gun's roots go straight back to the last days of the nineteenth century. The U.S. Army was deep in the jungles of the Philippine Islands, which they inherited after the Spanish-American War. Our soldiers were fighting a fierce counterinsurgency war against radical Islamist Moro tribesmen. The tribesmen had a habit of charging Americans with long knives while wearing wood-and-leather body armor. The Moro fanatics supposedly fought under the influence of powerful narcotics, which made them almost immune to pain. Shoot them, and they just kept coming. It was like something out of a zombie movie. The regulation firearms at the time, .38 Long Colt revolvers and .30 Krag rifles, didn't have the man-stopping power for this kind of an attack.

Humbled by the experience, the Army soon conducted experiments on some unfortunate live animals and human cadavers, and decided that American soldiers needed a larger caliber weapon on the hip. What they wanted was something that would stop a horse.

Literally.

"The cavalry doctrine of those days was if you could drop a horse in its tracks, you got rid of the rider as well," explained military historian Edward Ezell of the Smithsonian Institution. It was two for the price of one. So the military went looking for a handgun that could do the job. A historic "bake-off" was held by the Army. Weapons from five companies were put to the test. After years of trials, the championship match was conducted on March 3, 1911, when two finalist handguns faced off against each other in a competition

Philippines, 1899: "Kansas volunteers firing from trench."

somewhere between *Survivor* and *American Idol, Pistol Edition.*

At the end of the tests, one gun stood supreme: a semiautomatic, locked-breech, single-action Colt pistol. The handgun chambered .45-caliber, 230-grain, full metal jacket, smokeless rounds fed from a single stack, seven-shot magazine. The winning prototype had fired no less than six thousand rounds. It had been dunked in acid and salt water, and forced to handle deformed and misloaded rounds. The board of judges found that "the Colt is superior, because it is more reliable, more enduring, more easily disassembled when there are broken parts to be replaced, [and] more accurate."

In other words, it rocked.

The winning design was the brainchild of the Leonardo da Vinci of firearms design: John Moses Browning. The world of guns would be very different without Browning, and the M1911 was his baby. It became the official sidearm of the U.S. Army on March 29, 1911. The U.S. Navy and U.S. Marine Corps followed suit, adopting it in 1913.

When it was adopted, Browning's Colt was officially known as the "Colt Caliber .45 Automatic Pistol." The words "United States" were added to the title, along with the designation M1911 and then M1911A1 for the improved version that came out in 1924. The word "automatic" has remained, in one of the most common nicknames, the .45 Automatic. It's also in the name of the cartridge it takes, .45 ACP (Automatic Colt Pistol). The way we classify guns these days, though, the weapon is a semiautomatic; you have to pull the trigger for each bullet to fire.

It is no exaggeration to give John Browning credit for creating much of the modern world of guns. "To say he was the Edison of the modern firearms industry does not quite cover the case, for he was even greater than that," wrote Captain Paul Curtis in *Guns and Gunning*.

"Browning was unique. He stood alone, and there was in his time or before no one whose genius along those lines could remotely compare with his."

Browning came up with many of the big breakthroughs of the last century and a half in "a creative rampage unmatched in the history of firearms development," wrote authors Curtis Gentry and John Browning (the inventor's son) in their book, *John M. Browning: American Gunmaker.* "His speed and productivity made his accomplishments blur."

Born in 1855 to a Mormon gunsmith in Ogden, Utah, John Moses Browning quit school before seventh grade to work in his family's shop. He earned a hands-on education in firearms manufacturing and engineering from his dad, who'd developed a prototype "slide-action" repeating rifle. The younger Browning's inventive mind quickly showed itself: He created his first gun as a boy and earned a U.S. patent before he was twenty-five.

In 1883, a salesman for the Winchester Repeating Arms Company traveled through dusty Ogden and, by chance, tested Browning's newly patented rifle. The gun made its way to T.G. Bennet, the vice president and general manager of Winchester (Oliver Winchester had died in 1880), who was so impressed that he traveled to Ogden and personally bought Browning's

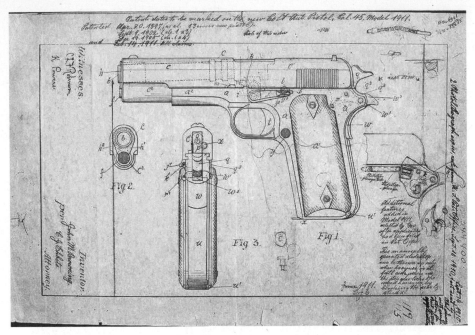

Above: John Browning's designs for his "Auto Pistol,
Cal .45, Model 1911," submitted to the U.S. Patent Office
in September 1910. Below: the finished product.

design for eight thousand dollars. The purchase began a two-decade relationship between the designer and the Connecticut manufacturing giant.

Browning's inventions were captured in 128 patents covering eighty weapons, including the classic Winchester Models 1886, 1892, and 1895 lever-action rifles; the Model 1894, and the 1893 and 1897 Winchester pump-action shotguns. After a break with Winchester, he produced a revolutionary series of semiautomatics and machine guns. Among them: the Browning Auto-5 Shotgun (produced under license as the Remington Model 11), the legendary Browning Automatic Rifle (BAR), the .50-caliber M2 Browning machine gun, and the M1911 pistol and its descendant, the 9mm Browning Hi Power. He also designed the .45 ACP (Automatic Colt Pistol) cartridge fired by the M1911.

Browning didn't use blueprints. According to his descendant Bruce W. Browning, he would dream up a weapon in his head, work out a bunch of problems and kinks, then build a prototype based on his ideas. Only when he had the model working would he turn it over to others to be drawn and "engineered."

This American genius was working for Colt when he designed the M1911. He had developed an earlier Colt pistol, the Colt Model 1900. Inspecting the weapon,

Above: Where the magic happened: John Moses
Browning's work bench. Below left: Browning's Ogden,
Utah, storefront. Below right: Ogden, 1874, still very
much the Old West.

you can see some of the ideas that would make the 1911 a classic. The older gun was a self-loaded weapon that fired a .38 ACP round. It looked something like a smaller M1911 with a longish barrel.

Inspect a Browning design—any Browning design—and you can see the influence of the American frontier. Survival in the West depended on keeping things simple, and making them tough. The simpler and more rugged, the better. It is the winning formula for a gun, or for any tool really.

"Make it strong enough—then double it," Browning said. "Anything that can happen with a gun, probably will happen, sooner or later."

Like the Model 1900 before it, the Model 1911 uses a small amount of the energy from the cartridge as it is fired to eject the spent shell and cycle a new round into place. The energy that causes the gun to recoil is used in the M1911 to slap out the old cartridge and put a new one in its place.

The idea of "self-loading" (or semiautomatic) is now common, but it was new at the turn of the century. That alone would have spooked the Army brass in years gone by, but the fresh faces at the top were no longer afraid of cutting-edge design . . . as long as it worked.

And the M1911 did.

To the shooter, the gun's brilliance starts with loading, where a spring-loaded magazine is easily filled with bullets. The mag slips vertically inside the pistol grip. Rack the pistol—pull back the slide (the top of the gun, sitting over the barrel). This chambers a round. Aim. Fire.

The recoil energy of the bullet pitches the slide back. The spent shell pops out quicker than you can see it. A new one pushes up from the magazine inside. Aim, and fire again. Nothing to it.

It's not just the action or its internals that make the gun so sweet. The trigger is short and comfortable. The pistol weighs just 2.4 pounds before you pop in the magazine. The recoil is manageable, so you can shoot with one hand reasonably well. The gun has both grip and manual safeties, so it's hard to fire accidentally.

Browning's design was simple enough that it could be mass-produced with good, steady results, unlike its main competitor from the era, the more complex German Luger. Fewer parts also meant less could go wrong in miserable combat conditions. Part of the reason it's tough as hell.

A Springfield TRP Operator 1911 took a frag for me in Fallujah back in 2004. My gun had a bull barrel, and I modified it with custom grips and a rail system. I doubt Browning would have recognized it at first glance. Still, at its very heart it was a M1911. The toughness he'd baked into the cake back a hundred years ago saved my hide. So I owe the man my gratitude—I might not have been able to walk after that if it weren't for him.

By the way, the very same .45 that went through those original torture tests in 1911 is still with us, looking none the worse for all that wear. It and a nearly identical hammerless prototype variation are housed at the John M. Browning Firearms Museum in Ogden, Utah.

The M1911 first saw combat in 1916 when General Pershing drove into Mexico in a fruitless search for rebel leader Pancho Villa, whose troops had looted and burned the town of Columbus, New Mexico.

In World War I, the sidearm was used by many American troops in close-quarter battles in the trenches, forests, and fields of Western Europe. "The bottom line was that when Americans shot Germans with Colt .45 automatics, the Germans tended to fall down and die," wrote historian Massad Ayoob. "When Germans shot Americans with their 9mm Luger pistols, the Americans tended to become indignant and kill the German who shot them, and then walk to an aid station to either die a lingering death or recover completely. Thus was born the reputation of the .45

automatic as a 'legendary man-stopper,' and the long-standing American conviction that the 9mm automatic was an impotent wimp thing that would make your wife a widow if you trusted your life to it."

The M1911 gained more hard-core battle experience in the hands of Marines and bluejacket sailors fighting in Latin America and the Caribbean during the "Banana Wars." In Haiti in 1919, guided by a turncoat Haitian general, a Marine sergeant named Herman Hanneken used a disguise to sneak into the lair of rebel chieftain Charlemagne Péralte. Hanneken gunned him down with a M1911 Colt .45 in front of hundreds of Péralte's followers. In the chaotic gunfight that followed, the tough Marine somehow managed to escape with his life. He was later awarded the Medal of Honor.

A few months later, a team of Marines snuck through the Haitian jungle to the headquarters of Benoît Batraville. Batraville had taken over after Charlemagne Péralte's death. The Marines were out for some payback for their fallen comrade Lieutenant Lawrence Muth, who had been killed and cannibalized by Batraville's gang. (The bandits cut out the Marine's heart and smeared his blood on their rifles to improve their marksmanship.)

Gunnery Sergeant Albert A. Taubert approached the entrance of the bandit's cave, clutching an M1911.

Taubert, a highly decorated World War I veteran, spotted Batraville. As the Haitian opened fire with a .38 revolver, the Marine calmly shot and killed him. The 1919–20 Second Caco War ended soon afterwards.

In World War II, the M1911 was the regulation side-arm for most Americans fighting in Europe and the Pacific. To meet the needs of war, the government contracted with numerous manufacturers—including some unusual folks like the Union Switch & Signal railroad company and the Singer sewing machine corporation—to produce almost two million pistols.

The gun became famous for keeping our guys alive in the hairiest situations. In 1942 on Guadalcanal—America's first offensive against Japan—Gunnery Sergeant John Basilone is said to have gone through the jungle armed only with a Colt M1911 as he fetched ammo for his machine gun unit in the middle of a Japanese attack. Pounded by the enemy, Basilone and his section were down to two machine guns and three men, one of whom had lost his hand. Basilone and his Marines held off screaming "banzai" charges by Japanese troops all night, waiting for reinforcements to arrive. Their stand helped the Marines hold Henderson Field, a key air-base in the campaign. The sergeant received the Medal

World War II poster featuring the G.I.'s
favorite sidearm, the M1911.

of Honor for his bravery; he later died in action on Iwo Jima. Basilone was one of only two Marines to receive both the Medal of Honor and the Navy Cross during the war.

On the other side of the war, American paratroopers found the weapon came in handy in the predawn assault behind the beaches on D-Day. In the cloudy and windy darkness, 2nd platoon, F Company of the 82nd Airborne's 505th Parachute Infantry Regiment began jumping from a C-47 aircraft. In the dark, windy night, the troopers descended over a wider area than planned. Several fell directly into the French town of Ste.-Mère-Église, one of their primary objectives, instead of outside the town.

Two, in fact, landed on the old Roman Catholic church at the center of town. Private Ken Russell slammed onto the church roof. Private John Steele's chute got tangled on the bell tower. A third paratrooper, Sergeant John Ray of Gretna, Louisiana, hit the ground on the church square nearby.

As Ray worked to detach his parachute equipment, a German soldier blasted him in the stomach with a submachine gun. Figuring that Ray was dead, the German spun toward Russell and Steele, who were trapped and defenseless. As the Nazi took aim with his MP40, a dying Sergeant Ray pulled up his M1911A1, aimed it at the back of the German soldier's head, and squeezed the trigger.

Bull's-eye.

Ray died, leaving a young widow, but Russell and Steele survived the invasion of France. Ste.-Mère-Église, which commanded an important crossroad on the way to the Normandy beaches, was the first French town freed on D-Day.

But maybe the most amazing feat performed by an American with an M1911 during World War II occurred not on land, but over the skies of Burma.

In March 1943, Texas-born Owen J. Baggett's B-24 heavy bomber was jumped by Japanese Zero fighters. The enemy's 20mm cannons set the big plane on fire.

As the B-24 filled with smoke and incoming bullets, Baggett and four crew members bailed out. Japanese Zeros circled the chutes and strafed the helpless American aviators as target practice, killing several and wounding Baggett's arm.

Between 4,000 and 5,000 feet, a Japanese pilot circled close to Baggett. The Zero's canopy was open, maybe so the pilot could get a better view of the American before finishing him off. At first Baggett played dead. Then, with the Zero throttled back close to a stall, he pulled up his M1911 pistol and fired directly at the Japanese pilot's head.

Baggett got off four shots before the Zero dove sharply away.

Probably wishing he had another shot, Baggett lost track of the plane as it disappeared below.

Baggett and another survivor were soon captured on the ground and sent to a POW camp near Singapore. Conditions were tough; the Texan's weight plunged from 180 to 90 pounds in the two years he spent there. And yet Baggett realized he was being treated as kind of a celebrity by the Japanese. He was even given the rare opportunity to end his captivity by committing hara-kiri, or suicide.

With honors like that, who needs Red Cross packages? He declined.

One day in the camp, Baggett met an American colonel of the 311th Fighter Group who had also been shot down. They got to talking, and soon Baggett heard an incredible tale. Before he was captured, the Colonel had met a Japanese POW who told him that the Japanese aviator Owen Baggett shot at had crashed his plane. The pilot's body was found with a bullet in the head.

The story of the GI who shot down a fighter plane with a handgun had apparently spread through the Japanese military. That may have explained why Baggett had gotten the VIP treatment—the guards were honored to be holding such a badass.

Did I mention he was from Texas?

The American POW colonel vowed to Baggett that he would write up a report, but he died in the camp. The tale was nearly lost to history, but in 1996, *Air Force* magazine recovered the story, reporting that "There appears to be no reasonable doubt that Owen Baggett performed a unique act of valor, unlikely to be repeated in the unfolding annals of air warfare."

Five years after the end of World War II, an American tank commander from Nebraska found himself inside a M26 Pershing tank, surrounded by a force of five hundred North Koreans.

Master Sergeant Ernest R. Kouma and his lone tank were the only thing blocking the path of a massive enemy assault on American infantry positions along the Nakdong River. He held his ground all through the night, issuing orders to his crew and repulsing enemy charges with fire from the turret.

At one point, surrounded by enemy troops, Kouma jumped up into a hail of gunfire, grabbed the externally mounted .50-caliber M2 machine gun—designed by none other than John Browning—and sprayed the enemy at point-blank range.

When he ran out of .50-cal ammo, he methodically picked off enemy troops with his M1911A1 pistol, then doused them with grenades. Wounded, after the nine-hour battle Sergeant Kouma and his crew drove eight miles through what was now enemy territory to reach American lines. His tank wiped out three communist machine gun batteries on the road down. He is estimated to have killed two hundred and fifty North Korean soldiers—but in doing so, saved many more American lives.

Master Sergeant Kouma's Congressional Medal of Honor citation says: "His magnificent stand allowed the infantry sufficient time to reestablish defensive positions. Rejoining his company, although suffering intensely from his wounds, he attempted to resupply his tank and return to the battle area. While being evacuated for medical treatment, his courage was again displayed when he requested to return to the front."

The M1911 went on to serve in the Vietnam War and beyond. The king of the combat pistols was finally retired from many branches of the U.S. military in 1985, when the Pentagon designated the NATO 9mm M9 Beretta as the standard sidearm. I didn't like the 9mm cartridge for combat, and I was far from alone. To this day, you hear a lot of complaints from fighting men about the lack of stopping power on their belts. Many special op warriors continue to use versions of the M1911, purchasing them out of their own pocket.

Back home in the States, the M1911 became the personal handgun of choice at federal law-enforcement agencies, including the FBI and Secret Service. While the official weapon was often another gun, many agents and officers chose the M1911 as their backup. It was also used by some state units like the Texas Rangers and the occasional local department. There's a famous story back home about a Texas Ranger named Charlie Miller, who carried his M1911 ready to fire in his holster.

"Isn't that dangerous?" asked a citizen one day.

"I wouldn't carry the son of a bitch if it wasn't dangerous," said the lawman. You've got to love the Rangers.

In cases where the local department allowed them to supply their own service weapon—not unusual in Texas—the M1911 was one of the more popular choices. But for a long time, the majority of local departments regarded semiautomatic pistols as too much gun for the situations their officers routinely faced. And they didn't have the money for it—not just to buy the guns, but to keep them up. The weapon required more care and attention than other revolvers, and the ammo wasn't free. To many police chiefs, there was hardly any reason to look into something else. What they had was tried, true, and trusted. The main police gun during this long stretch was the .38 Special, or some variation of that classic wheelgun. It's a weapon on our list—but first let's look at something that made a lot more noise.

7

The Thompson Submachine Gun

"The Thompson [is] the deadliest weapon, pound for pound, ever devised by man."

—Time, *June 26, 1939*

At 1:15 p.m. on September 20, 1926, the most powerful gangster in the United States sat with his back to the wall at his favorite restaurant on the first floor of the Hawthorne Hotel in Cicero, Illinois, just outside Chicago. He was about to have a sip of coffee when he heard a familiar, and very unwelcome sound: the tat-tat-tat of a Tommy gun blasting away outside.

Al Capone dove under the table. The sixty other patrons inside the restaurant shrieked and scattered. The waiters melted into the kitchen.

Frankie Rio, Capone's bodyguard and personal hit man, rose, waving his gun. He scanned the windows to the street. The shooting had stopped. Nothing inside the restaurant was damaged, and no one there was hurt.

Just a show?

Capone heard a car speed off. He got to his feet and started for the door to show he wasn't a pussy.

Frankie Rio flew through the air, tackling his employer and shoving his face to the floor.

"It's a stall, boss," grunted Rio. "The real stuff hasn't started. You stay down."

Moments later, nine sleek limousines and touring cars slid up in front of the hotel. The barrels of Thompson submachine guns poked through the windows and opened fire. More than a thousand bullets poured into the building. The gunmen were acting on orders of Capone's rivals, and they didn't stop until they ran out of ammunition.

As the others paused, a man wearing a khaki shirt and overalls got out of the next to last car. He kneeled down on the sidewalk in front of the hotel, and began spraying neat rows of gunfire across the interior and exterior of the building. Drum mag empty, he reloaded and fired some more. Then he got up and went back to his car. Slow and easy, like nothing had happened.

Three blasts on the horn and the limos burned rubber.

Not one of the bullets fired in Al Capone's direction hit him. Several other people were wounded, including a five-year-old boy and his mother who'd been outside in their car. Capone paid their medical and other bills, which totaled ten thousand dollars. It was a business expense.

The shooting spree would go down in history as the Siege of Cicero. Its target was overlord of the "Chicago Outfit," a one-hundred-million-dollar-a-year crime empire based on the three pillars of American vice: gambling, prostitution, and booze. "I am just a businessman, giving the people what they want," Al Capone once explained. "All I do is satisfy a public demand."

That was booze, mostly. Prohibition had become law the passage of the 18th Amendment and the Volstead Act in 1919. From then on, practically every drink a man or woman had put money in the pocket of a criminal somewhere.

Three weeks after his lunch was interrupted at the hotel, Capone got his revenge. Rival gangster Hymie Weiss, who Capone fingered for the attack, was gunned

Al Capone—nicknamed "Scarface"—made national headlines and inspired numerous films, such as this 1932 Howard Hughes production.

dead in downtown Chicago. The instrument of his execution: a Thompson submachine gun.

The Thompson went by many names. "Tommy Gun" is the one most of us know. It was called that pretty much from the beginning. But the Chopper, Trench Broom, Chicago Typewriter, and the Annihilator have all been popular at one time or another.

The gun has a reputation as being hard to handle. That's a case of the bark being worse than the bite, at least if you're prepared and know what you're doing. The drum mag gives it more balance than you're led to expect by the stories. The kick is there, sure, but it's no more serious than most other full autos. Hold on the trigger and the gun begins to climb, but again, that's pretty much what you'd expect. Most of the Tommy men, which is what they called the mobsters who made it famous, fired only in small bursts. That gave them a lot more control than you see in the movies. Lay on the trigger a bit and the flash is very noticeable in the dark, but it's really the sound you remember. The old '30s movies don't get it exactly right, but they are darn close.

Invented to help clear trenches in World War I, the gun came too late to be used there. Then the gangsters got a hold of it. So did the movies. Capone and his cronies—real and in the talkies—used the rapid-fire weapon so well and so often most of us still consider it a gangster gun. But in fact, the Thompson was a favorite among GIs in World War II, when something like a million and half were made. The gun and its bootleg clones even saw action in Korea and Vietnam.

And why not? It certainly looks cool, especially with the drum magazine. And while not exactly known for accuracy, there's no arguing with the results. The Tommy gun was far and away the most lethal handheld automatic weapon you could get in the first half of the twentieth century, and it's still no slouch.

The idea of a rapid-fire battle weapon had been around for centuries, but no one figured out how to make one work until the 1800s.

One of the first prototypes of a fast-firing, multiple-round field weapon was the "Union Repeating Gun." Nicknamed the "Coffee Mill Gun" by Abraham Lincoln after he viewed a sales demo in 1861, the hand-cranked contraption fired .58-caliber paper cartridges fed into a breech by a hopper. Lincoln, as he often did, spotted its potential.

"I saw this gun myself, and witnessed some experiments with it, and I really think it worth the attention of the Government," he told his Ordnance Department.

As usual, the department's chief—dinosaur and enemy of innovation General James Ripley—stalled. A handful were eventually ordered for the Union army's use, but they saw no use in battle. The Coffee Mill gun had a number of problems, most especially a nasty habit of overheating. So your guess is as good as mine about whether it might have helped the Yanks much.

The Gatling gun was a different story. The multi-barrel, hand-cranked weapon was patented in 1861 by North Carolina–born doctor Richard Jordan Gatling. Richard was a serious inventor and tinkerer. After settling in the Midwest in his thirties, he developed a revolutionary seed planter and a steam plow. When the Civil War started, his imagination turned to weapons. He aimed big, hoping to produce a gun that would do the work of many men.

He definitely got that part right. It took him a few versions and models over the years to perfect his vision and keep the Gatling bullet cannon at the cutting edge of the available technology. But for roughly twenty-five years it was the state of the art.

What it wasn't, technically speaking, was what we now think of as a machine gun. Because unlike every machine gun today, the Gatling required someone to turn the handle to make it work. It was kind of like an

Gatling battery, Fig. 1.

A six-barreled Gatling gun.

organ grinder, only the music you'd be making had a deadly downbeat.

Gatling guns played an insignificant role in the Civil War, and they didn't change the course of any battle. Maybe their most dramatic appearance was off the battlefield, when the weapons were mounted on the roof of the *New York Times* building in Times Square on July 17, 1863.

The good citizens of New York weren't too keen on being drafted to fight for the Union. They were especially angry at the latest provisions of the law, which allowed the rich to buy their way out of service. Mobs rampaged through the city streets. The *Times* was a vocal supporter of Lincoln and the Republicans, and the crowd decided that it had exercised its First Amendment rights a little too vigorously.

Journalists were different in those days. A *Times* editor passed out rifles to his staff, set up two Gatlings borrowed from the Army in the windows for all to see, and placed another one right on top of the building.

He took the trigger himself.

"Give them grape," he yelled loud enough to be heard over the approaching horde. "And plenty of it."

"Grape" was a type of shot or bullet fired from cannons, but the expression was basically slang for "cleared hot to fire." In modern English, his words meant, *Shoot the bastards, and do it a lot.*

The reporters didn't get the chance. Seeing the weapons, the crowd decided freedom of the press was an unalienable right, and took off.

Depending on the model, the Gatling had from six to ten rotating barrels that fired two hundred bullets a minute. The rifled barrels cooled just enough between shots to save them from overheating. Heat is a problem every rapid-fire weapon faces, and the reason things like water jackets were invented later on.

With up to 1,200 rounds spitting out in the space of a minute, the Gatling could put a serious hurt on an enemy. But the guns had some drawbacks, as we've touched on earlier. They were heavy and had to be carted around on two-wheel carriages like artillery pieces. Unlike artillery, they needed to be pretty close to the action, which made them and their crews conspicuous targets on the battlefield. The guns were mounted high, and a gun still hasn't been invented that can duck incoming fire.

Another early machine gun, the Hotchkiss "cannon-revolver," was similar to the Gatling though its firing mechanism worked on a different principle. The gun was designed in 1872 and manufactured by a company owned by Benjamin Berkeley Hotchkiss. Though he was American, he set up his factory in France, which is where the guns were produced. Société Anonyme des Anciens Etablissements Hotchkiss et Cie made a line of light cannons which were also used by the American Army.

The next leap forward in machine-gun technology was the Maxim gun, introduced in 1884 by Maine-born inventor Hiram Maxim, a farmer's son and inventor whose works included a better mouse-trap. Visiting the Paris Electrical Exhibition in 1881, Maxim ran into a friend who told him there was good money in war. "Hang your chemistry and electricity!"

said the friend. "If you want to make a pile of money, invent something that will enable these Europeans to cut each other's throats with greater efficiency."

Maxim apparently took the advice to heart, and gave up on his other inventions to concentrate on guns. Figuring that soldiers needed a portable, fast-reloading, rapid-fire gun, he developed a mechanism that used the recoil of the weapon to load the next cartridge. He came up with the world's first light, single-barrel automatic machine gun. The self-powered gun was water-cooled and could fire five hundred bullets per minute and more.

By the way, "light" is a relative term. Even the later models weighed forty pounds or more. You wouldn't have wanted to carry one on your back for very long.

As his friend predicted, Europe pounced on the weapon. In 1896, the British-owned Vickers corporation purchased Maxim's company and began producing the American-designed machine guns under its own name. During World War I, Vickers guns were standard equipment for British forces. They were even adapted for air combat on the first fighter planes.

Not to be outgunned, the Germans and Russians ripped off the Maxim design for themselves. The lethal firepower of the machine gun was one of the big reasons World War I became such a bloody mess. No war

A rare sight: U.S. troops operating
a Maxim machine gun. Texas, 1911.

is pretty, but trench warfare brought the ugliness to
new lows. Military commanders on both sides were
insanely slow to adapt to the new combat conditions
on the ground. Hundreds of thousands of troops were
mowed down in pointless assaults "over the top" as
they ran into the killing fields ruled by the machine
gun.

By the time the United States entered the war, there
were four fairly decent machine-gun options available on the open market, all conceived by Americans:
the Maxim, Lewis, Benet, and the Colt Model 1895,
designed by the great John Browning. If you wanted
to choose just one, the Lewis gun would have been a

pretty good bet, especially since it could be set up and handled by one man, with another toting the ammo. The earliest models of the Browning had performed well in limited service in the Spanish-American War of 1898. But the usual delays and muddled thinking at the Ordnance Department meant the Americans ended up with French machine guns at first; only toward the end of the war did the Lewis and Browning weapons start coming to the troops in any numbers.

Those French machine guns? Well, a few thousand were Hotchkiss machine guns, which were manufactured by the company Benjamin Hotchkiss had established in France the previous century. Modern descendants of his "cannon-revolver," the firm's family of machine guns were decent, though very heavy for infantry weapons.

But most of the guns the Americans ended up with were Chauchat light machine guns. These featured magazines with exposed cartridges that jammed every time they got into mud or dirt—pretty much an everyday thing in combat. Welcome to war!

There were a few cool things about the Chauchat, like the fact that it had a pistol grip and was lightweight—the "Pig" or Squad Automatic Weapon of its day. But if you were in the trenches depending on a Chauchat to save your hide, prayer might have been a better option.

Until this point, the machine gun was a stationary weapon. It was great at defending territory and providing cover fire for an advance. Nice guns, as long as you didn't have to move them: the best were heavy mothers. Most took two or more soldiers (and maybe even a horse) to operate, transport, and carry the ammo.

Anyone who thought about it, or busted his hump carrying one of them, knew the future of firearms lay in a fully portable, handheld machine gun. As it happened, one American figured out how to make it happen.

John Taliaferro Thompson was a rare thing: a brilliant and farsighted Army ordnance officer. A Kentucky boy, he headed north and graduated from West Point. A colonel by the time the Spanish-American War started, he did a reasonably good job as the chief ordnance officer attached to the commanding general of the Cuban campaign.

As a member of the Ordnance Department, Thompson played a key role in getting the M1903 Springfield rifle and the M1911 pistol made. He and Major Louis LaGarde supervised the torture tests that selected the winning M1911 pistol design. By 1914, he had automatic weapons on his mind. He retired from the Army and went over to Remington Arms as their chief engineer. He also started a company called Auto-Ordnance to manufacture an automatic rifle. Auto-Ordnance partnered up with a Navy man who had patented a delayed blowback breech system, and went to work adapting it to a rifle design.

The war convinced Uncle Sam that the Army needed Thompson back, and he was recalled to active duty. He was put in charge of American small arms production. But the automatic rifle was never far from his mind, and his company kept working on it.

The blowback breech system had a lot of promise, but the engineers Thompson hired discovered that using rifle cartridges caused too many problems. Bullets had a very nasty tendency of firing too soon, which can really put a dent in the day of the guy holding the gun, not to mention the people around him. Bullets that followed often didn't eject smoothly, which wasn't quite as bad a problem but still didn't make for a happy operator.

The engineers did some thinking and decided what they really needed was a shorter cartridge. Thompson and his team soon turned to one he knew very well: the .45 ACP rounds that did such a good job in the M1911 pistol.

While pistol rounds simply don't go as far as cartridges made for rifles, in the close quarters of a trench, maximum short-range stopping power trumps long-range accuracy. Since the gun was meant as a trench clearer, Thompson realized, the bullets were perfect.

Re-retired, Thompson went back to Auto-Ordnance. In 1919, the company began testing a prototype. They soon produced a production model unlike anything the world had seen. It could fire more than 600 rounds a minute. The weapon was fed from a 20-round stick magazine, or 50- or 100-round drum magazines. (Later versions had 30-round stick mags.) Because the powerful recoil from the .45 bullets tended to cause the Thompson to shoot high, a forward grip was added to help muscle the gun level.

They called it a submachine gun. Their reasoning was simple: the bullets it fired were smaller than what was in a regular machine gun, and the words "sub-calibre gun" had already been taken, thankfully.

Thompson contracted with Colt to produce 15,000 guns, and waited for the orders to pour in.

But Thompson had missed his moment. With the "War to End All Wars" over, no one needed a "trench sweeper." Sales stunk. Despite Thompson's insider connections and impressive live-fire demonstrations, the U.S. Army didn't bite. The Navy and Marines came through with small orders here and there, but Thompson's Auto-Ordnance Corporation limped along

General John T. Thompson and his legendary gun.

on the fringe of the firearms industry. Local police forces mostly shrugged. To them the gun looked like overkill, literally and figuratively. And at two hundred dollars, it wasn't an impulse buy, for them or most private citizens either.

Then, suddenly, the Tommy gun became popular for all the wrong reasons.

It turned out the Thompson was the perfect tool for gangsters hoping to make an impression on their rivals. Small, portable, the weapon made one man into an army. In the hands of hit men and bank robbers, the power and psychological shock of the spray gun could rearrange an underworld command chain in a heartbeat. Instead of the trenches for which it was designed, the Tommy gun came to rule the back alleys of American cities.

Thompson personally didn't like the association, but few gangsters took the time to ask his opinion. And as he gradually stepped back from running the firm, the corporation pretty much told dealers to sell the gun to whoever wanted it.

Mobsters in Chicago, New York, Philadelphia, and practically anywhere money was to be made from booze or gambling began shooting it out with submachine guns. The Tommy Gun Wars were fed by

"There's no getaway from a Thompson!" Above left: an ad promoting the Tommy Gun to police. Above right and below: John Dillinger and other gangsters were quick to adopt Thompson's gun. Dillinger even added the forward grip from a Tommy to his modified M1911 pistol.

wheelbarrows of money, and just as much anger. One killing encouraged three others; revenge became as important as control.

Al Capone certainly wasn't the only gangster whose boys relied on the Tommy gun, but his crew sure did have a Thompson fetish. In Brooklyn on July 1, 1927, Capone's old boss Frankie Yale was intercepted and drilled with a hundred bullets by men in a Lincoln chase car. Yale and Capone fell out after Yale started hijacking booze Capone had bought from him, giving new meaning to the word double-dealing. Overkill was part of Capone's payback: the message it sent, not so much to the dead Yale but everyone else, was *Cheat me and I'll shoot you dead, then kill you some more.*

It's thought that some of the same mobsters who murdered Yale were behind the St. Valentine's Day Massacre in Chicago on February 14, 1929. In a real headline moment for American gangsters, six thugs (including the guy who kneeled to spray his Tommy gun at the front of Capone's hotel) and one unlucky optometrist were lined up against a wall and machine-gunned to death, presumably on Capone's say-so.

America's most infamous public enemy of the era was undoubtedly John Dillinger, a Hollywood-handsome bank robber who used the Thompson as his withdrawal slip. The former Indiana farm boy was very polite when he robbed banks. He was even said to be genuinely sorry for the one policeman he'd killed with his Tommy gun. At least eleven others died during his crime spree at the hands of his fellow gang members.

But Dillinger had style.

"He liked to amuse bank customers with quips and wise cracks during holdups," wrote author Paul Maccabee. "He would leap over the counters to show off his athletic ability and sometimes fired his Thompson submachine gun into the ceiling just to get people's attention. Witnesses may have been robbed, but they got their money's worth."

The ceiling might have been about all Dillinger could hit—he's said to have been a bad shot.

Dillinger was gunned down by FBI agents on the night of Monday, July 22, 1934, after watching a movie at Chicago's Biograph theater. His big hardware wasn't with him; instead of the Thompson or his favorite Colt 1911 (modified with a Thompson grip), Dillinger started to pull a 1908 Pocket Model Colt .380. He never had the chance to use it. The G men were packing M1911s. The Bureau had Tommy guns, but they would have been too dangerous here. As it was, a stray bullet injured a bystander.

Dillinger's sometime partner in crime was another Tommy gun lover, a psychopathic cop-killer named Lester Gillis, better known as Baby Face Nelson. Baby Face staked his claim to fame by killing more FBI agents than any other criminal.

Les earned his nickname during a sidewalk stickup in 1930. He shoved a handgun in the gut of Chicago mayor "Big Bill" Thompson's wife and made off with jewelry valued at eighteen thousand dollars. "He had a baby face," she said, describing the thief. "He was good looking, hardly more than a boy."

Baby Face had a personal gunsmith who customized his weapons for maximum performance. He also had a short temper and a heavy trigger finger. During a bank robbery in Mason City, Iowa, he machine-gunned an innocent bystander. "Stupid son of a bitch," he told the man as he lay bleeding. "I thought you were a cop."

Baby Face was one sick pup, and I don't mean that in a good way. Like quite a few outlaws and criminals romanticized by the media and film, he was a psychotic nutjob in real life. After shooting a policeman during a robbery on March 6, 1934, in Sioux Falls, South Dakota, he yelled, "I got one of them! I got one of them!" and danced on top of the bank counter.

Dillinger and Baby Face blasted their way out of an FBI ambush at a Wisconsin resort called Little

Bohemia on April 20, 1934. One federal agent and a civilian were killed in the ruckus. Just before shooting one of the federal agents with his Tommy gun, Baby Face growled, "I know who you are! A bunch of fucking government cops with vests on! I can give it to you bastards high and low!"

And he did.

Ten days later in Bellwood, Indiana, three police officers recognized Baby Face and his gang. They stopped the car without waiting for backup.

That was a mistake.

The psycho jumped out with his Thompson and took them prisoner instead. He beat the driver down to the pavement, then told the other two lawmen to run away. According to author Jeffery King, "Nelson calmly aimed a machine gun at their backs. The other outlaws begged Baby Face not to shoot, telling him it would only make things worse for them. He lowered his weapon, then suddenly whirled and peppered the police car with machine-gun fire, completely destroying it and shooting out most of the glass."

Finally, on the afternoon of November 27, 1934, FBI agents and state police caught up with Baby Face in Barrington, Illinois. A wild shoot-out erupted.

Baby Face's Ford was a mobile weapons vault, stuffed with ammunition, loaded magazines, and guns—including a Tommy gun, a Winchester .351 carbine with extended magazine, and a civilian version of the Browning Automatic Rifle, or BAR. When Baby Face ordered a flunky to open fire with the BAR, he let loose straight through the front window. The roar of the gun in the car could have shattered a skull on its own.

The battle peaked with Baby Face charging the lawmen on foot, blazing away with his Winchester. "It was just like Jimmy Cagney," remembered eyewitness Robert Hayford. "I never seen nothing like it. That fellow just kept a-coming right at them two lawmen, and they must have hit him plenty, but nothing was going to stop that fellow."

The lawmen pumped Baby Face Nelson full of lead, but they couldn't stop him. The wounded outlaw managed to kill two federal agents and somehow drive off. Baby Face died in bed with his wife that night in a safe house, nursing no less than seventeen wounds. He was twenty-four.

On July 22, 1933, George Celino Barnes, aka "Machine Gun Kelly," took his shot at a big score. The bootlegger and bank robber kidnapped superrich oilman Charles Urschel at the point of a Thompson.

Machine Gun Kelly's reputation tended to outshine his actual abilities. Despite his nickname, he didn't use the Tommy gun on many of his outings. But in this case, there is no doubt that he picked his victim wisely. He also turned out to be a man of his word. When Urschel's family paid off the $200,000 in small bills, the Oklahoma City victim was released unharmed.

But Machine Gun probably hadn't counted on the FBI getting involved in the case. After a ninety-day nationwide investigation and seventeen-state dragnet, the FBI was able to trace a Tommy gun from a captured gang member. Piecing together other clues, they grabbed Kelly. He was tried, convicted, and put away for life.

Legend has it that Kelly gave FBI agents the nickname "G-men" when he pleaded for mercy during their raid. But that story is an urban legend. People had been using the term on their own for years. Not that facts ever really slow down a good story. Just ask Willie Sutton.

Sutton was one of the last Thompson-toting "gentleman bandits" to be caught. He had a simple reason for using a Tommy gun: "You can't rob a bank on charm and personality." Sutton would know: he robbed around one hundred financial institutions in the New York area between the 1920s and his final capture in 1952.

Sutton is the smart-ass who's supposed to have answered the question "Why do you rob banks?" with the answer "Because that's where the money is."

Great answer, but it's probably another urban legend.

But he did give an answer to the question in a book he wrote after his capture, and it makes just as much sense as the other one. "Because I enjoyed it," he said. "I loved it. I was more alive when I was inside a bank, robbing it, than at any other time in my life."

After the repeal of Prohibition in 1933, the Tommy Gun Wars petered out. Meanwhile the company was close to going bust pretty much through the 1930s. A few government contracts helped keep it alive, but the books were filled with red ink when John Thompson died in 1940. The majority shares of the company ended up with Russell Maguire, who reorganized the firm just in time for World War II.

After the Japanese attack on Pearl Harbor in December 1941, the company suddenly had more business than it could handle. The Tommy gun was the only proven light machine gun available, and in a reversal of fortune, soldiers embraced its bad-boy reputation. Great Britain ordered several thousand Thompsons; the compact guns became favorites in their elite commando units. Once when Prime Minister Winston Churchill spotted a British soldier with one, he borrowed it and posed for a photo. The picture became famous as an "F-U" to the Nazis.

The gun Churchill flashed had a drum magazine. Soldiers used both the drum and a smaller, though easier to carry, stick mag. The kits sold to the Brits came with two round drums and four stick magazines. There was also a thousand rounds of ammo, which probably lasted about as long as snow in south Texas. The contractor that supplied the cases, Savage Arms in New York, got $225 for each weapon set.

More than a million Thompsons were ordered by various branches of the American military, including new versions that were improved and tweaked for mass production. Despite occasional complaints of jamming and control problems, the Thompson proved to be a winner.

"It was the perfect weapon for close-defense," said one Army colonel. "Carrying one provided perhaps the best life insurance a man could have."

Short-barreled and firing the bruising .45 ammo, the Thompson was ideal for commando operations behind the lines. There were a lot of those missions. The commander in chief, Franklin D. Roosevelt, was a big booster of special-op forces, and seems never to

A dapper gangster? No, that's Winston Churchill
testing a Thompson, July 1940.

have heard of a commando raid he didn't like. Unlike some later presidents, he kept asking for more.

In the Pacific Theater, Thompsons were used by the 2nd Marine Raiders, nicknamed "Carlson's Raiders" after their commander, Major Evans Fordyce Carlson. The major explained to FDR that the ten-man squads were designed for "high mobility" and "maximum fire power." The squads packed five Thompson submachine guns, four M1 Garands, and one Browning Automatic Rifle. Often they would be deployed via submarines and inflatable rubber boats on missions that took them deep behind Japanese lines.

When landing at a target, the Raiders locked a circular 50-round ammo drum into their Thompsons. When it was empty, they chucked it and slapped in an easier-to-carry 20-round stick. The Raiders brought their Thompsons along on August 17, 1942, when they wiped out the Japanese base on Makin Island in one of the earliest ground attacks waged by U.S. forces in the war. And the Tommy gun was along on their legendary thirty-day "long patrol" through fiercely defended Japanese territory in the jungles of Guadalcanal in November and December 1942. The unit took down some five hundred enemy soldiers, at a loss of just eighteen of their own.

"A Marine of the 1st Marine Division draws a bead on a Japanese sniper with his tommy-gun." Okinawa, 1945.

Elsewhere in Asia and the Pacific, General Joseph Stilwell toted a Thompson through Burma, and General Frank Merrill's "Marauders" deployed Thompsons in commando attacks behind Japanese lines.

The Thompson served in Europe as well. On D-Day—June 6, 1944—First Lieutenant Harrison C. Summers and his brothers in the elite 502nd Airborne regiment liberated St.-Germain-de-Varreville, France, close to Utah Beach. Summers was then ordered to attack and capture a building complex simply called WXYZ on a field map.

Following orders, the paratrooper and two buddies located WXYZ and charged in. What they didn't know was that the building housed the barracks for at least a hundred German soldiers.

It took five hours, but when Summers emerged, thirty Nazi soldiers were dead, fifty were prisoner, and the building was secure. "Summers is a legend with American paratroopers," noted popular historian Stephen Ambrose, "the Sergeant York of World War II. His story has too much John Wayne/Hollywood in it to be believed, except that more than ten men saw and reported his exploits."

Harrison Summers, who died in 1983, was nominated twice for the Medal of Honor; it was denied him both times. But there are numerous Medal of Honor citations involving Tommy guns. One of the most incredible involved another paratrooper, First Sergeant Leonard A. Funk Jr. of the 82nd Airborne's 508th Parachute Infantry Regiment. During a blizzard in eastern Belgium on January 29, 1945, Sergeant Funk and his men humped fifteen miles through waist-deep snowdrifts before reaching their target—a village filled with Nazis near the German border. Despite artillery shelling and constant enemy fire, Funk's squad rapidly

cleared fifteen houses and took eighty enemy prisoners. Funk could only spare four of his troops to guard
the POWs while he took the rest of the unit to secure
the area.

While he was away, a Nazi patrol materialized.
They freed their comrades and took the American
guards captive. When Funk returned, he walked right
into the Nazis' trap. A German officer shoved his
Luger into the sergeant's stomach and ordered him to
surrender.

Funk slipped his Thompson off his shoulder,
moving very slowly. He was outnumbered something
like a hundred to one, and clearly knew the jig was up.

Except he didn't, and it wasn't. In a flash, he swung
the gun level and filled the building with that famous
rat-a-tat-tat roar. As the Nazi officer dropped to the
ground, Funk turned his Tommy gun on the remaining Germans, cutting down twenty-one of them and
taking the rest prisoner—this time for good.

"1st Sgt. Funk's bold action and heroic disregard
for his own safety," reads his Medal of Honor citation,
"were directly responsible for the recapture of a vastly
superior enemy force, which, if allowed to remain free,
could have taken the widespread units of Company C
by surprise and endangered the entire attack plan."
Funk survived the war and returned home to work

for the Veterans Administration, where he served his fellow vets for more than two decades.

In 1942, the British edition of *Yank* magazine printed the story of a U.S. Army Air Corps sergeant who seemed to be a pro with the submachine guns that had just been issued to his unit. He took a Tommy gun apart piece by piece, then quickly snapped it back together, and blasted away a target. When a major asked him where he learned the skill, the sergeant shrugged.

"Well, sir, you see," he said, "I once hadda take these things apart in the back of a car going seventy miles an hour."

He'd been a bootlegger before going to work for Uncle Sam.

Born out of the horror of WWI's trenches and made infamous by Prohibition-era gangsters, John Thompson's submachine gun had finally fullfilled its promise during WWII. The gun remained in the U.S. military inventory for years after the war. Some were still being used for special missions during the 1960s.

A friend of mine named Donnie Durbin runs the best gun store in Texas, in my opinion. Donnie is a Marine—I won't call him a retired Marine, because once you're a Marine, there is no such thing as retiring from the Corps.

Donnie did a stretch of fighting in Vietnam. While he was there, he happened across a Thompson submachine gun that had been dropped by a VC somewhere along the way. (VC means Viet Cong, aka the enemy, for y'all under thirty.)

He carried it around for a few days, and liked it. Even though from a different era, it still had plenty of power, wasn't really that hard to control, and best of all, it was just cool. A gangster gun.

But after a week or so, he decided to give it to someone else. The thing got to be heavy carrying through the jungle. It wasn't just the gun; the bullets and their drum magazine added several pounds to his kit. And if you don't think a couple of pounds make a difference to a warrior, you've never thrown on a loaded ruck and humped it ten miles.

At the same time, gun technology had given Donnie and his brother Marines rifles that could fire nearly as fast on full auto and were about two pounds lighter when empty. While those rifles had not yet been perfected, they clearly owned the future.

You might make an argument that the Tommy gun redeemed its reputation with all the good work it did in World War II. There's a lot of stock in that—it was the instrument of freedom for a lot of people. Of course, history is a complicated subject. The good sits right

next to the bad pretty much all the time. The same fella who was a bootlegger and might've used a Tommy gun against the police turned out to be a soldier who used it against death camps and extermination.

The Tommy gun defined the submachine gun category. But that definition has gotten narrower over the years. Today's true submachine guns, such as the MP5 family, are now mostly specialty weapons. In one direction, they've been replaced by squad-level machine guns that have the power of some of the heavy weapons of World War I and II. On the other side, they've seen lightweight carbines take up much of their territory.

Then again, as cool as it was, the Thompson was never the top gun in the American inventory, not even in World War II. Pride of place there belonged to a weapon that both continued old traditions, and broke new ground: the M1 Garand.

8

The M1 Garand

"In my opinion the M1 rifle is the greatest battle implement ever devised."

—*General George S. Patton*

In the early morning of August 18, 1942, Army Corporal Franklin "Zip" Koons was woken by a spray of water from the English Channel and the drone of airplanes in the distance. He jumped up.

One of the men with him put his hand out to steady him.

"Get ready, Yank," said the man, a British commando. "The beach is ahead."

Corporal Koons took a deep breath, then ran his hands over his rifle as he pulled himself to his feet in the boat. The weapon's wood was sleek and almost oily with the spray of the sea. It was a new gun: an M1 semi-automatic that fired eight shots, before reloading. The commandos were jealous.

Or would be, if it successfully proved itself. No one had used one in combat before.

Koons checked to make sure it was loaded—probably the twentieth time since he'd set out—then fixed his eyes on the shadows ahead. Two British Spitfires buzzed to his left and began firing. They were aiming their guns at the beam of a nearby lighthouse, trying to distract the defenders' attention as much as knock the light out.

It worked, in a way. Nazi anti-aircraft guns began to respond, shattering the peace of the tiny coastal village below Dieppe, France. The whole countryside was now awake, thank you very much.

I'm really in the war, Corporal Koons told himself. *Damn.*

Koons and forty-nine other American Army Rangers were about to become the first Americans to see combat in Europe. They'd been training with the British commandos for weeks, earning their respect bruise by bruise. But for all the live fire exercises, all the forced marches and the endless gun drills, none of the Rangers could say in his heart that he was completely ready for combat. That was something they'd have to experience firsthand to truly understand.

The shallow boat grounded hard against the rocks, and Koons jumped out behind his commando buddy, running like hell for the shadows under the cliffs ahead. His fate depended on three things—his resolve, the men he was with, and the untested rifle he held out of the water as he ran to shore.

He couldn't have made a better choice when it came to men. The commandos were the rock stars of World War II, badass warfighters who could do everything from take over an enemy town to blow up a docked warship. The Rangers were no slouches either; every man on the mission had volunteered three times, and most of them were as ballsy as the toughest commando.

The rifle—that was something special as well. It was the "U.S. Rifle, Caliber .30, M1," a ten-pound, eighty-five-dollar, gas-operated, air-cooled, clip-fed semi-automatic. It was new to the unit—Koons had only just wiped off the heavy protective grease it had been shipped in the other day. But it would soon prove to be one of the finest guns ever made.

The M1 Garand has been called "the gun that saved the world," and that's not an exaggeration. The rifle is without a doubt the most important in modern

American history. To the Greatest Generation, and even their kids, the M1 defined the word "rifle."

It was created by John Cantius Garand, a quiet, humble gun designer who worked for the U.S. government's Springfield Armory, in Massachusetts.

Garand was a native Canadian who, like a lot of gun designers, was a little odd. It's said he used to flood his basement during the winter so he could skate there after work.

Good thing he didn't live in Texas.

After World War I, the Army realized that a semi-automatic or self-loading rifle would give whoever used it a great advantage. Of course, being the Army, they wanted the weapon to be all things to all people—it had to be light, had to be accurate, and it had to take more abuse than a mule in winter.

The smartest thing the Army did was hire a bunch of people, including Garand, and told them to have at it. Garand had been discovered, more or less, because of a design for a machine gun he'd invented. It was an interesting arrangement: When fired, the primer moved back and hit the firing pin, which came back and unlocked the bolt. A cam and a spring combination kicked out the shell and brought in a new cartridge. It was different than any other mechanism around, and even more complicated than it sounds.

U.S. warriors and their M1 Garands
during the Pacific Island campaign.

But it did work—just not well enough to beat out other designs.

Garand tried using the same mechanism in a semi-automatic rifle. That performed a little better. But he didn't have a breakthrough until he let go of that idea entirely. Instead, he found a way to use the gas generated by the burning powder to do work in the rifle that, till now, had been done by hand or recoil.

As the bullet in the M1 Garand moves out of the barrel, the gas behind it finds its way to a small port. The pressure of the gas drives a piston back. This moves the operating rod and powers the mechanism that opens the bolt, kicks out a round, and feeds a new one. Cams, lugs, tangs—the mechanical pieces work together like the insides of an old-fashioned watch, but are tough enough to take the pounding and abuse involved in launching something at the speed of sound, or thereabouts.

New developments in powder propellant were key to making it all work, since the gas had to be produced in a certain volume and pressure. (Slow and steady in this design was better than all-at-once quick.)

Garand was not the first person to think of the idea. Browning had been there before, and the principle was being used for machine guns. Garand got it to work in a semi-automatic rifle that could be mass-produced.

His willingness to think about problems in a whole different direction put rifles on a new course.

While Garand was developing his designs, another genius, also a little peculiar, was working on his own project. John D. Pedersen's semi-automatic rifle had a different, more complicated mechanism. It also used a .276 caliber round. There were a few advantages to using the smaller cartridge in an infantry rifle, including weight and wear on the gun. Not to get too technical here, but one of the interesting sidelights of the workup on bullets for the new rifle showed that smaller bullets could do more damage at certain distances than the .30-06. That's a point to remember down the line.

Garand first produced his gun in .30 caliber. Then the Army brass heard the arguments in favor of the smaller rounds and decided the next infantry rifle should be chambered for .276. So he went back to the workbench and came up with a .276 version.

It was better than the .30. In fact, it was better than Pedersen's, too. The Garand .276 was easier to manufacture, and less prone to breakdown, at least according to the tests.

That's when Army Chief of Staff Douglas MacArthur stepped in. General MacArthur insisted that the next infantry rifle, whatever it might be, should be chambered in .30-06.

He didn't do it because of the bullet's impressive accuracy, range, or superior stopping power. Rather, the Army had been kicked in the gut with budget cuts, and adopting a gun with the same bullet they'd been using for twenty years was a lot cheaper than the alternative. It was the middle of the Depression, and things were tough everywhere.

There's a bright spot in every cloud.

It took a few more years to actually perfect the .30-06 version of Garand's gun, but the M1 Garand was offically tapped as the Army's rifle on January 9, 1936. Getting it into the hands of soldiers would take longer still—but it did get there. The rest, as we say, is history.

The M1 Garand was the world's first semi-automatic rifle issued as standard weapon to any army. It boosted the combat power of the American fighting man over his enemies, who at that point were pretty much all armed with World War I–type bolt-action rifles. The Japanese, for example, mostly used the Arisaka Type 99. The Type 99 was modeled after the Mauser and held only five rounds.

To load the M1, a soldier locks the bolt by pulling the operator rod on the side back. He wants to give it a good tug, making sure it locks; if he's gentle there's a chance the mechanism will slide back forward later and try and grab his thumb. He then takes the eight-round

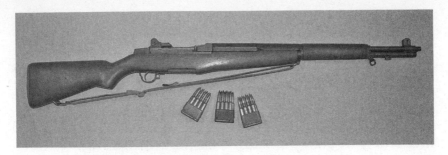

Top: the M1 Garand and its eight-round en-bloc clip. Middle: John Garand (left) presents his weapon to the U.S. Army's Chief of Ordnance (middle) and the commanding officer of the Springfield Armory (right). Bottom: M1s being loaded for the front; by 1944, almost 4,000 were being produced a day.

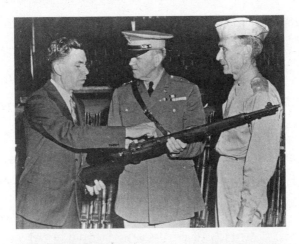

clip and pushes it down with some authority into the receiver. The bullets click into place. He removes his thumb—loading is always supposed to be done with the thumb, according to the manual and the old instructors. The bolt slaps forward.

Done. The first round is chambered and the gun is ready to go. From that point, the soldier can fire as quickly as he can pull the trigger. When the bullets are gone, the clip is ejected with a loud ping. The rifle is singing for new rounds.

General George Patton called the M1 "the greatest battle implement ever devised." Historian William Hallahan described the Garand as "one weapon that outgunned its counterparts in every other army in the field." It was tough and dependable no matter where or how it was used. "In surf and sand, dragged through the mud and rain of tropical rain forests, sunbaked, caked with volcanic ash, covered with European snows that melted, then refroze inside the breech, beset by rust and mildew, mold and dirt, the Garand still came out shooting."

But all this lay in the future back in 1942 near Dieppe, France.

As Zip Koons ran up the narrow path from the beach, he heard the muffled bang of a grenade exploding in a nearby house. Guided by some French spies, the commandos at the head of the team had run into a house where Germans were known to be sleeping. The Germans had tried to resist.

Most likely they wouldn't have been taken prisoner anyway, not by the French.

Koons kept running. His team was assigned to destroy a German gun battery so the main assault to the north could proceed without interference. His job was to help secure the farm that bordered the woods near the artillery. There was a barn on the property, and the commandos were just getting to it when Koons ran up. Another American Ranger, Sergeant Alex Szima, was already there with his Thompson.

"Go to it, Yanks," said the commandos.

Szima and Koons ducked in and started clearing the barn. It was empty, but in the dark they couldn't take that for granted. Sweat poured off the corporal as he followed Szima across the floor and then up to the loft. The place was empty.

They found a wide hay door on the second story and opened it. There in the dim light across from them sat the battery, no more than a few hundred yards away. The first Nazis, woken by the gunfire, were just now running to their posts.

Szima said something Koons didn't hear. He was too busy raising his rifle to his shoulder.

Across the way, the German reached his weapon and started getting it ready to fire. Koons pressed his trigger.

Bam!

The M1 jerked against his shoulder.

It felt good.

The man he'd aimed at was down. Another was running to take his place.

Bam. Koons fired again. *Bam.*

The M1 was as accurate as the Springfield at this distance. The recoil was easy to control. The sights, which he'd zeroed on the ranges back in Scotland, were steady and sturdy. But the real asset was the clip—eight bullets—and the fact that he didn't have to move his hand to reload, unlike the bolt-action Springfield he'd come to Britain with. He just moved to the next target, or steadied his aim if he missed.

Bam. Again and again. Reload.

Commandos were swarming into the battery area.

Bam. Koons nailed a German who was raising a gun to shoot.

Bam, another German fell. *Bam, bam, bam.* Until there were no more targets.

The commandos secured the artillery emplacement and began disabling the guns. They had no way of knowing, but their small part of the mission was one of the few things that went right for the Allies that day. The raid on Dieppe got a lot of people killed, Canadians mostly, and a handful of Americans as well.

But it was an important baptism of fire for the Rangers. In their first combat action they proved that Americans could fight as equal partners with the premiere warfighters of their generation. The lessons they learned there were soon used in Africa and Sicily, then back in France itself.

It also showed they had one hell of a gun in the M1, better in fact than any other on the battlefield. Koons and his friend Szima were accused of being sharpshooters, but they claimed they were no such thing. "I was a bartender, before the war," laughed Szima.

They figured out later that Corporal Franklin "Zip" Koons probably killed twenty Germans that day. But he simply shrugged. Koons told everyone he'd just been doing his bit. He smiled when the British pinned a Military Medal on his chest, making him one of the few foreigners to ever get the honor. He survived the war, and went home to Iowa, where he raised a family, worked as a banker, and lived the American dream without much of a fuss, just like millions of other members of the Greatest Generation.

Even before it was used in combat, the M1 Garand was recognized by America's British allies as a powerful and important weapon. Koons and his fellow Rangers had demonstrated the gun not only for the commandos, but for the Queen, who knew enough about guns to be impressed by the type of clip it used. But even with the Queen as an admirer, the M1 remained an American gun. There were a few exceptions, but mostly the Brits stuck with bolt-action versions of the Lee-Enfield as their standard infantry rifle. They were fine weapons, but they weren't Garands.

The British commandos wanted the Rangers' M1s for themselves, and tried to do some horse trading on the side. But the Rangers weren't buying. They knew what they had.

It wasn't only foreign soldiers who lusted for the semi-automatics. When they hit the beaches at Guadalcanal in August 1942, most of the U.S. Marines were still armed with weapons of the previous war, the superb but increasingly outdated M1903 Springfield bolt-action rifles. The Marine brass figured they were getting great results with the 1903 Springfield, and they just weren't so sure about the M1 Garands.

That thinking changed right quick. What rifleman worth his salt doesn't want his gun to hold as many bullets as possible in a firefight? And to reload fast? On Guadalcanal, it was not unusual for the Americans to face lightning banzai charges by Japanese troops. Reloading a Springfield under normal circumstances was not difficult, but a guy charging at you with a bayonet is not normal. You needed a bullet ready at all times.

Lieutenant Colonel John George remembered a time when a Marine struggled to reload after firing. With an enemy soldier charging in, two nearby army soldiers simply "pointed their Garands, still holding more than half-magazine capacity, at [the enemy's] chest. Then they pumped the triggers until both clips were ring-ingly ejected from their receivers. They lowered their aim to keep the stream of metal pouring through him as he fell to his knees, then his haunches, then on his face, clutching his rifle tightly to the last."

That only had to happen once for certain Marines to decide they had to have the new guns—by any means necessary.

"We had to keep ours tied down with wire," remembered Colonel George. "Leathernecks were appropriating all they could lay hands on by 'moon-light requisition.' In daylight, they would come over to our areas to barter souvenirs with the freshly landed doughboy units; any crooked supply sergeant who had an extra M1 rifle could get all the loot he wanted. When the Marines began to get a few Garands up to the front the demand proportionately increased. They quickly learned that the M1 did not jam any more often than the Springfield, and that it was equally easy to maintain."

There's a story told about a Marine corporal of the 2nd Marine Raider Battalion marching very tightly behind an Army sergeant leading an advance platoon during the campaign. The Army man asked the leatherneck what the deal was.

"You'll probably get yours on the first burst, Mac," answered the Marine, eying his companion's M1 Garand. "Before you hit the ground I'll throw this damn Springfield away and grab your rifle!"

If you were bound for combat, there was a lot to like about the M1 Garand. It had several more rounds than the Springfield. You could fire much faster than anything but a machine gun. It had less recoil than a bolt-action rifle. It had an excellent sighting system. You could drop it in salt water and sand with few ill effects. Fast-firing, fast-reloading, accurate, user-friendly, durable, and reliable—check, check, double-check. It was easy to disassemble, clean, and oil.

On the negative side, the "pinging" sound the weapon made when you fired your last round and the

"G.I. passes a roadside grave," a battlefield sketch
with M1 Garands. Guadalcanal, 1943.

clip flew out let the enemy know you had to reload. If you didn't push the operating rod back right or had something else miss its catch when you were loading, your thumb got slammed by the bolt, giving you the infamous "Garand thumb." Otherwise, properly maintained and handled with reasonable sense, the weapon was effective and about as soldier-proof as it is possible to make a gun. Of course, once men had eight shots without having to reload, they wanted more. Can't blame them for that.

On Guadalcanal, in a slow, grinding struggle, the American soldiers and Marines expelled the Japanese in February 1943.

It was an important turning point in the war. The American victory, combined with the U.S. Navy's earlier success at Coral Sea and Midway, shifted the momentum against the Japanese. They would never recover it.

"Guadalcanal is no longer merely a name of an island in Japanese military history," said Japanese infantry commander Major General Kiyotake Kawaguchi. "It is the name of the graveyard of the Japanese army."

In the European Theater, the M1 Garand offered U.S. infantrymen three more shots and less time between them than the standard German Karabiner K98

Mauser rifle. The Germans tried pretty hard to find a suitable semi-auto replacement for their bolt-guns, but couldn't quite hit the sweet spot with anything. So the K98s remained the main thing in German hands when they came up against Americans.

That's not to say that some of the German guns, including the Karabiner K98, weren't impressive. As a matter of fact, most people credit the Nazi StG44 with being the first assault rifle ever. That gun seems to have influenced the famous AK47, though the AK is a very different beast. And our M60 machine gun owes a lot to the German MG42, a battlefield bulldog that pretty much defined the term "suppressive fire." But as far as rifles went, the M1 was better than anything the Germans were fielding in serious numbers during the war.

The thing that seems to have impressed American soldiers the most wasn't the M1's accuracy or even the number of rounds it could fire. John Garand's baby was just as tough as they were, and cared about as much as they did for creature comforts. Which is a good thing, because they don't call war "being in the shit" for nothing.

"The most amazing thing about that M1 is you could throw that thing down in a mud hole, drag it through it, pick it up and it would fire," said Darrell "Shifty" Powers. He was one of the famous "Band of Brothers" of E Company, 506th Parachute Infantry Regiment of the 101st Airborne Division "It wouldn't jam; it would fire. What we did mostly was keep the outside of it as clean as we could with a rag or something. And we'd clean the bore out as often as we could. Any time we were off the line we'd clean the rifles well. In combat, when you were right on the line you don't take time out to clean the rifle. You just kept the mud and dirt wiped off the outside of it the best you can. They were outstanding weapons, that rifle worked all the time."

Interviews with German prisoners revealed that many of them were spooked by the superior firepower delivered by the Americans' M1 Garands. They were sometimes mistaken by green German infantrymen to be portable and terribly accurate high-powered machine guns.

The Battle of the Bulge, which started with a surprise attack in mid-December 1944, was Hitler's last-ditch counteroffensive to try to stop the Allied express. The Germans massed the best of their divisions along the Western front, which roughly coincided with the German border, then tried to drive a wedge through the American line. The plan was like a Hail Mary with ten seconds to go in a football game, but given where Germany found itself, they had to take some sort of gamble or just give up.

At first, the Nazis kicked the Americans all through the Ardennes Forest. The XLVII (47th) Panzer Corps ran through the weak sector in Omar Bradley's armies, punching so deeply into Belgium that Eisenhower thought he'd have to retreat to the other side of the Meuse. One of the reasons that didn't happen was the arrival of the 101st Airborne at the little crossroads town of Bastogne. The paratroopers, who'd just spent several weeks slugging through Holland, were supposed to be getting a little R&R. Instead, they were packed into trucks and driven to Belgium, where they were told to hold a key crossroad in front of the German advance. They were just about surrounded on December 22 when the German corps commander, General der Panzertruppe Heinrich Freiherr von Lüttwitz, gave them an offer he didn't think they could refuse: surrender, or we'll bulldoze you.

Brigadier General Anthony C. McAuliffe made his answer short and sweet:

> "To the German Commander,
>   Nuts!
> —The American Commander."

The Germans probably had a little trouble translating that until the paratroopers helped out with

An American aims his Garand at a Nazi.

some precision M1 shots from their hunkered-down positions.

Bastogne was relieved on December 26 when advance units from George Patton's army, diverted north by Bradley, punched through the German troops surrounding them. The German advance was running out of gas, but the Wehrmacht was not about to retreat without a fight. Bad weather and bad blood between the British and American commanders under Eisenhower hampered the counterstroke. When it finally got under way, it slogged slowly through frozen terrain. The Germans, their backs to their border, fought like cornered wolves.

Private Joseph M. Cicchinelli was part of A Company, 551st Parachute Infantry Battalion attached to the 82nd Airborne Division, near the Belgian village of Dairomont. Though the 82nd never got the press the 101st did, they had also rushed to the rescue at the start of the Battle of the Bulge. Holding the line on the northern side of the German advance, they had just as important a job, and took as bad a beating in some places.

As the Americans went from defense to offense, the unit joined the counterattack. Cicchinelli's platoon was told to take Dairomont, one of a series of small towns commanding the crossroads south of Spa and Leige. The woods were filled with snow and dead soldiers on both sides. It was so cold a private was discovered frozen to death that morning. Supplies were low; some guys hadn't eaten in two days.

The battalion commander ordered a frontal attack on the village. The Americans poured M1 and Thompson submachine gun fire at German positions, but their attack stalled. There was the danger of friendly fire as two squads encircled and rushed the enemy from two different directions in the late afternoon fog. So platoon leader Second Lieutenant Dick Durkee ordered a desperate maneuver.

"Fix bayonets!" came the command. The men pulled bayonets out and snapped them below the muzzles of their M1s.

Thirty American soldiers charged through knee-deep snow toward a German machine-gun nest. The position was guarded by foxholes. Durkee reached the first foxhole, swung his rifle around, and cracked an enemy soldier on the head with the butt end of his Garand. Then he moved on to the next. "We reached the enemy position, and leaped from foxhole to foxhole, thrusting our bayonets into the startled Germans," Cicchinelli remembered.

In less than thirty minutes of hand-to-hand combat, sixty-four Nazis were dead.

Some Germans thrust their hands up to surrender, but "they never had a chance," recalled Durkee. "The men, having seen so many of their buddies killed and wounded during the past twenty-four hours, were not in a forgiving mood." By the time the fighting was over, thirty half-frozen, half-starving American GIs with bayonet-tipped M1 Garands had liberated the village of Dairomont.

Later that spring, having repelled the Nazi's furious final counterpunch, American GIs hoisted beer mugs and bottles of wine inside the ruins of Hitler's luxury mountain retreat at Berchtesgaden. Their M1 Garands were stacked along the wall. On May 7, 1945, two weeks after Hitler used a Walther BPK 7.65 pistol on himself, General Eisenhower accepted the German surrender.

The M1 Garand saw action again in the Korean War, where its durability meant life or death during the coldest months of the war. One Marine veteran of the fight, Theo McLemore, said later that the trick to keeping the M1 Garands working was to run the weapon dry: wipe out all traces of oil and lubricant from the rifle, which otherwise froze and jammed the gun. That is definitely not something you want to try at home, but apparently the Garands could handle it.

"Not having any oil or grease was hard on the weapons," McLemore admitted, "but removing it allowed us to use our M1s even when the temperature got down to 40 below. The M1 was our best weapon, and we really relied on those rifles."

The M1 served faithfully, but its time had passed. Being able to squeeze off eight shots without reloading had been a godsend in the 1940s. Now it was not enough by half. More versatile automatic and semi-automatic weapons, made possible by gas systems, were clearly the way of the future.

The problem was how to get there.

The M1 was a proven weapon system, so it was natural to try to improve it. Different trials during and right after World War II gave test versions more rounds and the ability to fire fully automatic. The truth is,

Medal of Honor recipient Baldomero Lopez leading his Marines and their M1s in Korea, 1950.

none of these experiments was very successful. A much more promising rifle, known to history as the T25, was developed as an alternative. Despite its potential, the T25 didn't get far in development. Politics took over—there's a shock—and the eventual winner in the contest to replace the M1 was the M14, the next branch on the Garand's evolutionary tree.

The worst thing about the M14 was that it wasn't the AK47, which appeared in Russian hands shortly before the M14 was announced. The AK47 was a groundbreaker and an icon. It was the best gun of its day. Although it's a far cry from my favorite, it's still a deadly and popular weapon the world over.

The second worst thing about the M14 was that it tried to be all things to all people. It was specified that the gun had to meet a wide range of requirements—accuracy at distance, fully automatic fire, ruggedness, and all that. But they just didn't work together well in that platform or with the cartridges it was designed to fire.

The M14 was adopted in 1957 and served with frontline troops early in the Vietnam conflict. There were drawbacks and complaints right off. The rifle was difficult to control on automatic fire. The weight and size of the weapon made it a bit of a pain to use if you had to hump long distances in the jungle. Soldiers said the humidity swelled the wooden stocks, eroding the gun's accuracy.

But the gun was good at some things. For one, as long as you didn't use it on full-auto, it was very accurate. It fired a big, man-stopping round which could penetrate the thick jungle canopy. In fact, if you thought of it simply as an M1 on steroids, an improved semi-automatic that used a twenty-round magazine instead of a clip, it wasn't a bad gun. If you put a scope on it, or if you were truly skilled in the use of its iron sights, the M14 was a lethal and dependable infantry weapon. It wasn't an AK, and as long as you remembered that, you were good to go.

Some soldiers kept the gun, preferring it over its replacement, the M16. But there were plenty of critics. It didn't help that the government had spent millions in taxpayers' money to develop it, and another $140 million to produce it. And that was back in the days when a million dollars was a *million dollars.*

The editor of *Army Times* called the M14 "nothing more than the M1 Garand with a semi-automatic position and an uncontrollable fully automatic position." A report by the comptroller of the Department of Defense put it down as "completely inferior" to the World War II–era M1 in September 1962. The worst cut of all came from John Garand himself, who claimed the gas system was "bunk. I tested it and it doesn't work the way they claim."

But a funny thing happened to the M14 on the way to the scrap heap. The gun's accuracy and its ability to shoot a number of rounds without having to change the magazine suggested to some that it could be the basis of a good sniper weapon.

The M14's sniper brother, the M21, turned out to be a very useful sniper weapon. It served from the Vietnam War into the 1980s. A new and improved

An American on patrol in Vietnam with an M14.

version, the M25, started being used around the time of the first Gulf War.

SEALs used the M14 for different tasks, never completely letting go of the older gun and its powerful rounds. They did this despite the limitations: the weapon was designed at a time when body armor wasn't common, and things like lasers and night scopes were still mostly things in science fiction books.

Being SEALs, they couldn't leave well enough alone—they had to make it better. A much improved version, the SEAL CQB rifle, also known as the M14 Enhanced Battle Rifle, eventually emerged as a modern variant of the original. From the outside, the weapon looks nothing

An M14 Enhanced Battle Rifle in the hands of a U.S. Army soldier in Kunar province, Afghanistan, January 2013.

like the wooden framed gun of the 1960s. It's heavier, and there's not a wood grain in sight. But it still has the heart of the gun that won World War II deep inside.

Craig Sawyer is a security consultant and the star of a bunch of reality shows, including *Rhino Wars* and *Top Shot*. Back in the day, he was a SEAL sniper, and among his favorite weapons was an M14. We traded notes at a recent SHOT Show, and swapped stories.

In the Teams, Craig used a customed sniper rifle that was tailored to be mission specific. Today his sponsors give him access to the best gear he can find. But he still goes old school when he can. Having learned to shoot as a kid in Texas—yup, we're everywhere—Saw still feels comfortable doing things the old-fashioned way. No wonder: I've heard some incredible stories about shots he pulled off from helicopters using just an M14 with no scope.

Now, it's not just the rifle that matters. The guy at the trigger is important too. You don't just wake up one day and shoot a tight group at eight hundred yards. A man may have God-given talents, but without practice he won't be very good. That's something that all good shooters, whether they're snipers, Marines, or match competitors, have in common; they practice a lot, and they keep on practicing.

Then again, that philosophy applies to just about everything you do in life.

The M1 Garand is truly an American classic. But its day was shorter than just about every weapon we've hit on. The Garand showed the way of the future: more bullets, easy loading, rapid firing. Accuracy was important, durability more so. Past a certain point, range might or might not be a critical factor, depending on how the gun was being used.

Modern combat rifles had to be versatile and not too heavy. Cheap to produce was probably too much to ask, but that didn't stop the bean counters from trying.

All of that pointed in the direction of the modern battle rifle, a weapon that could be used in a variety of situations. If it wasn't exactly cheap, at least an army could use it for a bunch of jobs without having to purchase something else.

But before we talk about the gun that came to fill that wide niche, let's take a step back to something closer to home—a classic American wheelgun, the .38 Special.

9

The .38 Special
Police Revolver

"Well, we're not going to let you just walk out of
here."
"Who is we, sucker?"
"Smith, Wesson—and me."

—*Clint Eastwood as Inspector "Dirty" Harry Callahan,*
San Francisco Police Department, in Sudden Impact

President Harry S. Truman was in his underwear,
fast asleep. Fifty yards away, two men in pinstripe
suits approached, carrying hidden semi-automatic 9mm
pistols, one a Walther P38, and the other a Mauser-
produced Luger. They were going to kill the president.

They planned to storm the steps of the temporary
presidential residence at Blair House, across the street

from the White House, then undergoing renovations. They would shoot the guards, hunt down Truman, and execute him.

It was 2:20 p.m. on November 1, 1950. Truman was catching some rest as he often did in the afternoon, napping in a front bedroom on the second floor of Blair House. His room was just a short dash up two flights of stairs from the street and sidewalk. If the president had been looking out the room's window, he would have seen the two approaching assassins: Puerto Rican revolutionaries Oscar Collazo and Griselio Torresola as they walked from opposite directions toward the house.

Defending the building was a small force of White House Police and Secret Service officers, all carrying .38 caliber revolvers. The Secret Service had two-inch-barrel Colt Detective Specials, and the White House Police, who were under the command of the Secret Service, had four-inch Colt Official Police models on their hips. Both Colts were very good handguns, members of the .38 Special family used by police everywhere in the country. The wheel guns were reliable, nearly cop-proof, and best of all, inexpensive.

The Blair House property was actually two buildings; the Lee House sat on the Blair's west, attached inside though from outside they looked separate. They were close to the sidewalk and the street, both of which were open to the public. A tiny guard house stood on the sidewalk at each end of the property. A decorative wrought-iron fence flanked the sidewalk. Canopies covered the stairs in front of both houses.

Seeing his accomplice approaching the western guard house, Oscar Collazo walked past the post on the east side and took out his Walther P38. Walking toward the steps, he pointed it at uniformed White House police officer Donald Birdzell who was standing on the sidewalk near the street, his back to him.

Collazo pulled the trigger.

The pistol didn't fire. Collazo didn't know the gun well, and in his rush he'd gotten all confused. Most likely he had accidentally flicked on the safety; the hammer snapped down without doing anything but making a loud click.

The assassin struggled with the gun. The officer turned to face him. Finally the German-made Walther fired, and Officer Birdzell fell, bullet in his knee. Stumbling as he tried to get up, Birdzell pulled his gun and tried to answer Collazo's shots with his own. Another White House Police officer and a Secret Service officer drew their guns and opened fire, but their bullets were wild or deflected by the bars of a wrought-iron fence between the assassin and themselves. Then a bullet ripped through Collazo's hat, grazing his scalp.

"Crack shot of White House police force." A colleague of the officers who defended President Truman on November 1, 1950, displays the pistol he used to hit 294 out of 300 bull's-eyes during a competition. .38s remain popular marksmanship weapons.

He didn't seem to notice it, pulling the trigger to return fire.

Meanwhile, Griselio Torresola stepped in the guard house on the west side and fired three times point-blank into White House policeman Leslie Coffelt's chest and stomach. Torresola then spun from the guard house and walked on toward the steps to help Collazo. Along the way he shot a plainclothes White House policeman in the hip, chest, and neck.

Inside Blair House, a Secret Service agent heard the gunfire and ran to fetch the Tommy gun from the gun cabinet. It was locked, and he fumbled with the key.

In the middle of Pennsylvania Avenue, Birdzell regrouped. He saw Torresola coming at him, and tried to line up a shot. Torresola was quicker. He fired a bullet into the policeman's other knee. Birdzell collapsed, out of the fight. Torresola calmly reloaded his Luger and kept moving toward the steps.

His accomplice, Collazo, suddenly realized he was out of bullets. He sat down and started to reload.

It's never good to have to reload when people are shooting at you, but it's especially bad when you have no cover and are extremely close to your enemy. The president's guards kept firing. One of their bullets finally made him stand up, wobble, then slam face-first to the pavement.

Harry Truman, startled awake by the gunshots, went to his second-story bedroom window. The president raised the window and looked down at the scene, trying to figure out what was going on.

Torresola was slapping a fresh magazine into his pistol some thirty feet away. It was an easy pistol shot. But before Torresola spotted him, Leslie Coffelt staggered out of his guardhouse. The severely wounded officer raised his .38 and fired.

The forty-year-old officer's aim was true. A 158-grain lead bullet spun into the skull of Griselio

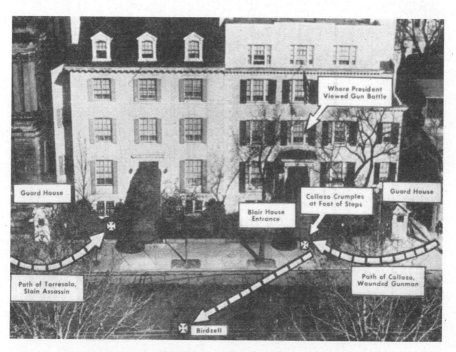

A diagram of the attempted assassination of
President Truman.

Torresola. His body shook as if it were possessed by the devil as he fell.

It was the last of about thirty shots fired during the forty-second gunfight. Someone saw the President at the window, and yelled at him to move away. But it was all over.

Leslie Coffelt died of his wounds. He is the only officer serving under the command of the U.S. Secret Service to ever have died while protecting a president. Oscar Collazo survived and was sentenced to death for the murder of Coffelt. Harry Truman commuted his sentence to life so he'd stew in jail for the rest of his days, instead of becoming a martyr to Puerto Rican nationalists. For reasons I haven't been able to understand, Jimmy Carter pardoned him in 1979, and Collazo returned to Puerto Rico to a hero's welcome.

Truman was said to have been deeply shaken by the close call, and haunted by the memory of Leslie Coffelt sacrificing his life for him. It's been argued that the bloody events contributed to his decision not to run for reelection to a full second term.

Given what the Secret Service goes through today to protect the President, the security around the Blair House that day in 1950 looks ridiculously thin. If

Collazo knew his weapon better or packed two pistols instead of one, odds are he would have been inside Truman's bedroom before the President pulled on his trousers. But consider this—America was the kind of place in 1950 where the president could walk around Washington, D.C., with only a single Secret Service agent tagging along. Usually he went with four, but Truman took a walk just about every day and didn't like waiting; the rest of the detail had to catch up or catch hell. The buck stopped on Truman's desk, but he didn't stop for anything, and didn't think much about his personal security.

That was all going to change. America was becoming a different place. And the police were the ones who'd be caught in the middle.

The first full-fledged municipal police force in America was started in New York City in 1844. The police started carrying pistols in the late 1850s. For the next forty years or so, they armed themselves with a hodgepodge of guns. The officers got about as much training as a SEAL gets dance lessons. When he came on as police commissioner, Teddy Roosevelt made the .32-caliber Colt New Police revolver the regulation police handgun. He also set up a marksmanship program, led by national shooting champion Sergeant William Petty.

Other big cities moved in the same direction. They were all dealing with similar problems: booming population, crowded living conditions, corruption, vice, immigration, criminal gangs—the entire dark side of an increasingly urban nation.

Once police departments decided to arm their officers, they faced difficulties armies don't have. Like the military, they needed weapons that were dependable and could stop a bad guy cold. But whatever they picked had to be suited to everyone on the force, big or small. That might not seem like much when a police force has mostly oversized Irishmen who like to crack heads, but step away from the cliché to modern forces with officers of every size, shape, and gender, and you see the dimensions of the problem.

In "traditional" warfare, armies didn't waste much thought worrying about civilians getting hurt. Police departments, on the other hand, spend all their time around civilians. They have to suit their weapons to the threat they face, but not go overboard. A bullet that stops a criminal and then goes into the next building can turn a clean collar into a tragedy.

Even in the worst crime pits, most police officers never have to fire on a suspect. Many officers usually only fire a handful of times in their career, if that. So they need guns handy, but still tucked away. Last and not least, whatever they get has to be inexpensive. Not cheap, but a good value. A buddy of mine from San Diego, Mark Hanten, is the commanding officer of the SDPD SWAT team. Mark pointed out recently that his department has some eighteen-hundred-plus cops, and some, like the LAPD, well over eight thousand. Buying a weapon for all of them can put quite a dent in the taxpayers' pockets.

The money isn't just in the weapons. The officers need ammo, both to use the gun and, just as important, to practice with. And practice takes time—every hour a policeman spends on the firing range is one less hour on the street, which means someone else has to do his job there.

So police weapons evolved toward efficiency, and just enough stopping power to get the job done. While rifles, shotguns, and automatic weapons fill certain roles, the sum of what a policeman needed meant a pistol would be his primary weapon. And if you were thinking about a pistol for most of the nineteenth and twentieth centuries, odds are you were calling to mind a product from one of two companies: Colt, or its chief competitor, Smith & Wesson.

Colt scored big with their revolvers in the mid-nineteenth century, but Horace Smith and Daniel

Wesson were right up there with them. The New England gunmakers teamed up in 1852 in a failed attempt to launch the lever-action "Volcanic" repeating pistol and rifle with a fully self-contained cartridge. As we've seen, the business flopped and Oliver Winchester ended up with the company. But Smith and Wesson didn't ride off into the sunset. The pair patented a rimfire cartridge in 1854, then used it to design a new revolver. In 1856, their new company, Smith & Wesson, unveiled the Model One Revolver. The .22-caliber seven-shooter launched the company on a road that would include a number of historic guns.

Coke versus Pepsi, Chevy versus Ford, Colt versus Smith & Wesson: the all-American pair duked it out for decades. Their guns got better thanks to old-fashioned competition. After making improved versions of the Model One, Smith & Wesson topped itself in 1867 with the Model 3 .44, the first big-bore cartridge-firing revolver. Colt came back with the classic Single-Action Army revolver of 1873. Then they followed up with the first successful double-action revolver, the Model 1877. In 1889, Colt unveiled a new line of Army and Navy revolvers, the first double-action revolvers with swing-out cylinders.

On a swing-out frame, the cylinder pivots away from the body, making it faster to load than a fixed frame

Toughest in the Block

Hammer blocks on all Smith & Wesson revolvers are strong, simple, and sure—no fragile stampings, no complicated link motions, no dependence on minute pins. We will be glad to send full details of our various models on request.

(No. 10 of 12 points which give sure-fire precision to all Smith & Wesson revolvers.)

10 POINT

SMITH & WESSON
Springfield Massachusetts
SINCE 1854

gun. At the same time, the frame is stronger than the break-top, a design which also makes for quick reloading by letting the cylinder and the front of the gun forward.

In 1899, Smith & Wesson came out with Model 10, also known as the Military and Police revolver. Colt followed with the New Police, the Police Positive, and then the Colt Official Police.

The weapons from both companies have a lot in common. Together they defined the category of police handgun, and even the word "revolver" for sixty or seventy years. And through most of that time, they shared one critical ingredient: the .38 Special cartridge.

The family of .38-caliber bullets can be almost as confusing as the guns that use them. It probably won't help to mention that the rounds were first supplied to replace the old ammo used by .36-caliber Navy revolvers. It *especially* won't help to point out that the .38 round's diameter is *really* .357—exactly because of that heritage. But those are the facts. The family includes the .38 Special, the .38 Short, .38 Long, and .357 Magnum, all at the same diameter. There are a bunch of cousins and near-strangers under each heading.

The .38 Special cartridge was one answer to the question of how to stop raging maniacs, the same problem the Colt 1911 was invented to solve. The .38 Special was more powerful than the .38 Long, which was a bit stronger than the .38 Short. First filled with black powder, smokeless powder became the standard about a year later. The .38 Special cartridges packed enough wallop for a while. But when stopping power became an issue again, improvements led to the .38 Special +P and .357 Magnum rounds.

Colt's history gave it a leg up in the police market. The Colt 1911 also helped with what marketers call a halo effect. It was like Ford or Chevy with NASCAR. Associating with a wartime hero made the other guns look that much better.

But it wasn't just the weapon's marketing that made it popular. "As a personal defense weapon, Colt's Official Police with a four-inch barrel is as dependable a gun as you could find," wrote police weapons expert Chic Gaylord. "The Colt Official Police revolver in .38 Special caliber with a four inch barrel and rounded butt is an ideal service weapon for densely populated metropolitan areas. The Colt Official Police is probably the most famous police service arm in the world. It is rugged, dependable, and thoroughly tested by time. It has good sights and a smooth, trouble-free action. This gun can fire high-speed armor-piercing loads. It can safely handle hand loads that would turn its competitors into flying shards of steel. When loaded with the Winchester Western 200-grain Super Police loads, it is an effective man-stopper."

By 1933 the Colt Official Police was standard issue for the police forces of New York, Chicago, San Francisco, Kansas City, St. Louis, and Los Angeles, plus the state police of New Jersey, Pennsylvania,

Maryland, Delaware, and Connecticut. The FBI issued the gun to its agents.

The standard pistols were meant to be carried in holsters at a policeman's hip, and had barrel lengths varied from four to six inches. As a general rule, the longer the barrel, the more accurate the gun was likely to be in the average policeman's hands. On the other hand, the longer the barrel, the harder it was to get out of the holster.

Both Colt and Smith & Wesson also came out with short-barreled "snub-nosed" pistols. These were usually meant to be carried under clothes or in a hidden holster as a backup weapon. In his patrol days, my SDPD friend Mark Hanten carried a Smith & Wesson 342PD in an ankle holster as a backup weapon, and frequently carries it as an off-duty gun as well. The J frame—the company's generic term for the small size, post-WWII guns—was popular with police chiefs, detectives, and others who needed a weapon with them but didn't want one that was too conspicuous.

The downside of the smaller guns is the kick that they have when firing. Mark used a .38 +P; think of it as a .38 Special round on steroids. It let you know you'd fired when it went off. "It's the kind of gun that you want to have but never want to shoot," as Mark puts it.

NYPD officers, 1964.

The granddaddy of the snub-nosed guns was the Colt Detective Special, also known as the "Dick gun" since it was first worn by detectives who were carrying it in concealed holsters. Introduced in 1927, the little wheel gun, like its big brothers, was popular in a lot of old movies. Edward G. Robinson, James Cagney, Charlton Heston, Chuck Connors, Burt Lancaster—all packed the snub nose. A lot of the same stars had the bigger Colt Official Police or some other version of the .38 Special in different films.

The .38 Specials were solid and reliable guns. They worked well for most police forces right through the 1950s and early 1960s. They were also more or less the weapons the police faced, when they encountered weapons at all. But little by little, more powerful guns popped up in the hands of criminals. Most police didn't realize it, but by the late sixties they had fallen behind the times.

Then one day they got a wakeup call in the form of a radio bulletin: Officers Down.

A number of serious shoot-outs and cold-blooded murders had a big impact on police thinking. One of the most famous happened in 1970, when four California Highway Patrol officers were killed in a shoot-out with suspects from a road rage incident. The two men who were stopped turned out to have a wide range of weapons, from a .38 Special to a sawed-off shotgun. After that, police departments began rethinking weapons and procedures, both.

Things kept ratcheting up. Like a lot of other police officers, Bob Owens, a lieutenant with the Dallas City Police Department, points to an FBI shoot-out in 1986 as the real turning point. Two Florida felons took on

eight FBI agents in a gunfight outside Miami and outgunned them with a shotgun and a Ruger Mini-14
semi-automatic rifle. Before the fugitives were finally
put down, two FBI agents were killed and five others
wounded.

While .38 Specials were used by lawmen in both
incidents, even more powerful weapons were outclassed. Rounds from automatics and .357 Magnums
didn't do the damage that police thought they would.
More importantly, the training that even the FBI agents
received was faulted.

"Training's a key thing," says Lieutenant Owens,
who as you might have guessed is a friend of mine. "It's
time-consuming, though, and it takes officers off the
street. It's hard to keep things balanced."

Owens's department uses training that is a lot more
realistic than in the old days, when policemen busted
paper firing at targets on the range. Trainers now try
to anticipate what situations officers might encounter,
and try to make things as realistic as possible.

The other half of the equation is getting law enforcement the tools they need to do the job.

Gun manufacturers had seen the problem coming.
Smith & Wesson introduced the .357 Magnum car-
tridge and the large-frame .357 Combat Magnum/
Registered Magnum revolver in the 1930s. Colt cooked

up the .38 Super Automatic round, capable of penetrating both bullet-resistant vests and automobiles. But many departments didn't have the money to refit their forces.

"At a time when full-power 'big-bore' handgun rounds ran in the 300 to 350 ft/lb. muzzle energy range, S&W upped the ante to over 500 ft/lbs," wrote NRA firearms historian Jim Supica in 2005. "Results of actual law-enforcement shootings suggest that the .357 magnum round, with 125 grain hollow-point loads, may be the most effective 'stopper' still today." Maybe, but .357s were used in both the California and Miami incidents, with mixed results. While training was absolutely part of the problem, police not only needed bigger bullets, but they needed more of them. Revolvers carried too few bullets and were too slow to reload when you were facing a determined criminal.

Owens carried a .357 Magnum for a while on the force, and remembers that some departments used what are called dump pouches to carry speedloaders. The speedloader held an extra set of bullets, and a practiced cop could slide them into his revolver fairly quick under the best conditions. The problem is, few gunfights are ever held under the best conditions. Owens would often find the bullets fell out of the loader during a patrol. Luckily for him, he never needed to use it.

Semi-automatic pistols were the obvious solution. They held more cartridges and were quicker to reload. Equipped with the right bullets, they had sufficient stopping power against all but the most well-armored opponents.

But getting new guns for an entire police force was an expensive proposition. In Dallas, officers were helped by H. Ross Perot, who after hearing how the locals were outgunned, bought every officer an automatic of his choice. My friend Rich Emberlin still remembers the Sig Sauer Mr. Perot bought him; it was a 9mm semi, and certainly a fine weapon. But even the semi-automatics were soon outclassed. Rich tells a vivid tale of the day 9mm subsonic rounds from a friend's gun simply bounced off the head and body suspect during a desperate shoot-out. So it's no surprise he traded his original Sig for a model that fires larger rounds. It's almost like a chess match—the bad guys counter every move the good guys make.

There is no one universal police gun or caliber anymore. Police departments use a wide range of pistols, including ones made by Smith & Wesson and Colt. But given its popularity, we can't take off without mentioning the big ugly that changed a lot of minds about what a pistol should look like when it first came to the public's attention in the mid-1980s: the Glock 17.

In the late 1970s and early 1980s, Gaston Glock was a plastics expert in Austria. He ran a company whose main products included curtain rods. An engineer by trade, he was talking to some Austrian military officers one day and heard them bad-mouth gunmakers for failing to produce a handgun that could meet their requirements. That got him thinking: Why not make a gun? Not just any gun, but the *perfect* gun.

Glock bought a bunch of pistols, stripped them down and put them back together. He checked every detail. He tinkered and researched, asked questions and messed around some more. It was easy to list what military people wanted in a handgun: a high-capacity magazine, light weight, accuracy, safety, and simplicity. It should be ready to fire at any time, but be safe otherwise.

Glock came up with a game-changer, the Glock 17. It was a super-light semi-automatic pistol with just thirty-four parts. Learning the gun took one day. It held seventeen rounds of 9 × 19mm Parabellum in its double-stack magazine, more than any other pistol at the time.

The thing about the Glock though—it didn't look quite like any other weapon that had come before,

unless you happened to be shopping in the toy department. Because the block-shaped body of the semi-auto
was made of "synthetic material" or "polymer"—what
you and I call plastic.

But it held up. Police and military buyers around
the world subjected the Glock 17 to torture tests. The
gun aced them. You can submerge it, subject it to high
temperatures and massive sequences of firing, and the
thing just keeps on working. The Glock is so rugged
that some salesmen drop it on the floor to impress
customers.

Glock bagged the Austrian army contract, and a firearms empire was born. American police and military
officers loved the new black-plastic gun, and started
swamping the company with orders starting in the
late 1980s. Glock gave excellent trial discounts to the
police. "This was smart," noted author Paul Barrett,
"because the point was to get the police departments
to adopt the gun, and that would give the gun cred-
ibility in the much larger, much more lucrative civilian
market, where you can charge full price and get your
full profit margin."

Glocks popped up in Hollywood movies and rap
songs. It became a pop culture hit. It also found its way
to criminals, who liked the Glocks for much the same
reasons the law did.

Above: The iconic Glock 17.

Below: On the right, taking it for a test-drive at a range in Poland.

There's an urban myth, still popular in some quarters, that the Glock can't be detected by X-ray machines. The myth was spread by a Bruce Willis line in the 1990 movie *Die Hard 2:* "That punk pulled a Glock 7 on me. You know what that is? It's a porcelain gun, made in Germany. Doesn't show up on your airport X-ray machines." Every bit of the line was false: there was no such thing as a "Glock 7"; Glocks are made of polymer, not porcelain; it was made in Austria, not Germany; and they do show up on X-ray machines. But in a strange twist, the firestorm of controversy triggered by the false rumors may have helped goose publicity and aid Glock sales.

Today, more than four million Glocks have been sold, and at least two-thirds of American police departments use Glocks, including the nation's biggest, the NYPD, plus federal agencies like the FBI and the Drug Enforcement Administration, and some military special-operations units also use Glocks as their standard sidearm.

As for myself, I prefer the M1911. To me, a Glock is about as good-looking as a lump of coal.

I started this chapter with a presidential assassination attempt. It's hard for a Texan to do that without thinking of Lee Harvey Oswald and that awful day back in 1963 when John F. Kennedy was shot down here. There are still plenty of folks around who were there and remember what all happened.

One of them is Jim Leavelle, who was walking Oswald down the ramp of the garage under police headquarters two days later when Jack Ruby shot him.

Jim, a friend of a friend, was a Dallas police officer for going on twenty-six years. If you've ever studied the JFK assassination, or even spent a bit of time looking at the photos, you've seen him at Oswald's right in the light suit on the garage ramp as they walk down to take Oswald to court. Just as they come into view in the famous TV footage, Ruby ducks past an army of reporters and policemen. Leavelle starts to yank Oswald toward him out of the way, but Ruby's too close. He fires into Oswald's middle, then gets gang tackled.

Leavelle says he spotted Ruby's pistol in the half-second after Ruby ducked around one of the other officers near the car. The retired officer is often asked by people why he didn't shoot Ruby.

"It just happens so fast," he tells them. "It always does. Sometimes you don't have time to draw. You just react. That's all you can do."

That's some hard-earned experience talking there. Training helps, good weapons help, but nothing beats dumb luck.

Leavelle was in a bunch of close scrapes over his career. He packed a number of weapons—a lot of .38s in just about every barrel length, a .45 Colt, a .38 Super, a .357 that he thought was a bit too heavy for an everyday carry. The day he escorted Oswald, he had two Colt .45s with him, but never had the chance to use them.

Ruby, by the way, killed Oswald with a .38 Special.

10

The M16 Rifle

"Brave soldiers and the M16 brought this victory."

—*Lieutenant Colonel Harold Moore*

The world shook as they rode to battle. The sky around them was filled with helicopters. Vietnam was green and light brown, peaceful from a few hundred feet above. But the drum of rotors were the call to war.

The American Hueys squatted into the elephant grass. Dust and dirt flew everywhere. They were in.

"Let's go!" yelled Lt. Colonel Hal Moore, grabbing his rifle as he leaned to jump out of the bird. "Let's go."

It was November 14, 1965. The forty-two-year-old lieutenant colonel was leading the soldiers of 1st Battalion,

7th Cavalry Regiment into a battle like none the world had ever seen. But as he and his men ran toward the edge of the jungle bordering Landing Zone X-Ray, I'd wager not one of them was contemplating history, or even the new tactics they were employing. They were thinking about their guns, maybe, and staying alive, mostly.

First Battalion had just put down in a remote jungle clearing in the Central Highlands of South Vietnam. It was the start of the Battle of Ia Drang Valley, an epic chapter in the Vietnam War.

Ia Drang—pronounced "ja drang"—is famous today as the first combined-arms air assault ever. Never before had a large group of soldiers been airlifted by helicopter and dropped down into battle miles from any support elements, or what you might call a traditional battlefront. Air support—not only from ground-pounders like the A-1 Skyraider but from strategic bombers like the B-52—played a critical role in the battle. The fight was also the first large-scale engagement between the U.S. Army and the People's Army of Vietnam—the North Vietnamese. It was as close to a "set piece" battle as the conflict ever got.

But Ia Drang was important because of another "first," one that's often forgotten today: It was the first time U.S. military personnel waged war with a fully automatic assault rifle as their standard weapon.

The rifle Moore held as he leapt from the helo was a new select-fire gun officially called the XM16E1. Soon to be known as the M16, the weapon had an immediate impact on the way Americans fought. It looked nothing like anything anyone had used in war before. The NVA regulars and Viet Cong took to calling it the "Black Rifle."

"What we fear most is the B-52 and the new little black weapon," said one of the Cong captured during the battle.

The Battle of Ia Drang was a baptism of hellfire for the men of the 7th Cavalry and the new M16. When

"The new little black weapon."

it was over four days later, the U.S. had won. A large number of North Vietnamese had been killed, and they had been chased from the battlefield. But the fight also taught the enemy what tactics might be most useful against American firepower. Americans saw the enemy was tough, and wouldn't give up easily, even when they were being slaughtered. And maybe most frustrating for regular U.S. GIs, they soon learned that while the new rifle they had was pretty good, it was not yet the weapon it could be.

Assault rifles, which we'll define as rifles that can be selected to fire single shots, bursts, or full automatic, had been around for more than twenty years. The Germans used a number of early versions, including the FG42 and the StG44 or MO-44. "StG" stood for "Sturmgewehr" or "storm gun," which is how we got the term "assault rifle." The weapon could fire five hundred rounds a minute but weighed only eleven and a quarter pounds empty. It used 7.92 × 33mm Kurz ammo fed from a 30-round magazine.

The StG44 appeared way too late to make any difference in the war. But it did influence the development of a weapon that today remains a classic: the AK47. Designed by Mikhail Kalashnikov in the Soviet Union in the early postwar years, the AK was—and is—a rugged, dependable gun that's cheap, easy to use, and no problem to maintain.

By the time World War II ended, the U.S. Army was working on its own automatic weapon. The most promising models were offspring of the M1. As we've said, these led to the M14, which despite its other qualities turned out to be less than the best choice for an assault rifle.

Among the roads not traveled by the brain trust at the Ordnance Department and the Springfield Armory was an odd little gun that some called "the aluminum rifle." That's because the weapon had an aluminum barrel with a steel liner. Instead of wood, the stock was made of fiberglass and foam. From the outside, the rifle looked about like any other .308 hunting gun. Pick it up, though, and you were in for a shock—it weighed six pounds, and that was with the scope.

The gun was an AR-1, made by a tiny division of Fairchild Engine and Airplane Corporation called ArmaLite located in of all places Hollywood, California. Only a handful of the prototypes were made, but you've got to start somewhere. That design helped convince Fairchild to give ArmaLite enough funding to get down to serious weapons design.

The company's first big weapon was a little one— the AR-5 survival rifle, bought by the Air Force

and designated the MA-1 Survival rifle. This was a
.22-caliber peashooter meant to be carried by aircrews
and used in desperation—great desperation—if shot
down. It wasn't designed to kill enemy soldiers, though
it could have been used for that if necessary. The MA-1
was more your basic varmint gun, good for rabbits,
beer cans, and not much more.

The theme running through ArmaLite's early
work was their willingness to work outside the box—
far outside. Lightweight guns? Guns made with aluminum or fiberglass? A .22 in a warrior's hands? All
novel ideas.

But being different doesn't get you anywhere on its
own. You also have to be good. And ArmaLite really
didn't arrive at that point until it hired, almost by
chance, Eugene Stoner. The self-taught gun maker was
an amateur in the best sense of the word—he loved the
art of making weapons, and he devoted himself to it. It
became a very productive relationship.

One of its earliest results was the AR-10, a seven-
pound automatic rifle that fired NATO 7.62 × 51mm
rounds. The AR-10 had a pistol grip and a carrying handle. Its receiver was made of aluminum and
its stock from phenol formaldehyde resins—another
of those fancy words for something most of us call
plastic.

If it sounds like I'm describing the M16, I am, pretty much, except for the rifle rounds.

The AR-10 was a unique gun. It was good, but it wasn't a perfect design. The barrel overheated, and there were a number of other nits and nags that would've had to be corrected before the gun went into production. But even if it *had* been perfect, the powers-that-were in the Army had pretty much already settled on what they wanted: the M14. In 1955, the Stoner ArmaLite contribution was shoved aside.

But not forgotten.

Pushed by Colonel Henry Nielsen, the head of the Army's Infantry Board, and General Willard Wyman, ArmaLite went to work on a version of the gun that used a smaller cartridge. The thinking was that a lot of smaller rounds would be more lethal in combat than fewer larger rounds.

One of the main points in the argument, which raged through the military and civilian think tanks, was how much ammo a rifleman could carry into battle. Would 650 smaller bullets trump 220 larger cartridges? If most battles are fought at 100 yards, does every rifle-man need a gun that can fire twenty times that far? If a small bullet can be made to do more damage than a larger one at combat range, which is better? And if most soldiers are crappy shots when the you-know-what hits the fan, isn't it better to increase their odds by giving them more chances to hit something every time they press the trigger?

The gun Stoner and ArmaLite produced was the AR-15. Its rounds were 5.56 × 45mm—which frankly sounds a heck of a lot more deadly than .22, which is what they were—Stoner used a .223 variant of Remington .222, the same round a lot of farmers favored to get rid of prairie dogs.

The AR-15 was ready for Army testing in 1957. You already know that it lost out to the M14. By then, Fairchild gave up arguing with the Army about the AR-15 and sold the weapon in 1959 to Colt's Patent Firearms Manufacturing Company for $75,000, and 4.5 percent royalties on any future units sold. The price was a bargain.

ArmaLite was spun off from its parent company. It's still in business making guns today. Colt, meanwhile, started showing the AR-15 around to potential buyers. Most people think the U.S. Air Force doesn't have much call for rifles. And it's true pilots aren't going to pop their canopy at Mach 2 and take shots with a rifle. But the service does have a need for security at its bases, and after trying the AR-15 in 1960, Air Force vice chief of staff Curtis LeMay wanted it for his troops. LeMay didn't get them until he was promoted to chief of staff, and even then had to deal with a lot of politics to receive his order of 8,500 placed. But he got them.

Army Special Forces also wanted the rifles; regular Army generals sought to keep M14s. Arguments went back and forth debating the pluses and minuses, until finally in 1963, Defense Secretary Robert McNamara put the M14 on hold and placed an order for more than 100,000 AR-15s, soon to be known as the M16.

The M16 had several advantages over the M14. It was much easier to control in full-auto. In fact, it was easy to operate overall. It was light as a feather by automatic weapons' standards—barely nine pounds with a full mag. It wasn't as long and heavy as the M14, and it had a lighter recoil, kind of like a gentle push when compared to the hard kick of the original M14. It was pretty accurate up to 460 meters. It was ideal for soldiers with small body builds, like our South Vietnamese allies. Its smaller rounds meant you could carry more. It even had the unique potential to make Pentagon bean counters happy, because it was relatively cheap and easy to produce.

The XM16E1 and the variations that followed all operate basically the same way. Loading is easy enough—slip the mag up into the receiver until you hear and feel a click. Pull back the charging handle and let go to chamber a round. You're good to fire.

Fire rate—single and auto, or single and three-round burst, depending on the model—is set by a switch on the left side above the trigger.

The gun was designed to lessen the effect of recoil. There are stories about trainers showing off the smooth-firing weapon for green recruits by putting the M16's butt in their crotch while firing.

Colonel Moore jumped from the helicopter and ran across a deep, dry creek bed at Ia Drang. The rest of his command group trotted behind. Though the Americans occasionally fired into the nearby brush, so far they had not drawn enemy fire. Moore found a spot between some giant anthills, and set up his command post.

Chu Pong, a large crust of a mountain, sat across the way. In geological terms, the 1,500 foot high-point was a "massif"—a large crust of the earth that remains fixed despite other changes around it. In military terms, it was high ground. Moore knew the Vietnamese were sitting up there, watching him and his hundred and seventy-five Americans. He was ready to rumble.

The enemy had the same idea. There were 1,600 of them.

By 12:30, several American platoons had contacted the enemy. Gunfire sprayed in fits around the hills between the landing zone and the mountain. The fight built slow, like charcoal just gradually warming in a grill. Squads engaged groups of NVA; the Vietnamese ducked and weaved. The Americans pursued. The Vietnamese countered; the Americans rolled with the punch.

Gradually, some of Moore's platoons stretched to the point where they lost contact with each other. Waves of enemy soldiers began to appear, intensifying the attack. Forty or fifty Vietnamese ran out of a tree line into a pair of American squads. The Americans fired their M16s. The NVA kept coming. Grenades, rifles—it was sheer hell for three or four minutes. Then quiet. Then it stoked up again.

Minutes turned to hours. The Vietnamese brought machine guns up; rockets and mortars began striking the Americans. One of Moore's platoons was cut off. The battle went into high gear.

American reinforcements flew in and were quickly committed. Suddenly, Moore himself was under attack. The colonel fought against his instincts to run into the woods and shoot the NVA himself. His job was to direct the battle, not get pinned down in the middle of it. He let his soldiers do their job, and stuck to his.

The men fired their M16s as quickly as they could load them. Skyraider attack planes rode in, striking small clusters of enemy soldiers. A medic kept his rifle

A 1st Cavalry platoon and their M16s hit
the ground in Vietnam, April 1967.

in hand as he went from patient to patient, pausing to
douse the enemy with automatic rifle fire while tending
the wounded.

The dry creek Moore had crossed earlier became
the center of fighting in the afternoon. Captain Louis
Lefebvre blew through two mags of M16 rounds in a
matter of seconds as sixteen or seventeen NAV regulars tried rushing from the trees. Between the rifle
fire, grenades, and a nearby machine gun, the enemy
vaporized.

But the Americans were taking big casualties as well.. Lefebvre was hit, and the machine gunner near him killed.

Moore could see the enemy easily now. The men at the trees were excellent shots; Americans were being taken in the head. The soldiers poured bullets into the Vietnamese, firing a dozen shots for every one the enemy sent. Their superior firepower cut down the enemy charges, but it was anything but pretty. The battle had deteriorated, said Moore, into a "vulgar brawl."

There were bizarre moments; thinking they were safely behind the lines, three NVA soldiers walked into the middle of an American group. M16s cut them down before the Vietnamese got their AKs off their shoulders.

Lieutenant Joe Marm found himself near an enemy machine gun nest in the middle of a massive anthill. He tried blowing it up with a LAW rocket. No dice. Grenade. Nothing. He reared back, lobbed another grenade over the back of the hill, then charged forward, M16 roaring. He ran some thirty yards right at the gun. When he was finished, the machine gun was out of action. Eleven NV enlisted and a North Vietnamese officer were all dead. Wounded, he continued to fight. Marm was later presented with a Medal of Honor in recognition of his bravery.

The battle continued with small-scale attacks through the night, then got hot again the next day. Severely outnumbered, the Americans poured lead into their enemies, got resupplied, fired more ammo. Planes strafed and bombed the surrounding jungle, staving off attack after attack.

For the Americans, the worst part of the fight came at a nearby landing zone, when companies that had moved away from the mountain to avoid being hit by a B-52 attack stumbled into a much larger Vietnamese force. One hundred and fifty-five American heroes would die or be listed as missing, and another 124 were wounded in that part of the battle. Overall, some 236 Americans lost their lives in the action at Ia Drang. According to Vietnamese figures, 555 NVA soldiers died, and 669 were wounded; the American estimates were slightly higher.

The engagement was a success for the Americans, even with the casualties. It proved air assault works. It also showed how chaotic war in the Vietnamese jungle could be.

And it demonstrated that the theories behind the new black gun made sense in real life. The M16 had made a critical difference in the battle. The large number of bullets it could fire helped turn back the Vietnamese several times.

"Brave American soldiers and the M16 rifle won a victory here," Colonel Moore concluded after the battle at LZ X-Ray.

But even inside Moore's unit, the rifle had not been flawless. There were scattered reports of problems.

Captain John Herren, the commander of Bravo Company, was surprised by a North Vietnamese soldier just after he had radioed in a report to another officer. He grabbed his M16 and fired at him; the gun fell apart with the burst, the trigger assembly coming out in his hand. Herren grabbed a grenade and tossed it over the embankment where the NVA soldier had run. Unfortunately, the grenade bounced off some brush and fell away. Herren and the two radio operators he was with didn't stick around to find out what would happen next. Other soldiers found weapons on the battlefield that were useless, whether because they'd been hit or had jammed was hard to say.

Flaws in the M16 started to become public soon after they reached the troops in large numbers in 1965 and '66. To that point, the only problem was getting enough of them out the door. But gradually, trial and error revealed that the gun had a fatal weakness as a combat rifle: It was not very forgiving if you fouled it or got it full of dirt. And a change in the powder used by the initial cartridges greatly increased the gun's failure rate.

In other words, the damn thing had this bad tendency to jam at the worst possible time.

Not always, certainly, but it only has to happen to you once to get you killed. In 1965, soldiers were said to be selling their M14s on the black market so they could buy the new M16 out of their own pocket. By 1967, a lot of them must have been thinking about getting their money back.

The M16 wasn't junk. It was a promising gun that needed improvements—which should have been fixed before being adopted.

In the years that followed, major revisions were made to the weapon. The M16 was tweaked as the M16A1 very shortly after it was introduced. A forward assist was added, which helped the shooter make sure the bolt was closed—useful when trying to clear a jam. The powder was changed. Instructions emphasized that the weapon needed to be maintained and cleaned often. There had been a lot of hype that it didn't, which added to the jamming problems.

In the 1980s, a much improved version, the M16A2, became the new standard. Among the improvements from the M16A1 to the M16A2 were a heavier and stiffer barrel, a new hand guard, a new butt stock, a better pistol grip, an improved sight, a redesign of the upper receiver that improved cartridge ejection—you get the idea.

Most critical for the troops using it was a change replacing full-auto with a three-round burst. The M16A3 switched back to semi-auto and full auto. Newer M16A4s and the M4 carbine have a flat-top receiver, which allows devices to be attached via Picatinny rails. As a general rule, the M16A4 is used by the Marines and the M4 Carbine by the Army. They have their limitations, as all guns do, but they are now world-class battle rifles.

If you want to know about a rifle, ask a rifleman. It happens that I have one handy—my brother, Jeff.

Jeff served in the Marines around the time I did, and besides deploying to Iraq, served in Marine Recon and put in time as a weapons instructor. He used several versions of the M16 platform during his military career, including a few old M16A1s that had been kicked around quite a bit.

For Jeff, "Learning the history of that weapon was pretty cool." We'd been shooting since we were kids so he was right at home when the drill instructor finally let them use the gun they'd been marching around

Above: the M4, a direct descendant of the M16. Below:
the Russian AK47, the M16's lifelong rival.

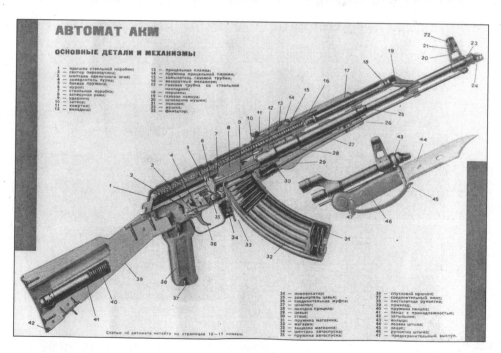

with forever. "It was a piece of junk in Vietnam, but it was built up to what it is now. It's impressive, and they keep making them better. Even in my first four years, they transitioned to A3. Then in Recon, we had the M4."

His preferences depended on the job that had to be done. The shorter-barreled M4 was a better weapon for clearing a building; the smaller length meant it was easier to maneuver in tight quarters. It was also a little less trouble carrying. But both versions shot more or less the same. "I didn't see a whole lot of difference in the effect of the rounds when it came to distances," says Jeff. "And most of our action was pretty close up."

Getting used to full auto took some practice, but after a few eight to ten-hour days of training, most of the men got to the point where they could squeeze off two or three rounds if they wanted to from the full auto version of the M4. That fire control gave them the advantage of both worlds—they could save ammo with a quick burst, and have full auto instantly if they needed it. But it was only something you could get with a lot of practice.

Where the first generation of M16s had twenty-round mags, thirty go in the boxes under today's guns. But the improvement my brother felt was the most important over those earlier models were on the rails. They let him hang all manner of gear on them.

Back in World War I, battle rifles were naked, except for the bayonet and strap. The first M16s were pretty naked themselves, though a bayonet was designed to be attached to the tip. Soon, though, someone figured out you could slap a grenade launcher to the bottom of that sucker, and give the average infantry squad a lot more firepower. The 203 grenade launcher became very popular with squads needing a little more oomph in battle—and what rifle squad doesn't?

With the latest versions of the gun, you can put gear on the top as well as the bottom, thanks to the rails. Scopes and laser sights are the most common; bipods, vertical grips—it's getting to the point where anything you can think up, someone has found a way to get it onto the gun. All that gear makes the gun heavier, taking away one of its advantages. On the other hand, its light weight to begin with makes the package lighter than it might have been.

Optics and laser sights are now pretty much necessities. Being able to fight well at night gives you an advantage over most if not all enemies. And while the M4 and M16 are not sniper weapons, scopes can help soldiers reach out and touch their enemy at a decent range.

U.S. Marines and an M16A4 in Afghanistan, 2009.

Incidentally, I used a Marine M16 rifle in Fallujah, Iraq. It was a standard infantry rifle, but I got it in an unusual way—I traded a Marine for it.

How do you get a Marine to give up his rifle? Give him a bigger one.

In 2004, I was part of a SEAL sniper unit attached to the Marines as they worked to clear the city of insurgents. After our first few days in the city, the enemy started getting smart and avoiding areas where the snipers were working. Meanwhile, the Marines on the ground going into houses were taking all the risks. It was hard to stand up on a roof feeling useless while they were getting shot inside the buildings. So I offered one of the Marines who was providing security for my sniper post a deal he couldn't refuse: Take my sniper rifle, I told him, and I'll use your M16.

I don't know that he got any kills with my gun, but I used his to shoot some Chechens who'd come to Iraq to help wipe out us infidels. The whole thing was a bit of a shock, for them and for me. We'd just breached the house and I stepped into the front room where they were gathered. I don't know what I expected to see, but whatever it was, it wasn't them. I looked at these white faces and blinked—they were the first white guys I saw on the enemy's side of the fence since I'd been in the country.

They were still dazed from our entry. But that only lasted a second. They started to react, grabbing for guns. So did I. Full auto never felt so good.

The gun that I had traded the Marine was a Mk11, an automatic decked out in a style not unlike an M16. My brother Jeff used the same weapon when he was working as a spotter and secondary shooter on a two-man sniper team as a Marine. Carrying the gun meant he only had to hump one rifle into battle. Because it was a semi-automatic, the Mk11 gave him the ability to provide cover at close range. But it also had long-range accuracy. And the gun's scope doubled as a spotting scope.

I liked the SEAL version of the gun myself for pretty much the same reasons. Mine didn't have a collapsible stock, but that was a small tradeoff. The 7.62 × .51mm rounds meant more stopping power, less sweat on my side of the weapon.

The AR-15 family has its own sniper version in use by SEALs, the U.S. Navy Mk 12 Special Purpose Rifle. The rifle has a sixteen-inch barrel but other than that is very similar to an M4. It fires a 5.56 × 45mm round from a thirty-bullet magazine. While the gun could be selected for full auto, I never fired it that way. I suppose it would have been handy to have if the situation came up where I needed it, whether to get the enemy's head down in a hurry, or to deal with a mass attack.

After the first wave of developers, other manufacturers like HK, Sig, you name it, began working on their own variations of the AR-15 design, knowing that the U.S. military wouldn't adopt anything else. The process has resulted in a much better gun family. HK's 416 is a phenomenal weapon, accurate and durable. Sig's 516 is another excellent development of the original concept, burnished with touches from the Sig brain trust.

Because the weapon has been adapted and adopted by so many countries and large manufacturers, it's opened the way for small companies to offer add-ons and improvements. That's become especially big as civilian versions have been adapted by recreational shooters. To some, the civilian version of the AR15 is now a "Barbie Doll for guys"—the platform can be customized any way you want it. Vertical grips, sight systems, rail systems, trigger systems are now a big part of the market.

But customization has been important for one segment of weapons community that probably no one thought would need a high-powered rifle back in the late 1950s or early 1960s—law enforcement.

A series of shootouts in the late 1980s and 1990s convinced police departments they had to change the way they did things, and bring more firepower to the streets. One of the worst incidents occurred February 28, 1997, in North Hollywood, California. Larry Phillips Jr. and Emil Mătăsăreanu picked that day to rob the Bank of America in North Hollywood. It wasn't a spur of the moment decision—the pair had been scouting the place for months. They had a number of violent crimes on their resume. They came prepared for their forced withdrawal with five rifles, a pistol, and over three thousand rounds of ammo. They were also wearing body armor.

Confronted by the police as they tried to escape, the pair easily outgunned the first officers on the scene, who had only 9mm handguns and a shotgun between them. While the criminals were cut off and trapped outside the bank, it took the police roughly forty-five minutes before they were finally able to kill them. In the meantime, eighteen officers were wounded out of the nearly three hundred involved.

The two men's rifles included an HK-91 with a drum magazine and AKMs. Their armor-piercing bullets were capable of slicing through the vests the police wore.

"It was a watershed," says Mark Hanten, my SWAT commander friend. The shoot-out was studied by his and other police forces all across the country. Among

Top: With my M4 on our first deployment in Iraq.
Bottom: Hunting feral hogs in Texas with a favorite AR15.

the more obvious conclusions: the police needed to be better armed.

Automatic rifles were part of the solution. While SWAT teams were common by the 1990s, North Hollywood and incidents like it showed that the specialty units were not the only ones who need high-powered rifles. As Rich Emberlin, who's worked both SWAT and high-level protection roles in the Dallas police department points out, the first guys on the scene are often the ones who have the best chance to contain a situation before it gets ugly.

I can attest to the fact that criminals are seriously armed these days. A while back, the Dallas police department allowed me to tag along when they served a warrant on some suspected bad guys. The weapons stash they had would have made a SEAL's eyes water. In fact, it did—I couldn't believe the range of handguns and rifles the criminals had massed. The confiscated weapons filled a large van.

Dallas has started a program to equip patrolmen with AR15 variants. Besides finding the money, one of their biggest problems is making sure that the officers have enough time to train—which means they have to worry about having enough officers to fill their patrol spots while they're on the range. Out in San Diego, Mark's department spent five thousand dollars on ammo alone when half the SWAT team trained with new AR15-style rifles.

About those new guns: I worked with Mark as he went about putting the new kits together. They're Sig Sauer 516s with ten-inch barrels and some very nice optics. It is a great package for perimeter and containment work, as well as being compact enough for interior work. There were smiles all around the range when the team was done.

On the other hand, I don't think anyone in the department will be sorry if they're never used anywhere but the target range.

Whether they're used in war or for keeping the peace, guns are just tools. And like any tool, the way they're used reflects the society they're part of. As times change, guns have evolved. If you don't like guns, blame it on the society they're part of.

One of the interesting things about the AR15 is its size. Next to the rifle we started this book with, the American long rifle, the modern AR15 combat rifle is small. There's an advantage in that: it can also be handled by a wide range of people.

Back when our friend Sergeant Murphy was shooting officers out of their saddles, the Continental Army and the American militias were almost exclusively

Artist James Deitz's depiction of the events of March 20, 2005, in Salman Pak, Iraq. Sgt. Leigh Ann Hester—and her M4—is pictured in the foreground at bottom right.

male. Now women are an important part of the military and law enforcement forces.

And so maybe it's appropriate we end this little tour of the modern combat rifle with the story of Leigh Ann Hester

In civilian life, Leigh Ann Hester was a petite, twenty-three-year-old woman who helped manage a shoe store in Nashville, Tennessee. At 9 a.m. on Sunday, March 20, 2005, she was a U.S. Army sergeant with the 617th Military Police Company, Kentucky National Guard stationed in a combat zone in Iraq. She and her squad of eight men and another woman were patrolling a road south of Baghdad and just north of Salman Pak. As usual, she had her short-barreled M4 within easy reach inside her up-armored Humvee.

Suddenly, Hester heard gunshots and explosions ahead. The patrol sped up, reaching a convoy of thirty civilian supply trucks and tractor-trailers. The vehicles were being ambushed with intense small-arms fire from the side of the road. An unusually large force of insurgents had filled trenches along the highway and were firing at the trucks. Bullets were flying everywhere.

Staff Sergeant Timothy Nein, in the lead Humvee, saw the civilian trucks trying to scatter. "Flank 'em down the road!" hollered Nein to the rest of the squad. A moment later, a rocket-propelled grenade slammed into the top of his vehicle. Waves of rifle fire punched into the grill and side door as the Hummer ground to a halt.

The others stopped and began engaging the insurgents. The Humvees took multiple hits. In the third truck, all the soldiers except Specialist Jason Mike were wounded. Mike grabbed an M4 assault rifle and an M249 light machine gun and began firing in two different directions to push back the attackers.

Hester spotted a convoy of seven parked cars not far away. The enemy was planning a fast getaway—and more than likely a kidnapping as well. Nein, who was still fighting despite the hits his vehicle had taken, decided their best bet was to go on the offense. He took his rifle and started walking directly toward the enemy positions in the trenches and behind trees and piles of dirt.

Hester jumped from her Humvee to back him up. Carrying her M4 and attached grenade launcher, she ran up alongside Nein as he took cover behind a berm. Nein plugged an insurgent as he popped his head out from behind a tree. Hester zeroed in on a man with a machine gun. She put him in her sights and squeezed the trigger.

"It's not like you see in the movies," she said later on. "They don't get shot and get blown back five feet. They just take a round and they collapse."

Hester gunned down another insurgent, then she and Sergeant Nein jumped into a nearby drainage ditch to get a better angle on the enemy. They started working their way down, pushing the insurgents back, step by step, using rifle fire and a grenade from Hester's launcher. When they started running low on ammo, Hester ran on back to her Humvee to get more. The firefight went on for more than thirty minutes until other U.S. forces arrived. The wounded were evacuated by helicopter, and the area was eventually secured. The Americans killed twenty-seven insurgents, wounded six, and took one prisoner. Hester personally killed at least three Iraqis with rifle and grenade fire from her M4. She received the first Silver Star given to a woman since World War II. Six other soldiers in her unit were decorated, including Specialist Jason Mike, Sergeant Timothy Nein, and Specialist Ashley Pullen.

Sergeant Hester "maneuvered her team through the kill zone into a flanking position where she assaulted a trench line with grenades and M203 rounds," according to the Army citation that accompanied her Silver Star. "She then cleared two trenches with her squad leader where she engaged and eliminated three AIF [anti-Iraqi forces] with her M4 rifle. Her actions saved the lives of numerous convoy members."

"It was either me or them, and I wasn't going to choose the latter," she said. "Adrenaline was pumping, bullets were flying, and I didn't have a choice but fight back.

"I think about March 20 at least a couple times a day, every day, and I probably will for the rest of my life," admitted Hester. "It's taken its toll. Every night I'm lucky if I don't see the picture of it in my mind before I go to sleep, and then even if I don't, I'm dreaming about what we did."

Leigh Ann Hester says she doesn't feel like a hero. "I did my job."

Amen to that.

Epilogue

Pick up a rifle, a pistol, a shotgun, and you're handling a piece of American history. What you hold is not just a finely engineered instrument, but an object that connects you to people who fought for their freedom in the backwoods of Saratoga, New York, died on the rolling hills of Gettysburg, and cornered criminals in the canyons of big cities across the country. Each gun has its own story to tell, its own connection not just to the past, but the American spirit.

Guns are a product of their time. An American long rifle, stock smooth and silky, frame lightweight, barrel long and sleek—the man who made this gun worked in the dim light of a small forge, and chose carefully the wood to use. His fingers went raw as he honed the stock, and the iron from a nearby mine stained his hands and the water he used to cool the parts as he finished.

Take the gun up now, and the smell of black powder and saltpeter sting the air. Raise the rifle to your shoulder and look into the distance. You see not a target but a whole continent of potential, of great things to come, a promising future . . . but also toil, trial, and hardship. The firearm in your hands is a tool to help you through it.

A Spencer—now here is an intricate machine, a clockwork of a gun finely thought out, each piece doing many different parts of the job as the weapon is aimed and gotten ready to fire. This is a gun of a time when imagination sprang forward, when the brain was a storm of ideas, one leading to another, then more, and others beyond that. This is a machine of pieces in a complicated dance, made to work as one; a machine no stronger than its weakest part. It is a sum far more than the simple addition of stamped metal bits and honed edges. The Spencer and its contemporaries come from a time not just of cleverness, or the birth of great industry. All of those, yes, but the weapons were also born in a time of disruption, of fear, of our better selves wrestling with weakness and temptation. Would we be one nation? Would we be several? What future would we have?

Preserving the Union was just one job the Spencer and the other repeaters, revolvers, and early machine guns were invented to solve. They had other, even bigger questions to help us answer: Would we conquer nature, or be conquered by it? If we could tame the wild, could we tame ourselves? Would we overcome our worst impulses and make a better America, then take a leading place in the world?

And once there, what of it?

The answers were positive, on the whole. But they were not given without great struggle and missteps. There were terrible detours: injustices, unnecessary violence, and criminals who found a way to use for evil what should have been, what were, instruments of progress.

In the end, those same tools helped us endure. They faced down the worst evil of our times. They stopped genocide and the enslavement of a people. The Thompson submachine gun didn't just redeem its own reputation fighting evil in World War II; it helped all of us redeem man's potential. After the darkest shadows spread over Europe and Asia, after insanity pushed away common sense and decency, we were able to recover. Weapons did not do it; guns were just helpers, tools as they always are. Men and women did it. But the tools that men and women made, that they carried in their arms and slung on their backs, were a necessary and important part of the struggle.

A gun today is a wonder of high-tech plastic, metal, and compounds too long and complicated to pronounce. Building on the past, gun makers have skimmed away every excess possible, until their products weigh no more than necessary for the job at hand. They pack into a tiny chamber the power of jet engines and rocket ships. They split the world into minute fractions of inches and degrees, measuring what lies before them with the precision and detail of a microscope, finding distinctions where previous generations might have found only blurs. Yet, each gun they produce carries within it the sum of the past. The powder that each cartridge contains can trace its evolution back two, three, four hundred years and more. The machine that molds the cheekpiece has roots in the wooden wheel and the forge that stood at the side of the crooked creek where long rifles were made by hand.

There are always numbers to talk about when discussing about guns. Four billion dollars' worth of wages directly involved in manufacturing alone; ten billion overall in the industry. Nearly fourteen million hunters in America, who together spend some $38 billion a year on their pursuit. Six million—the number of guns manufactured in the U.S. in a single year.

But numbers mean nothing without people: the woman in the factory at Colt, inspecting the latest example of the gun that won the West; the guy truing a Remington 700 action in his garage workshop for a soldier going overseas; the hunter stalking deer in the Minnesota woods.

You can get a little fancy talking about guns. You can become a bit starry-eyed thinking about history. You can forget the rough spots.

That's not fair. Real life has been messy, bloody, complicated. Not a straight line.

That doesn't mean it hasn't been triumphant, victorious, glorious, and wonderful along the same way. Good has triumphed over evil; we have come to terms with our darker selves. America has won its freedom, preserved it, and extended it to others. Guns are not perfect—no model in our history has come to market fully finished without flaw. Neither have we. Man and gun have improved together, sometimes with ease, more often with great struggle and sacrifice.

Our victories in the past are no guarantee for the future. What has been won can always be lost. But the past can show us the way to the future. It can give us hope: The men and women in this book did it; we can too.

When you pick up a gun, whatever model, think a little on Sergeant Murphy taking aim on the battlefield, then going home to start a new life with his young wife, busting the forest into productive land, raising kids. Think about the policemen braving the insanity that was Baby Face Nelson, taking bullets so that others might live. Think about Zip Koons, nervous and fearful in that barn in rural France, yet always doing his job, and just his job. Think of the SWAT team guy trying to put the hostage taker in his crosshairs so he can't kill the child he's dragging by the hair. Think about the soldier on the front line preserving freedom.

Think of yourself, and your connection to history. Ask yourself: What do you owe to the American soul you're tied to, and how are you going to pay it forward?

Afterword

by Taya Kyle

This book has been a real journey for me. It began more than a year ago, when Chris shared with me the idea for *American Gun*. He was energized by the project. I loved seeing his passion grow as he dove into the research and discovered fascinating facts. And then, after his death, I was honored to be involved in carrying out his vision. Working on it, I felt deeply connected not just to American history, but to Chris himself. I hope you felt the same.

Traveling through the past with Chris in *American Gun* brought to life incredible turning points in history, from the streets of the old West to the battlefields of the Civil War, right up to the modern day. It strikes me that while times and guns change, the human experience remains constant. There will always be good.

There will always be evil. There comes a time when honest debate, serious diplomatic efforts, and logical arguments have been exhausted and only men and women willing to take up arms against evil will suffice to save the freedom of a nation or a continent.

What makes us uniquely American is that when the chips are down and freedom is threatened, our men and women have always answered this call and have been willing to put it all on the line to fight battles both here and abroad. I find their stories inspirational. The world is full of people tempted to live not on their own merit, but on a path forged by others. Still others maliciously prey on the defenseless and the innocent. I feel blessed to have been reminded by this project of the humanity and strength of those who believe in giving their all to protect and serve the greater good.

I had the honor of living with and loving one of these men.

Chris Kyle was a multifaceted man who was not only capable of rising up when the chips were down, but who also had personality and character to spare. His humor, passion, depth of love, and dedication, combined with his intelligence, easy-going confidence, and down-to-earth manner, came in an exciting package wrapped in a veritable ribbon of unsurpassed humility.

Visit www.chriskylefrog.com for
more on Chris and his legacy.

American Gun is just one of the many projects Chris was working on in February 2013. Please join me on www.chriskylefrog.com and be a part of the other irons Chris had in the fire.

On behalf of Chris, and from the bottom of my heart, to all the men and women who have served in law enforcement and in the United States military, thank you.

To all of you who support our military and law enforcement communities, in word and deed, Chris would be proud to know you.

Much love,
Taya
April 2013

Acknowledgments

C hris had an essence that was larger than life. His big personality, boisterous laugh, and laid-back style drew people in. He knew the meaning of true friendship. One of the best parts of working on this book was finding out just how blessed Chris was by his friends in return. This book depended on many people who without hesitation offered their time, energy, and knowledge to help fulfill Chris's vision for *American Gun*.

Jim DeFelice: You jumped into the trenches with us in *American Sniper*. You weathered the following storm. And when the chips were down again, you rolled up your sleeves, reached out your capable hand, and helped me out of the ditch. You prove that in life, and even in death, friendship endures. This book would not be what it is today without you.

Kevin Lacz: You embody the meaning of brother-hood. That is one of the highest compliments I can give. Thank you for being you and always having our backs. Jeff Kyle, you are the brother every man should be so lucky to have. Thank you for answering my questions. We love you. Mark Hanten, we treasure your support and friendship over the years. Thank you for devoting your time and keen eye to the guns and stories in this book. Rich Emberlin, in addition to being a great friend, you have a wonderful ability to bring people together. It certainly helped with *American Gun*.

Doug Wicklund of the National Firearms Museum, Bob Owens, Steven Young, John Navarro, Jim Leavelle, Chris McIntyre, Jim Galvin, Monty LeClair, and Craig "Saw" Sawyer, thank you for answering our calls quickly and lending your support.

Brad Juneau, your quiet, strong, generous support of veterans is awe-inspiring. It seems your huge heart knows no limits. I am not sure I can ever adequately express the difference you and your beautiful daughter and my dear friend Melanie Luttrell have made in my life. Melanie, you seem to see my needs before even I'm aware of them. Brad, the term "available day or night" comes to mind when I think of you and this book. My last-minute requests for help were answered every time I asked, no matter what time of day or night. Your insight and comments gave me confidence and made *American Gun* better. I am convinced you have a special place in heaven waiting for you—but you will have to wait at least another fifty years to see it, okay?

Jay Mandel and Mel Berger of William Morris Endeavor and Bill Doyle, thank you for the time you put into getting this project off the ground with Chris. He thoroughly enjoyed working on it with you.

Peter Hubbard, editor extraordinaire, your support and enthusiasm for Chris's books, coupled with your desire to get it right, have made all the difference. Thanks also to Sharyn Rosenblum and the entire staff at William Morrow/HarperCollins.

To my parents, Kim and Kent Studebaker, to Chris's parents, Wayne and Deby Kyle, and to my beautiful and supportive sister, Ashley Purvis-Smith, thank you. To Karen Hanten, Jennifer Lee, Kim Essary, Deanne Hall, Sarah Dyer, Jennifer Bullinger, and Lauren Staub, thank you for your tireless, selfless support of our family.

To my amazing children, your patience and maturity far surpass your age. Your light, laughter, and love are the best reason I know of to take this bull of life by the horns and ride it all the way.

To Chris, our love fuels the fire igniting my passion to carry out your vision and work.

In closing, if you will take a couple extra minutes with me to acknowledge the life of Ryan Job, I think it may help sum up the drive and passion of the men and women both in the stories and those who helped bring *American Gun* full circle. Once you hear about Ryan, you will know why I *need* to take the time to mention him.

The photograph here shows Ryan, Chris's SEAL teammate, living life to its fullest after being critically wounded in Ramadi, Iraq, in August 2006. Ryan is shown in October 2008 with a Winchester Model 70, .300 Weatherby mag, shooting a record-setting elk with the help of a computer-assisted scope and a close friend.

Despite having been blinded and enduring multiple surgeries, Ryan went hunting, climbed Mt. Rainier, and completed college with a 4.0 grade-point average. He married Kelly, who had been with him before his injuries. They had an eagerly anticipated baby on the way when he inexplicably and tragically lost his life following one of his multiple surgeries. He was a man of great character and strength.

Chris and Ryan were on a rooftop in Ramadi when Ryan was shot and blinded. One of the worst moments of Chris's life came when he realized Ryan was down.

Ryan Job hunting elk with a Winchester Model 70
equipped with a Carl Zeiss Conquest scope and
an in-line camera system.

Chris ran to him and radioed for the corpsman.
Immediately he and his Teammates picked Ryan up
and started down the stairs with him. Ryan was tough.
Face shattered, spitting massive amounts of blood, he
demanded that Chris and the others who came to help
let him walk on his own: not because he was too proud
to be carried, but because he didn't want to take other
guys out of the fight.

Years later I choked back tears as Ryan apologized
for the time it took them to get him to safety. He felt
somehow that he had let them down.

Ryan was too humble to realize how much they loved him. On the patio of a restaurant in Arizona in 2009, Ryan, with his beautiful wife, Kelly, sitting across the table and his guide dog curled at his feet, casually mentioned that while he wasn't happy to have been blinded, he was glad that it had happened to him and not anyone else. With grit, humor, determination, and the love of an amazing woman, Ryan took what hardships he was given and made his life amazing.

That undefeatable spirit shows why Ryan, my husband, and countless others answer the call of the country they love.

But there was one other moment in particular that sums up what these men are all about. Badly injured, Ryan was flown to Germany for stabilization and then to Bethesda for multiple surgeries and a gruesome introduction to the next chapter of his life. He had every right to be bitter and perhaps even hateful toward everyone and everything around him, including the country that sent him to war. But in that time of crisis, with his head bandaged, multiple surgeries behind and in front of him, and the knowledge he would never see again, he asked someone to push his wheelchair to a flag outside. On a windy day in Maryland while on hospital grounds, Ryan Job sat still in full salute to the American flag. He held the salute for quite some time, as the wind whipped the flag and clanged the rope against the hard metal flagpole. I imagine an unspoken communication between flag and warrior, each thanking the other for what they had given them.

Patriotism is not an antiquated ideal. It beats strongly in many an American heart.

I am eternally grateful to the men and women who have such strength and character that they are willing to go to distant lands and write a blank check to this country. Because of them, our lives here in America are full of opportunity and enduring freedom.

When you see an American flag and when you hear the National Anthem, I hope you stop and show your respect, not for the fabric flying in the wind, but for Ryan and the other men and women who like him and my husband have lived the literal meaning of the words "the land of the free and the home of the brave."

—T.K.

Appendix
The Ten Guns, by the Numbers

AMERICAN LONG RIFLE

Other names: Kentucky Long Rifle, Pennsylvania Long Rifle, long hunter

First designed: Eighteenth century, exact date and inventor unknown

Type: Precision rifle, single-shot

Predecessor: Most likely evolved from Jaeger hunting rifles

Caliber: Varied with gun maker, but roughly .50

Primary use: Hunting, military sniping

Notable features: Sleek and long, surprisingly light, slow to load

When used: Eighteenth and nineteenth centuries, especially during and after the American Revolution

Current use: Genuine long rifles are historical antiques of considerable value. Authentic guns and replicas are used for sport and reenactments

SPENCER REPEATER

First designed by: Christopher Spencer

Type: Repeating rifle, manually cocked

Caliber: .52

Rounds: 7 metal rimfire cartridges, loaded through butt magazine

When used: American Civil War, Indian Wars

Used by: American Army soldiers, primarily cavalry and mounted infantry

Of historical note: The Spencer was a key development on the road to the modern combat rifle

Trivia: Following the Civil War, Spencer rifles and carbines were sold overseas to France and Japan

Abe Lincoln tested the Spencer himself before approving its use.

COLT SINGLE-ACTION ARMY

Nicknames & other titles: Peacemaker, Model P., M1873, Colt .45

First designed by: William Mason and Charles Brinckerhoff Richards for Colt's Patent Fire Arms Manufacturing Co.

Type: Pistol, 6-shot revolver

Predecessor: Colt Army 1860; there were many other earlier influences

Caliber: .45 Colt

Variations: Many, but among the most notable is the Colt Frontier, chambered in .44–40 to be compatible with Winchester 1873 Repeater

When used: First introduced in 1873, the .45 is still available from Colt

Used by: Everyone from Teddy Roosevelt to George C. Patton, Pat Garrett to Buffalo Bill Cody

Trivia: While Colt .45 is the best-known caliber, many revolvers were chambered for other calibers, including the .44-40, so that the ammunition could be used in both the Colt handgun as well as Winchester Model 1873 abd 1892 rifles

WINCHESTER 1873 RIFLE

Nickname: The Gun that Won the West

Type: Rifle, lever-action repeater

Predecessor: Volition Repeating Rifle, Henry Repeater

Caliber: .44

Historical note: One of the key members of a family that was the iconic frontier tool for settling the American West

When used: First introduced in 1873, the gun is still offered for sale by Winchester (although they're actually manufactured by Miroku in Japan)

Variations: Among the most important was a carbine version with a shorter barrel and rifles chambered in .38 WCF, .32 WCF, and .22 rimfire. Later Winchester models built on the 1873, even as they added improvements

Trivia: A musket version with a 30-inch round barrel was among the family's lesser-known members

TV & movies: The gun has its own movie: *Winchester '73*, produced in 1950 and starring James Stewart. Various other Winchesters have been featured in TV and movies; Chuck Connors used a .44–40 Winchester 1892 in the *Rifleman*.

SPRINGFIELD MODEL 1903 RIFLE

Nickname: Springfield

Origin: The rifle was designed at the Springfield Armory immediately after the Spanish-American War

Type: Bolt-action rifle

Predecessor: Mauser bolt-action rifles, 1889–91 & Spanish M93

Caliber: .30

Notable features: Bolt-action, five-shot magazine

Cartridge: The gun fires a .30-06 round. The "aught-six" refers to the year the cartridge was introduced.

When used: The Springfield 1903 was the standard American Army rifle from its introduction in 1903 until 1936. A large number of Springfields were used in WWII. The weapon is still used for recreation

Trivia: The cartridge was changed and the gun rechambered after it was discovered that the original cartridge burned too hot. The .30–06 has a slightly shorter case and bullet.

COLT M1911 PISTOL

First designed by: John Moses Browning

Type: Pistol, semi-automatic

Predecessor: The M1911 evolved from a series of designs by Browning in the years before 1911

Caliber: .45

Notable features: 7-round detachable box; works on recoil principle

When used: Continuously, from its introduction in 1911 to the present day

Primary users: Military, police, civilian

Major conflicts involved in: World War I, World War II, Korea and Vietnam

Trivia: In WWII, the U.S. military designated the gun "Automatic Pistol, Caliber .45, M1911." (Current terminology deems the gun a semi-automatic.)

A .22 caliber version was developed as a training aid for the Army.

THOMPSON SUBMACHINE GUN

Nickname: Tommy Gun, Trench Broom, The Chopper, Chicago Typewriter, The Gun That Made the '20s Roar

First designed by: John T. Thompson

Type: Submachine gun

Predecessor: While large machine guns predate the Thompson, the weapon defined the submachine gun category when introduced in 1919

Caliber: .45

Notable features: Forward grip, drum magazine (interchangeable with stick magazine on most but not all models)

When used: Developed in 1919, most popular during Prohibition and WWII

Variants: The first production model was the M1921. Various improvements and refinements continued over the years, especially with the advent of war. The main military variants were the 1928A1 and M1.

Rivals: The Browning Automatic Rifle or BAR is sometimes cited as a competitor for the title of first submachine gun. But the weight and length of the BAR, along with its selective fire mode, make it more a processor of the assault rifle or, alternatively, what today is commonly called a "squad level machine gun"—a light machine gun that can be carried and operated by one man, such as the FN Minimi.

Trivia: It is estimated that 1.5 million Thompsons were produced for the U.S. military during WWII

M1 GARAND

First designed by: John Garand

Type: rifle, gas-operated, semi-automatic

Predecessor: The M1 was selected after a competition with another Garand design and a rifle by John D. Pedersen. It was the first truly successful gas-operated semi-automatic infantry rifle in the world

Caliber: .30–06

Magazine/clip size: 8 bullets

Notable features: Loads from the top; can be field-stripped with no tools

When used: Primarily WWII and Korea. Recreational use continues to the present day. The M1 is also used by some color guards and drill teams.

Countries where used: U.S., West Germany, Italy, Japan, Denmark, Greece, Turkey, Iran, South Korea

Trivia: The gun's inventor was Canadian

.38 SPECIAL POLICE REVOLVER

Nickname: ".38 Special" is a generic nickname for revolvers chamber in .38 Special and related calibers

Type: Revolver, double action, 5 or 6 shots

Predecessor: Assorted revolvers; the most famous was probably the Colt New Army Special, chambered for .38 Long

Caliber: .38

Notable features: Easy to load, simple to maintain, rugged and dependable, available in a number of barrel lengths and sizes

When used: Early 20th century to present day

Used by: Police and recreational users as well as for personal-protection

Major manufacturers: The classic examples are from Colt and Smith & Wesson. But many other manufacturers have had success with pistols chambered for different .38 caliber rounds and continue to offer them, most notably Ruger and Taurus International.

M16 RIFLE

First designed by: Eugene Stoner for ArmaLite

Type: Assault rifle, gas-operated, selective fire, automatic

Predecessor: AR-10

Caliber: 5.56 mm (.223 caliber)

Notable features: Selectable three-round burst or full automatic (depending on model). Current military-issue magazine holds 30 rounds; original held 20.

When used: First introduced in 1963, the gun has been the standard military rifle for American soldiers ever since.

Notable family members: AR-15, M16A1, M16A2, M16A3, M16A4, M4 carbine, MK12 Special Purpose Rifle (SPR)

Manufacturer: Colt's Manufacturing Company, Colt Defense LLC. Members of the AR15 family are produced by a number of other companies

Materials: Aluminum, plastic, steel

Trivia: The Marine Corps' current bayonet for the M16 is the OKC-3S, which replaced the M7. A version of the M16 is made specifically to fire from the ports of the Bradley Fighting Vehicle; it is the M231.

Source Notes

Key sources for this book include the resources of the National Firearms Museum in Fairfax, Virginia; the publications *American Rifleman, Guns and Ammo, Gun Digest,* and *American Handgunner;* and the research and historical collections of the New York Public Library. Interviews with Doug Wicklund, senior curator of the National Firearms Museum, also provided valuable historical detail, as did *American Rifle, A Biography* by Alexander Rose, 2008. In addition, *The Sinews of War, Army Logistic, 1775–1953,* by James A. Huston, 1997, provided information on problems with U.S. Army Ordnance and weapon selection through the years.

Chapter 1: The American Long Rifle

"I never in my life saw better rifles": Henry J. Kauffman, *The Pennsylvania-Kentucky Rifle* (1960), p. 24.

Timothy Murphy and Battle of Saratoga detail: Richard M. Ketchum, *Saratoga: Turning Point of America's Revolutionary War* (1997); Richard Worth, *Saratoga* (2002); Timothy Murphy: Frontier Rifleman, New York State Military Museum and Veterans Research Center website; William Conant Church, "General Burgoyne's Original Order Book," *The Galaxy Magazine*, June 1876/January 1877. Note: there is some historical dispute over whether the sniper's actual name was Timothy Murphy.

In his autobiography, Sam Houston described his father as having served with Daniel Morgan's riflemen. I have not yet located additional records to pinpoint exactly when and where this service took place, as unit rosters from the Revolutionary War are often incomplete or lost to history, and units were periodically attached to various different units and commands. Also, American "after-action reports" in that war were very spotty, and do not often contain precise inventories of weapons used.

"when they understood they were opposed": Roger D. McGrath, The American Rifleman in the Revolutionary War, *The New American*, September 13, 2010.

Detail of the Battle of Cowpens is mainly from Lawrence E. Babits, *Devil of a Whipping: The Battle of Cowpens* (1998); and Kenneth Lewis Roberts, *The Battle of Cowpens* (1958). I'm most grateful to Cowpens historians Lawrence Babits and John Robertson for additional details and perspective they shared with me.

"The enemy front is not the goal": Roman Johann Jarymowycz, *Cavalry from Hoof to Track* (2008), p. 18.

"seldom has a battle": John Marshall, *The Life of George Washington* (1843), p. 404.

"an unbroken chain of consequences": George Otto Trevelyan, *George the Third and Charles Fox, Volume 2* (1915), p. 141.

"a tall man with flowing hair": Wallace O. Chariton, *Exploring Alamo Legends* (1992), p. 470.

"Now hold your fire, men": Louis Wiltz Kemp, Edward W. Kilman; *The Battle of San Jacinto and the San Jacinto Campaign* (1947), p. 13.

"Take prisoners like the Meskins do!": T. R. Fehrenbach, *Lone Star: A History of Texas and the Texans* (2000), p. 232.

"Parade! Parade!": James W. Pohl, *The Battle of San Jacinto* (1989), p. 43.

"San Jacinto! San Jacinto!" "The scene that followed": Ferenbach, *Lone Star*, p. 234.

"be generous to the vanquished", "You should have remembered": Charles Edwards Lester, *The Life of Sam Houston* (1860), p. 147.

Chapter 2: The Spencer Repeater

"What kind of Hell-fired guns have your men got?" Alexander Rose, *American Rifle: A Biography* (2009), p. 147.

Details and dialogue of Lincoln's shooting guns in spring of 1861: ibid., page 143; and William Osborn Stoddard, *Inside the White House in War Times* (1890), p. 41–44.

"I believe I can make this gun shoot better." Robert V. Bruce, *Lincoln and the Tools of War* (1956), p. 115.

"handled the rifle like a veteran marksman", "Boys, this reminds me": Charles Augustus Stevens, *Berdan's United States Sharpshooters in the Army of the Potomac* (1892), p. 10.

"newfangled gimcracks": Phil Leigh, The Union's 'Newfangled Gimcracks,' " *NYT Blogs*, January 23, 2012.

"Hoover's Gap was the first battle where the Spencer": Larry M. Strayer, Richard A. Baumgartner, *Echoes of Battle* (1996), p. 18.

"Those Yankees have got rifles", "What kind of Hell-fired guns have your men got?": Alexander Rose, American Rifle: A Biography (2009), p. 147.

"a circus rider gone mad": James Welch, Paul Stekler, *Killing Custer* (1997), p. 57.

"come on, you Wolverines!": Edward G. Longacre, *Custer And His Wolverines* (2004), p. 143.

"the most dramatic, largest man-to-man": Paul D. Walker, *The Cavalry Battle That Saved the Union* (2002), p. 15.

"the inwardness of the thing": ibid. p. 147.

"you are younger than I am": Bruce, *Lincoln and the Tools of War*, p. 263.

"This evening and yesterday evening": John Hay, *Letters of John Hay and Extracts From Diary* (1908), p. 93.

"There is no doubt that the Spencer carbine": Bruce, *Lincoln and the Tools of War*, p. 290.

"If a large part of the Union Army": ibid., p. 102.

Valuable information on the Ordnance Department and other facets of Army supply were provided by *The Sinews of War: Army Logistics, 1775–1953*, by James A. Huston, Center of Military History, 1997.

Chapter 3: The Colt Single-Action Army Revolver

"The good people of this world": Herbert G. Houze, *Samuel Colt: Arms, Art, and Invention* (2006), p. 1.

"yonder comes a thousand Indians!": Andrew Sowell, *Early Settlers and Indian Fighters of Southwest Texas* (1900), p. 319.

"They are fixin' to charge us": Frederic Remington, "How the Law Got Into the Chaparral," *Harper's* magazine, December 1896, p. 60.

"Crowd them!": Sowell, *Early Settlers and Indian Fighters of Southwest Texas,* p. 320.

"Any man who has a load" Mary A. Maverick, *Memoirs of Mary A. Maverick* (1921), p. 83.

"Sometimes a bad horse would blow up": "Glocks vs. Peacemakers," *American Handgunner,* May 1, 2005.

Davis incident: Massad Ayoob, "The Jonathan Davis Incident," published online in *American Handgunner,* The Ayoob Files, February 21, 2013.

Butch and Sundance dialogue: Massad Ayoob, "Butch Cassidy and the Sundance Kid: How did They Really Die?", *American Handgunner,* January/February 2011, p. 74–5.

"strange character,": Joseph G. Rosa, *They Called Him Wild Bill* (2011), p. 111.

"He was a broad-shouldered": Joseph G. Rosa, "Wild Bill Hickok: Pistoleer, Peace Officer and Folk Hero," originally published by *Wild West* magazine, published online by historynet.com: June 12, 2006.

"Bill beat them to it": Helen Cody Wetmore, *Zane Grey, Last of the Great Scouts* (1918), p. 329.

"The secret of Bill's success": Joseph G. Rosa, *Wild Bill Hickok, Gunfighter* (2001), p. 48.

"Whenever you get into a row": George Ward Nichols, *Wild Bill* (1867), p. 285.

"Charlie, I hope you never have to shoot": Eugene Cunningham, *Triggernometry: A Gallery of Gunfighters* (1941), Introduction, p. xx.

Hickok-Tutt gunfight details: William Connelley, *Wild Bill and His Era* (1933), pp. 84–5; Rosa, *Wild Bill Hickok* (1996), pp. 116–23.

"I never allowed a man to get the drop on me": Joseph Rosa, *Wild Bill Hickok,* p. 109.

"Seven men shoot at each other": Massad Ayoob, "The OK Corral Shootout," *American Handgunner,* May 1, 2007.

"The gunfight came in bursts": Casey Tefertiller, *Wyatt Earp* (1997), p. 122

Additional detail for this chapter is from John Taffin, *John Taffin's Book of the .44,* published online at sixguns.com.

Chapter 4: The Winchester 1873 Rifle

"The Winchester stocked and sighted": Theodore Roosevelt, *The Works of Theodore Roosevelt—Volume 3* (1902), p. 38.

Dalton Gang's raid on Coffeyville banks: Robert Barr Smith, *Daltons! The Raid on Coffeyville, Kansas* (1999), pp. 83–150.

Like many others, newspaper editor David Elliott spelled Bill Power's name as "Powers." Powers may in fact have been the actual spelling, as many relatives before and after styled it that way. But it's Power on the official tombstone, and that's what I used here.

"The Sharps was a different kind": Keith McCafferty, "Guns of the Frontier," *Field & Stream,* February 1997, p. 35.

Little Bighorn details: Thomas Powers, "How the Battle of Little Bighorn Was Won," *Smithsonian* magazine, November 2010; Hamlin Garland, "General Custer's Last Fight as Seen by Two Moon," *McClure's* magazine, September 1898, p. 446; Richard G. Hardorff, *Lakota Recollections of the Custer Fight* (1991), p. 44; Doug Scott, email to the authors.

"is by all odds the best weapon": Theodore Roosevelt, *Hunting Trips of a Ranchman* (1904), p. 39.

"carries far and straight": Theodore Roosevelt, "Ranch-life and Game-shooting in the West," *Outing* magazine, March 1886, p. 616.

"No one but he who has partaken": Lamar Underwood, *Theodore Roosevelt on Hunting* (2006).

Chapter 5: The M1903 Springfield

"The French told us": Alan Axelrod, *Miracle at Belleau Wood* (2007), p. 2.

Details of the Battle at San Juan Heights, Cuba are from: Theodore Roosevelt, *The Rough Riders* (1899); Richard Harding Davis, *Notes of a War Correspondent* (1911); Herschel V. Cashin, *Under Fire With the 10th U.S. Cavalry* (1902); and Peggy Samuels, Harold Samuels, *Teddy Roosevelt at San Juan* (1997).

"The armory also spawned a culture": John Lehman, "Bookshelf: Save Ammunition, Lose Wars," *Wall Street Journal,* March 9, 1995.

"I think that ramrod bayonet": United States Army Ordnance Department, *Report of the Chief of Ordnance,* 1905, p. 129.

One British general: See John S. D. Eisenhower, *Yanks, the Epic Story of the American Army in World War I* (2002), page 17.

Details of the Battle at Belleau Wood are from Axelrod, *Miracle at Belleau Wood*; Albertus Wright Catlin, Walter Alden Dyer, *With the Help of God and a Few Marines* (1919); and David Bonk, *Chateau Thierry & Belleau Wood, 1918* (2012).

For more information on the Springfield's use as a sniper rifle, see "No Drill" 1903A4 Sniper Rifle—1903 Springfield at the GunsAmerica .com website: http://www.gunsamerica.com/blog/no-drill-1903a4-sniper-rifle-1903-springfield/.

One of the first companies to use the bullet: www.lapua .com/en/story-of --338-lapua-magnum.html.

Chapter 6: The M1911 Pistol

"Beyond a doubt": NRA Staff, *AR's Top 10 Handguns*, http://www.american rifleman.org.

Details of Alvin York episode are from Alvin York, *Sergeant York, His Own Life Story and War Diary* (1928); David D. Lee, *Sergeant York: An American Hero* (1985); Sam Cowan, *Sergeant York and His People* (1922); and John Perry, *Sergeant York, His Life, Legend & Legacy* (1997).

"It fits the hand like a trusted tool": Brian Sheetz's Top 10 Handguns, http://www.americanrifleman.org.

"The cavalry doctrine of those days": Eduardo Lachica, "The Cavalry is Gone," *Wall Street Journal*, June 20, 1984.

"the Colt is superior": "The .45 Automatic," *American Rifleman*, March 20, 1911, cited in Charles Bennett, "The 1911," *Law Enforcement Technology*, August 1, 2012.

"To say he was the Edison": Scott S. Smith, "John Browning's Guns Hit The Bull's-Eye," *Investor's Business Daily*, December 13, 2010.

"Make it strong enough—then double it": Anthony Smith, *Machine Gun* (2003), p. 260.

John M. Browning, American Gunmaker by John Browning & Curt Gentry, 1964, gave insight into Browning and his inventions.

Chapter 7: The Thompson Submachine Gun

Attack on Al Capone in Cicero: Laurence Bergreen, *Capone: The Man and the Era* (1996), pp. 205–6.

"I am just a businessman": Selwyn Raab, *Five Families* (2007), p. 42.

"I saw this gun myself": Robert V. Bruce, *Lincoln and the Tools of War* (1956), p. 120.

"Give them grape": C. J. Chivers, *The Gun* (2010), p. 32.

"Hang your chemistry": John Ellis, *The Social History of the Machine Gun,* (1975), p. 34.

John Dillinger detail: Mark Holtz, *Public Enemy #1,* (2013).

"He liked to amuse bank customers": Allen Barra, "A Gangster With Star Appeal," *Wall Street Journal,* June 25, 2009.

"He had a baby face": Bryan Burrough, *Public Enemies* (2004), pp. 102–3.

"Stupid son of a bitch": Steven Nickel, William J. Helmer, *Baby Face Nelson* (2002), p. 173.

"I got one of them!": Jay Robert Nash, *Bloodletters and Badmen* (1995), p. 212.

"I know who you are!", "Nelson calmly aimed a machine gun": Massad Ayoob, "Learning from a Cop-killer," *American Handgunner*, July 2007.

"It was just like Jimmy Cagney": Nickel and Helmer, *Baby Face Nelson*, p. 337.

"finally reaching the point": J. Edgar Hoover, Persons in Hiding (1938), p. 149.

Willie Sutton quotes: Willie Sutton, Edward Linn, *Where the Money Was* (2004).

"It was the perfect weapon": Mark Keefe, *The Echo of the Thompson Gun*, September 21, 2012, www.americanrifleman.org

Details of Thompson's company and the gun's development: Martin Pegler, *The Thompson Submachine Gun*, (2010). Additional information on the background of machine gun development was drawn from John Ellis, *The Social History of the Machine Gun*.

"Summers is a legend": Stephen E. Ambrose, *D-Day: June 6, 1944* (1994), p. 299.

Chapter 8: The M1 Garand

Franklin Koons at Dieppe: The account of Franklin Koons and the other action at Dieppe, France is based on Rangers at Dieppe, Jim DeFelice (2008), especially pp 116, 146, 153–8, 224.

Garand was not the first person to think of the idea: See some of the discussion, and how Garand's machine gun worked, in Julian S. Hatcher, *Book of the Garand* (2012).

The U.S. Army produced an excellent film detailing the inner workings of an M1 Garand: *M1 Garand— Principles of Operation,* which is available on YouTube. Additional information on the Garand was drawn from the Army field manual for the weapon, "FM 23–5."

"In my opinion the M1 rifle": Jim Supica, *Guns* (2005), p. 186.

"one weapon that outgunned": William H. Hallahan, *Misfire* (1994), p. 390.

Fetched ammo: See "Battle for Henderson Field," article posted at Raritan -online.com: http://www.raritan -online.com/jb-henderson-field.htm. Basilone came from Raritan, N.J., which continues to honor his memory.

"You'll probably get yours": Leroy Thompson, *The M1 Garand* (2012), p. 55.

"Guadalcanal is no longer": Robert Leckie, *Challenge for the Pacific* (1965). P. viii.

"The most amazing thing about that M1": Mark G. Goodwin, *U.S. Infantry Weapons in Combat,* http:// www.scott-duff.com.

Battle of the Bulge detail: Martin K.A. Morgan, "The Men & Guns of the Battle of the Bulge," http://www .americanrifleman.org; Gregory Orfalea, *Messengers of the Lost Battalion* (2010). Joe Cicchinelli's memories of his war service are collected in an oral history collection online at http://www.joecicchinelli.com/ home.htm.

M1 in Korea: Bruce Canfield, Arms of the Chosin Few, http://www.american rifleman.org.

"bunk": Springfield (Mass.) *Daily News*, March 19, 1963.

Chapter 9: The .38 Special Police Revolver

Attack on Blair House: Stephen Hunter and John Bainbridge Jr., *American Gunfight: The Plot to Kill Harry Truman—and the Shoot-out That Stopped It* (2005).

Valuable background for this chapter was provided by Massad Ayoob, *Massad Ayoob's Greatest Handguns of the World* (2010).

"As a personal defense weapon": ibid., p. 68.

"at a time when full power": Jim Supica, *Guns* (2005), p. 31.

"This was smart": "How the Glock Became America's Weapon of Choice," *Fresh Air*, National Public Radio, January 24, 2012.

Some information regarding the different pistols and their offerings is drawn from the catalogs of Smith & Wesson and Colt. Both companies also offer brief accounts of their history on the websites. General information on Smith & Wesson .38 Special revolvers was drawn from *The History of Smith and Wesson Firearms* by Dean Boorman. In addition, Patrick Sweeney's *Gunsmithing Pistols & Revolvers, 3rd Edition* (1986), was very useful for understanding the evolution of some of the weapons. Some information on the Glock 17 is from the "Glock Instruction for Use" manual, and the Glock catalog.

Chapter 10: The M16 Rifle

"Brave soldiers and the M16": Russell W. Glenn, *Reading Athena's Dance Card* (2000), p. 172.

Ia Drang battle details are drawn extensively from Harold G. Moore, Joseph L. Galloway, We Were Soldiers Once . . . and Young (1992); and also from *The Battle of Ia Drang Valley, 1965,* a documentary by CBS News that is available on YouTube.

"What we fear most": *Popular Science*, August 1967, p. 70.

Information on the early political struggles and development of the AR-15/ M16 is drawn from *American Rifle: a Biography* by Alexander Rose.

Details of events of March 20, 2005 involving Leigh Ann Hester and her colleagues are from contemporaneous press accounts, especially: Steve Fainaru, "The Everyday Heroics of a Woman in Combat," *New York Sun,* June 27, 2005; Multinational Corps Iraq Public Affairs videotape of Hester interview with CBS reporter posted on YouTube titled "Sergeant Leigh Ann Hester—First female soldier to win Silver Star since WW2"; and Recon Intelligence Report, "Conspicuous Courage Under Fire, Part 4," posted on YouTube.

Technical data on the StG44 varies depending on source. These numbers here are from Ian V. Hogg and John Weeks, *Military Small Arms of the 20th Century.* There were a number of variations in the rifle family, which is one reason for the discrepancies.

Additional information on ArmaLite and the improvements in the various M16/M4 models is drawn from "A Historical Review of ArmaLite: Edition of 4 January 2010," available online at: http://www.armalite.com/ images/Library/History.pdf; and Ian V. Hogg and John Weeks, *Military Small Arms of the 20th Century* (2000).

HARPER LUXE

THE NEW LUXURY IN READING

We hope you enjoyed reading
our new, comfortable print size and found it
an experience you would like to repeat.

Well – you're in luck!

HarperLuxe offers the finest in fiction and
nonfiction books in this same larger print size and
paperback format. Light and easy to read, HarperLuxe
paperbacks are for book lovers who want to see
what they are reading without the strain.

For a full listing of titles and
new releases to come, please visit our website:

www.HarperLuxe.com